Scapegoat

'… even now his [Winston Churchill's] treatment of some officers, and his invariable search for scapegoats when anything went wrong, leaves an impression almost amounting to vindictiveness…'

Stephen Roskill; *Churchill and the Admirals*

This book is dedicated to Admiral Sir Tom Phillips and all those who lost their lives in the sinking of HMS *Prince of Wales* and *Repulse* and to Commander T.V.G. Phillips – a fine man, a fine officer and a loving and dutiful son

Scapegoat

The Death of HMS *Prince of Wales* and *Repulse*

Martin Stephen

Pen & Sword
MARITIME

First published in Great Britain in 2014 by
Pen & Sword Maritime
an imprint of
Pen & Sword Books Ltd
47 Church Street
Barnsley
South Yorkshire
S70 2AS

Copyright © Martin Stephen 2014

ISBN 978 1 78383 178 4

The right of Martin Stephen to be identified as the Author of this
Work has been asserted by him in accordance with the Copyright,
Designs and Patents Act 1988.

A CIP catalogue record for this book is available from the British
Library

Typeset in Ehrhardt by
Mac Style Ltd, Bridlington, East Yorkshire
Printed and bound in the UK by CPI Group (UK) Ltd, Croydon,
CRO 4YY

Pen & Sword Books Ltd incorporates the imprints of Pen & Sword
Archaeology, Atlas, Aviation, Battleground, Discovery, Family
History, History, Maritime, Military, Naval, Politics, Railways, Select,
Transport, True Crime, and Fiction, Frontline Books, Leo Cooper,
Praetorian Press, Seaforth Publishing and Wharncliffe.

For a complete list of Pen & Sword titles please contact
PEN & SWORD BOOKS LIMITED
47 Church Street, Barnsley, South Yorkshire, S70 2AS, England
E-mail: enquiries@pen-and-sword.co.uk
Website: www.pen-and-sword.co.uk

Contents

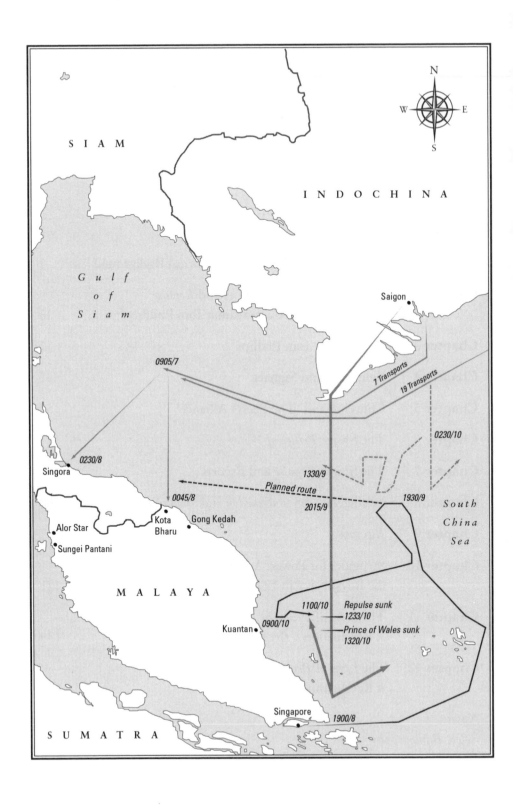

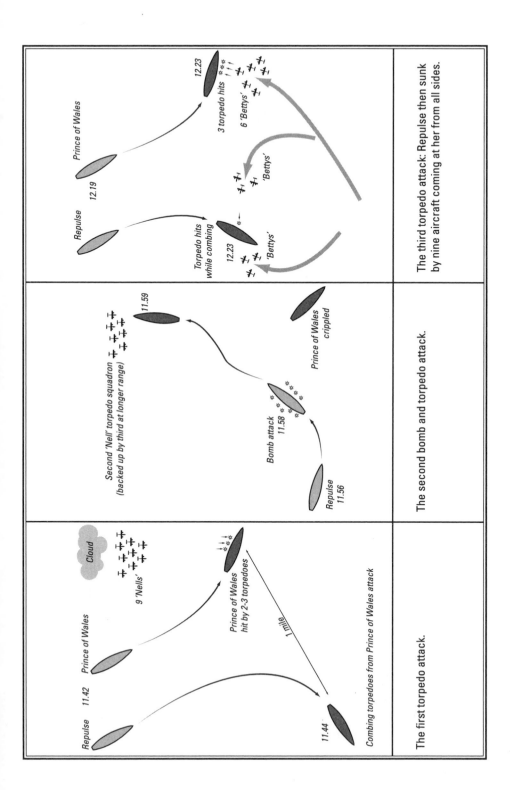

Repulse 11.42 **Prince of Wales**

Cloud

9 'Nells'

Prince of Wales hit by 2-3 torpedoes

1 mile

11.44

Combing torpedoes from Prince of Wales attack

The first torpedo attack.

Second 'Nell' torpedo squadron (backed up by third at longer range) 11.59

Repulse 11.56

Bomb attack 11.58

Prince of Wales crippled

The second bomb and torpedo attack.

Repulse 12.19 **Prince of Wales**

12.23

3 torpedo hits 6 'Bettys'

Torpedo hits while combing

12.23 'Bettys'

'Bettys'

The third torpedo attack: Repulse then sunk by nine aircraft coming at her from all sides.

Acknowledgments

I owe a great debt for this and my other books to the research facilities offered by the Cambridge University Library. I am also grateful to The National Maritime Museum, the British Museum, the Imperial War Museum and Churchill College, Cambridge. In particular I would like to thank Helen Mavin, Assistant Curator (Photographs) and Parveen Kaur Sodhi (Commercial Sales & Licensing Executive, Image Sales and Licensing) both of the Imperial War Museum.

I am grateful to Sir Tom Phillips, Sheila Gregory and the family of Admiral Sir Tom Phillips for allowing me access to his papers and the extensive collection of material collected and kept by the family and friends after the loss of Force Z. Similar thanks go to Jennifer Leach. I am also extremely grateful to Alan Matthews of the *Prince of Wales* and *Repulse* Survivors' Association.

Note on Methodology

Wherever possible I have referenced quotations to the most readily available source in which they have been published. For the occasional item which is not thus available I have given the original Public Records Office (PRO) reference, or that applying to the British Museum and Churchill College Archives (CA), otherwise known as the Roskill Collection.

Original naval records present something of a nightmare for the researcher. The official records suffered by virtue of having been generated in wartime conditions, and things were seriously confused further by the methodology adopted by those responsible for the writing of the official naval history of the war which saw considerable re-arrangement of the material that may have been helpful to the authors but was not helpful to subsequent researchers. One of my fondest recollections is calling up a file which I believed to be full of details of requisitions for the naval base at Alexandria, and having fall out of it an extraordinary statement from Admiral Vian taking full responsibility for something a junior officer was about to be blamed for. Several years and at least one ocean separated this document from those actually listed as being in the file and this was only the most extreme example of a not uncommon event. I regret I do not speak Japanese and have relied on secondary sources for all Japanese material.

Introduction

On 10 December 1941 two Royal Navy warships, the newly constructed King George V class battleship *Prince of Wales* and the First World War battle cruiser *Repulse,* were sunk by land based Japanese bombers and torpedo bombers while attempting to disrupt Japanese landings on British held territories, the length of what was then Malaya and is now Sri Lanka. Admiral Sir Tom Phillips, the commander of the ill-fated Force Z, was criticized by many post-war authorities for the disaster, which, along with the raids on Taranto and Pearl Harbor, is deemed to have marked the end of the battleship as the dominant force in naval warfare. The loss of these two great ships is associated with more than the end of the battleship era. A few weeks later Singapore, from whence the ships had set sail on their last voyage, was to fall to the Japanese, an event that to many people marked the effective end of the British Empire.

Prince of Wales and *Repulse* had embarked on their mission with no accompanying aircraft carrier. When spotted by a Japanese aircraft, Phillips failed to call up air cover from RAF air bases on the Malaysian Peninsular. As someone with no combat experience, and a man who had professed his faith in the ability of a well-handled surface ship to survive air attack, Phillips was held responsible in greater or lesser measure for the sinking of the two ships. In some quarters the image was cultivated of a man who combined some of the worst features of martinet and dinosaur. Phillips, who lost his life in the engagement, as did the captain of *Prince of Wales*, was therefore not able to defend himself and had no friends among the remaining senior Admirals such as A.B. Cunningham or James Somerville to fight on his behalf. Phillips had fallen out with Churchill, having once been a favourite, and in the aftermath of the debacle of the fall of Singapore and a mass stampede by some of those involved to cover their own backs, Phillips's reputation was never even a starter in the race for rehabilitation.

My own interest in Admiral Sir Tom Phillips was kindled when I was commissioned to write a book, *Sea Battles in Close Up*, looking at ten of the major naval engagements of the Second World War. I dutifully wrote a chapter on the sinking of *Prince of Wales* and *Repulse* that took what was then something of a middle ground, not totally condemning Phillips but at the same time finding little reason to exonerate him. I was left feeling edgy about what I had written for reasons of intuition I still do not clearly understand. The edge persisted to the extent of my badgering the long-suffering Leo Cooper to commission a book titled *The Fighting Admirals. British Admirals of the Second World War*. He thought it was about British Admirals of the Second World War. I thought it had given me a good cover story for writing a book about Admiral Sir Tom Phillips. I needed the cover story because I believed no one would commission a book on Phillips alone.

Then things started to go wrong. Try as I might, I could find no trace of the private or family papers of Tom Phillips. Admirals always leave these and they are an invaluable insight for any proper historian who wishes to work from primary sources. With two naval history books under my belt by then I knew the various archives where any such papers ought to be. Yet despite everything I found Tom Phillips might as well not have existed. After six months of increasingly frantic letters and 'phone calls, I had resigned myself to the fact that *The Fighting Admirals: British Admirals of the First World War* would more or less have to omit the one Admiral who had caused me to want to write it in the first place. Then one evening I came home to find my wife chatting in our drawing room to Sheila, a woman she had met earlier and invited round for a drink. Her surname bore not even the remotest connection to anyone or anything in the Royal Navy. Sheila commented on how the walls were lined with quite a lot of naval history books. I told her this was a hobby and that I was working on what was meant to be a book about a man she would never have heard of, Admiral Sir Tom Phillips, but that I would have to take another direction because I had failed to track down any of the man's private papers. A funny expression crossed Sheila's face, and she said: 'I do know who he was, actually; he was my grandfather. And I can tell you why you can't find the papers.'

It transpired that Tom Phillips's son, who tended to be known as 'Tom' after he left the Navy but prior to that was known as 'Gerry' to his father and

'Gerald' to the world in general, had inherited all the family papers on the death of Lady Phillips, Admiral Sir Tom Phillips's widow, in the 1970s. Lady Phillips had been responsible for the creation of an extremely interesting archive containing not only letters but also other contemporary material. Gerald Phillips had trusted the brilliant naval historian Arthur Marder to look inside the huge, old suitcase containing the papers but Marder had died before he could make full use of them. Following an invitation to Sunday lunch with the family, I was allowed access to the material in one of the most extraordinary experiences of my life. There were unpublished letters from Churchill, a string of tributes to Admiral Sir Tom Phillips and personal letters that gave a very different impression of the man from that found in most available books. Reading through this material I gained the sense of a man radically different from that generally portrayed, and infinitely more attractive. There were also some crucial corrections to the standard historical version of what happened, some of which I was able to include in *The Fighting Admirals*.

There is always a danger that a historian in contact with the family of his subject can be influenced emotionally to be kinder than purely intellectual considerations might allow for. When writing an earlier book I had an extremely cordial relationship with the son of a Second World War Admiral I previously believed to be a charlatan. And I have written extremely warmly about another whose family I regret to say I did not like at all. I believe my view of Admiral Sir Tom Phillips is as objective as it is unfashionable and is formed from a straightforward analysis of the facts.

Much more has emerged in the past years to merit a new book on both the loss of the two ships and the Admiral in overall command. Much more has been released or become known about the fall of Singapore, some of which has a direct bearing on the sinkings. The wrecks of both vessels have been thoroughly examined and battle damage assessed, and there is considerably more information available about the design of *Prince of Wales* in particular, which has a crucial bearing on the ship's loss. So too does an increasing store of knowledge about *material* on both the British and the Japanese side, new intelligence *material* in general, the increasing information available on Churchill's role in the incident and the fall of Singapore itself. As stated above, the private Phillips papers give a completely different picture of his character and personality to the stereotype presented in many books and allow for a revisionary book on the loss of the two ships and the reputation of their commander.

It is frequently said that history is written by the victors. So it is for around a hundred years after the events. Beyond that time the stranglehold on history exerted by those who won and survived to write the tale lessens and the truth will out. It is time the truth was revealed about Admiral Sir Tom Phillips, the man who was probably least responsible of any for the sinking of *Prince of Wales* and *Repulse*. To this day those most responsible for what happened on 10 December 1941 have not been called to account.

There is another factor behind my interest in Admiral Sir Tom Phillips. As with many people before and after him whose reputations have been traduced by history, there is a strong possibility that he was a scapegoat, a convenient figure to absorb the blame that should more properly have been placed on the shoulders of others. When I have not been writing books I have been privileged to be Head of three of England's leading independent schools. The Head of such schools has the rather strange experience of sitting at tables for which he does not qualify in terms of wealth, birth or social status. I imagine being something like the country vicar asked to make up the numbers for dinner at the big house in the eighteenth and nineteenth centuries. I have listened to, and even been treated as a confidante of, some leading figures in the Church, politics, the military, commerce and industry. It has made me extremely cynical and left me convinced that vast power is exercised by those who are neither elected nor accountable. It has also suggested strongly that many people elected to positions of real power do not use that power in the first instance to promulgate the Gospel, win the election or war or sell more widgets. Instead, their first and overriding priority is to use that power to guard their own backs. They exist in any organization I have known, but there is also a separate group of people who actually do the job and keep the business afloat (or who are simply naïve) and are far too busy to guard their backs. These are the most vulnerable when the fur starts to fly and are prime candidates to be made scapegoats for whatever has gone wrong. The more I read about Admiral Sir Tom Phillips the more I came to believe that of all the people who could be blamed for the sinking of *Prince of Wales* and *Repulse* he was the least liable and a classic example of the scapegoat – the person blamed for the faults of others.

A further factor that has helped to damn him was neither his own fault nor of his own making. Writers and journalists face a terrible pressure not to let the truth stand in the way of a good story. What makes a good story – Shakespeare's *Richard III* or the final moments of the First World War in the *Blackadder* television series – is often bad history. An antediluvian Admiral who did not believe in air power and had his two battleships sunk under him by aircraft is a classic good story, a headline from Heaven, and so good a story that it ought to be true. It wasn't of course, but that wasn't the point.

Phillips made a crucial mistake in getting himself killed. It meant the coast was clear for his detractors, those in power in the hierarchy of the Royal Navy who disliked or were jealous of him and those who might otherwise have shared the blame. The Royal Navy, as is common in any institution, had its own internal wars and jealousies in 1941 and tragedy can bring the best and the worst out of an institution. Being zealous of one's own reputation in the eyes of some senior naval officers became confused with being rather less zealous for the reputation of others. And, of course, just as everyone wants to jump on the bandwagon, so does everyone want to jump off when it threatens to crash.

In the battle to rescue the reputation of Admiral Sir Tom Phillips a number of forces have gathered in recent years and scouting missions been sent out. Perhaps now is the time for those forces to be gathered together for a major offensive, which I hope is what this book represents.

Chapter 1

The Military, Political and Historical Background

The Royal Navy in 1939

When war broke out in 1939 the Royal Navy was better prepared than the politicians who had denied it money and resources in the inter-war years deserved, but still very inadequately equipped for the challenges it would face. It had made great strides in naval aviation in the inter-war years, culminating in the Admiralty taking over control of the Fleet Air Arm in mid-1939. It had developed sonar or ASDIC to counteract the submarine threat. It had developed what was, for the time, state-of-the-art radar. It saw the multi-barrelled pom-pom as an effective counter to close-range air attack[1] and had five new King George V class battleships being built or about to enter service. It had a proud tradition and a self-belief that had survived surprisingly well the disappointment of the Battle of Jutland, the lower-deck discontent and mutiny of the 1920s, and the Geddes Axe, which removed thousands of officers as a cost-saving measure. Its twelve battleships, three battle-cruisers and six aircraft carriers dwarfed Germany's surface navy.

Many of these advantages were more apparent than real. The majority of the Navy's battleships were First World War designs, and the battle-cruiser *Hood* was effectively so, though completed just after the war. The decision to modernize six capital ships in the inter-war period, in itself a very wise move, meant them being in dockyard hands for many months, with the result that the Royal Navy never had more than thirteen of its capital ships available at any one time in the 1930s, and the number frequently went down to ten or fewer. For obvious reasons, the modernization plan had not allowed for the outbreak of war in September 1939, and so ran over into it. The battleship *Queen Elizabeth* did not finish her modernization until 1941. The situation was complicated by the fact that older ships needed increasing amounts of time for refit and repair. Corners could be cut in wartime, and were, but it was a dangerous game to play, and there were very practical limitations on how much time could be saved, or how much things could be speeded up.

Even the two 'modern' battleships built in the 1920s – *Nelson* and *Rodney* – were very slow by the standards of other navies and arguably obsolete the minute they were launched because they lacked the speed to escort aircraft carriers which were flying off aircraft. Although the Navy had carriers, and in *Hermes* built one of the very first purpose-built vessels, many of its carriers were conversions. It had developed an excellent all-round aircraft carrier design in HMS *Ark Royal* whose eventual loss to a single torpedo hit was due to poor damage control more than poor design, but it had then gone down the path of developing carriers with armoured flight decks, initially seriously reducing the number of aircraft that could be carried. The newly-commissioned carrier *Indomitable* that we have been led to believe should have accompanied *Prince of Wales* and *Repulse* to the Far East, was a belated recognition of the self-created problem of the first armoured flight-deck carriers, and sacrificed some armour in order to carry an increased number of aircraft. In addition, the Royal Navy was conditioned to see its carriers as working in the north Atlantic, and had much to learn from the USA who developed 'deck parking' on aircraft in the more clement conditions of the Pacific in order to increase aircraft carrying capacity. Yet advances in ship design had not been matched by equal attention to aircraft design, and the Royal Navy had no effective carrier-borne fighter or dive bomber in 1939. In fairness, this was a better situation than that which prevailed in Nazi Germany where Goering's Air Ministry provided no aircraft at all for Germany's one and only aircraft carrier, the *Graf Zeppelin*, with the result that the vessel never came into service.

The hope that the new undersea radar ASDIC (or sonar as we would now know it) would solve the threat from submarines proved flawed. It had serious limitations. It could not reveal the depth of a submerged submarine and depth charges had to be set to explode at a given depth. Furthermore, contact with the submarine was lost when the attacking vessel was over the target. Nor at the start of the war did the Royal Navy have the weaponry to launch depth-charges ahead of the attacking craft when it was still being 'held' by ASDIC. Depth charges launched over the stern of an attacking vessel were in effect a guess at where a submarine might be as well as a guess at its depth. Similarly with anti-aircraft defences, the pom-pom was prone to jamming and its capacity to destroy an aircraft often came in to play only after an attacking aircraft had launched its bombs or torpedoes.

Only two KGVs were active in the early war years, and one of those – *Prince of Wales* – was never fully worked up. These 'unsinkable' battleships were to prove in combat that they had serious design flaws, many of which were driven home by the loss of *Prince of Wales*. The Royal Navy had built fleet destroyers in preference to cheap rudimentary escorts, meaning a significant shortfall that took time it could ill afford to fill with the Flower class corvettes. Even more crucial was a shortage of trained men, to the extent that when *Prince of Wales* set sail to meet *Bismarck* nearly eighty per cent of her crew were new, hostilities-only men. The Royal Navy rose to the challenge of training a staggering number of raw recruits but it faced a massive shortage of what in the civilian world would be known as skilled labour. It was not unique in the manpower problems it faced. It was the Canadian Navy that was deemed the worst hit by the need for rapid expansion, leading to the no doubt apocryphal story of an escort group coming across a forlorn Canadian corvette circling round in foul Atlantic weather with the church pennant hoisted to signal a church service taking place on board, and the interrogatory pennant, the flag equivalent of the question mark. When asked to explain the meaning of this novel display, the corvette signalled that it meant, 'Dear God. Where Am I?'

There were other areas where the test of war would show weaknesses in the inter-war Navy. Its capital ships were by and large unable to refuel at sea, a failure that nearly got the *Bismarck* off the hook. Even ships as small as the 6-inch gun light cruisers of the Southampton class were designed to carry three of their own aircraft. Some commentators, including Admiral A.B. Cunningham, believed that the typical gap in the middle of the superstructure and the large, unarmoured aircraft hangar that this requirement demanded, acted as an aiming point for attacking aircraft and made ships so equipped more vulnerable. The lumbering Walrus aircraft carried by surface ships were rendered redundant once ships worked with aircraft carriers, and as ships had virtually to stop dead in the water to pick up the aircraft once it had finished its patrol any ship in a danger zone would steam on and instruct its aircraft to land at the nearest airfield, as happened with Force Z. However, the Japanese were good spotters of the aircraft carried on their cruisers, as shown when they spotted Force Z.

Yet even more serious than any of the above was the impossible vastness of the task facing the Royal Navy. Unlike its German equivalent, it faced multiple demands on its men and its ships. It had to defend the homeland not only against invasion but also against starvation and was always going to have to extend its reach across the Atlantic in convoy escort. This alone was a major task but it had two more major commitments, one to the Mediterranean theatre in the event of war and one to the outposts of Empire in the Far East. Britain in 1939 could find work for three navies.

There were other ominous omens for the mission Tom Phillips was to be sent on. In matters discussed at length later in this work, the supposed 'island fortress' of Singapore was a disaster waiting to happen, a fact that the Japanese almost certainly knew as a result of the loss of the merchant vessel *Automedon*. British intelligence severely underestimated the strength of both Japanese fighting men and their *materiel*. There was no significant tradition of inter-service co-operation and considerable enmity and rivalry between the Navy, Army and RAF, and a working partnership was not really formed until D-Day and the irresistible force of Admiral Sir Bertram Home Ramsay. Singapore and the Far East exemplified the lack of effective co-operation between Army, Navy and Air Force. Historians have tended to focus on the maverick influence of Winston Churchill on naval affairs during the war and perhaps as a result ignored the in-fighting, feuding and rival camps of the senior Admirals of the time. As is so often the case with great institutions, the Royal Navy was fighting its own internal wars at the same time as fighting an external enemy. Human jealousies, bickering and rivalry do not cease simply because a uniform is donned or has more gold braid thrust upon it.

The inter-war period was dominated by the Washington Naval Treaty signed in 1922 and modified by the London Naval Treaty of 1930 and thereafter. The treaty was designed to stop a new naval race and in essence sought to dictate the number and size of capital ships held by the world's major navies and the tonnage of smaller vessels such as cruisers. Britain came out the loser from these treaties. It suffered because its numerical superiority after the First World War hid the fact that most of its battleships were worn out by active service. It suffered also because unlike the German and Japanese navies it tried to stick to the treaty limitations. It suffered too because its ship designers failed to produce designs to match those of foreign navies, and not only because of the various treaty limitations. There were some triumphs, most notably the effective rebuilding of the First World War Queen Elizabeth class which though still too slow were tough and useful ships. The two 1920s battleships *Rodney* and *Nelson* approached an old problem in a novel way by massing engineering and armament, and hence armour, together and astern, producing ungainly ships that bore such a resemblance to Fleet Oilers that the sailors christened them 'Rodnol' and 'Nelsol'. Armed to American standard with an impressive nine 16-inch guns in triple turrets, all three situated forward of the superstructure, they came nowhere near the speed of American, Japanese, French, Italian or German rivals, reaching 23.5 knots on trials as distinct from the industry norm of thirty knots. As for the other new battleships for Britain, the KGVs, they provoked Churchill to rail that it apparently needed three KGVs to take on the *Tirpitz*[2] and as mentioned above, the sinking of *Prince of Wales* was to show up serious weaknesses in all aspects of their design. Here as everywhere else is illustrated the truth that navies can only fight with what they are given, and by 1939 the Royal Navy had not been given enough by world leaders, its own politicians or its own designers. If war is indeed politics carried forward by other means, war can only be carried forward if politicians give those who fight it the necessary means.

There were other problems that were to emerge as the war progressed. Winston Churchill had been First Lord of the Admiralty in the First World War and was to be briefly so again at the start of the Second World War (hence the famous 'Winston is back!' signal from the Admiralty to the fleet on 3 September 1939, the day war broke out), before becoming Prime Minister. Though a soldier by training and service he had, or felt he had, a special affinity to the Royal Navy, choosing among other things to describe himself in letters to the American President as 'Former Naval Person'. If one is a supporter of Churchill he took a close interest in naval affairs. If one is a critic he interfered far too much. Churchill runs more like a rope than a thread through the story of Force Z and its commander. It was Tom Phillips's flagship *Prince of Wales* that took Churchill across the Atlantic to meet Roosevelt in the early years of the war (Churchill flew back, to save time), and he spent longer on board her than he did on any other Royal Navy warship. Churchill had also been friendly with Tom Phillips and was instrumental both in choosing him to command Force Z and insisting that its flagship was *Prince of Wales*.

This was also the first war in which modern communications – the radio – meant far greater contact between the Admiralty at home and the commander out at sea. This caused both problems and resentment in the Norwegian campaign, and badly-worded or misinformed signals were to play a crucial part in the sinking of *Prince of Wales* and *Repulse*.

The Royal Navy came to the Second World War with a significant number of new ideas that showed it had done far more than stand still in the years after 1918. Yet it also came to the war with far fewer new ships than it needed and with some of the new ideas developed in the inter-war years hampered by shortages of cash and resources. One example was radar. The Royal Navy had a significant lead in this area over any other navy in the world and the German and Japanese navies in particular. The sinking of the German *Scharnhorst* by the *Prince of Wales*'s, sister ship *Duke of York* was largely the result of her superior radar fit and radar-controlled gunnery which allowed her to smash *Scharnhorst* despite experiencing serious problems with her main armament. Yet radar in its most advanced form was not fitted to many Royal Navy ships at the start of the war, and when it was the technical back-up and know-how to work the radar and keep it in service was not always there. *Prince of Wales* called specialists in to fix one of her radars before she left Singapore on her last voyage but she sailed without a repair being completed. *Repulse* had only one surface warning radar fitted – on a makeshift mounting that reduced its effectiveness.

Perhaps crucially for *Prince of Wales* and *Repulse,* what the inter-war years had not produced was any foray into inter-service co-operation. One nadir of such 'co-operation' was the escape of the *Scharnhorst, Gneisenau* and *Prince Eugen* from France back to Germany in February 1942 when large numbers of RAF aircraft were flung without proper coordination or fighter support against the well-escorted German ships. In fairness to the RAF, this was a very rare example of fruitful co-operation between the German Navy and the Luftwaffe. The destruction of Force Z has rarely been seen as in any way connected to this lack of any real tradition of inter-service cooperation, yet the need to liaise with the RAF was always going to be crucial to the success or failure of the mission.

With the above list of weaknesses and frailties it might be wondered that the Royal Navy in 1939 was able to fight at all. Rather than being a criticism of the Navy, the list of the problems it faced in 1939 is a huge tribute to the spirit with which it fought the war, and a remarkable illustration of just how much it did achieve and had to overcome to fight as successfully as it did. It was just unfortunate that so many pre-war chickens were to come home to roost in the rigging of *Prince of Wales* and *Repulse* in December 1941.

The Political and Historical Background

There is a body of opinion that sees Japan in the inter-war period as a wanton aggressor. Another camp, although acknowledging its failings, sees it as much put-upon and perhaps even driven to war by the USA. An ally of Britain in the First World War, Japan posed a real problem to both Britain and America in the post- and inter-war years. It seemed clear to many contemporary observers that Japan was intent on building a new order in East Asia. Rather like someone who had decided it owned a house it needed to kick out the existing tenants, in this case the colonial powers including America. It was clearly in Japan's interests to create a large closed area from which it could draw nearly all the raw materials it needed, which in turn would allow it to gain sufficient power to threaten major parts of the British Empire in Australia, New Zealand, Borneo, Malaya and New Guinea and American links with the Philippines, as well as being poised to disrupt the crucial trade in tin and raw rubber, with south-east Asia supplying over two-thirds of both commodities to the west. It was not lost on western commentators that an alliance with Germany and Italy was a logical step on the route to a new position of dominance, which increased the threat to Britain even more. British Chiefs of Staff wrote on 12 November 1937: '... we cannot foresee the time when our defence forces will be strong enough to safeguard our entire territory, trade and vital interests against Germany, Italy and Japan simultaneously.'[3]

An increasingly expansionist Japan, desperate for sources of raw materials, saw a General as its Prime Minister in 1928 and there was growing resentment at what it saw as racist attitudes and western determination to limit its power. In 1936 a strident book written by an officer of the Imperial Japanese Navy, titled *Japan Must Fight Britain*, sold 11,000 copies in translation. It is true that Britain and America might have handled Japan more tactfully, but a major problem in their doing so was Japanese warmongering in Indo-China and the atrocities conducted by their forces. They did nothing to make the voting populace sympathetic towards Japan, and to that extent the hands of the politicians were tied.

As war with Germany grew more and more likely so did the possibility of war with Japan, if only because war in Europe presented a classic opportunist opening. It was not that the British Government did not know of the threat, rather that it simply did not have the naval resources to deal with it or to leave a significant enough deterrent threat in Singapore. Some would argue that it was the First World War that brought an end to the British Empire with an impoverished nation simply unable to afford to defend itself to the four corners of the world.

If economic hardships in the inter-war years meant that the British would be hard-pushed in the event of war to send anything other than a token naval force to the Far East, political necessity demanded that such a force would be sent. To that extent Tom Phillips's fate and that of his men had been sealed before the keel of his flagship touched the water for the first time. Great Britain's Empire was not about waving the flag, colouring the map red or even promulgating the Gospel. It was about trade and raw materials. Following the ruinous cost of the First World War, the greatest recession the world had ever seen and with an ageing industrial plant, Britain was nearly broke, more dependent than ever on its Empire as a cheap market for its goods, not to mention its petrol, rubber and tin. It would have been economic suicide to lose the Empire and political suicide as well. It is difficult for us now to conceive of a country that defined so much of itself through Empire, but that was what it did.

In fact that Empire in the Far East posed two quite different problems. To some countries Britain was simply the occupying power exerting supremacy over an indigenous population by virtue of visible military strength and an ability to keep other nations out of its patch. Singapore was just such a colony which was why its fall was a death-knell to Empire. Never mind that it eventually regained what it had lost: the Japanese had broken not just an army when they took Singapore in 1941, but also the credibility of the colonial rulers and the myth of British invincibility.

Countries such as Australia and New Zealand were different. The majority of their population was not indigenous but could trace their ethnic origins back to the home country of Great Britain. Such countries were not retained as paid-up members of the British Empire by military force and indeed made a significant contribution to Britain's military strength themselves. However, these were countries increasingly maturing into nation states with their own identity and culture. Japanese militarism and expansionism posed a real threat to them – one Australian Prime Minister described his country as being but 'a stone's throw' away from Japan – and they exerted continuous pressure on the British to station a permanent fleet in Singapore. A naval force in Singapore to deter or impress Japan was essential to persuade Australia and New Zealand that London cared and mattered. *Repulse* was actually on its way to Australia when it was recalled to sail with *Prince of Wales* to disrupt Japanese invasion forces. Politics and economics placed two nails in the coffin of Phillips and his men before 1941. A further practical factor was the need for Britain's war effort to be reinforced by Australian troops, something it was made clear would not happen unless Britain in turn showed tangible support for its colonies. There was persistent pressure from the governments of Australia and New Zealand throughout the 1930s for Britain to station a fleet at Singapore. Unable to do so, but desperate to reassure, British policy was to build Singapore up into a major naval base complete with massive defensive 15-inch guns (which contrary to post-war belief did not only point out to sea), and to evolve the 'main fleet to Singapore' plan whereby Singapore would be organized so as to defend itself before the ninety or so days it would take for a 'main fleet' to be mobilized and sail there. All these factors dictated that a naval force would be sent to Singapore if war with Japan threatened, yet politics and economics dictated that the force would be inadequate. The main fleet promise was a cheque written against an account which simply did not have enough funds to meet it.

Certain facts about the decision to send *Prince of Wales* and *Repulse* to Singapore have been well-documented for years, though there may have been a completely different undercurrent of political intrigue that has not been nearly so well documented. If a force was to be sent at all, the Admiralty wished it to be composed of the Royal Navy's old and obsolete 'R' class battleships, watered-down versions of the Queen Elizabeth class and ships that had not been deemed worthy of significant modernization post-war. The Admiralty was overruled, not just by Churchill but by partners in the Coalition such as Anthony Eden, and the new KGV battleship *Prince of Wales* was sent instead, joining the old battle-cruiser *Repulse* (which unlike her sister *Renown* had not received a full modernization) which was already in the Indian Ocean. It was long thought that it was always a part of the plan to add a modern carrier – *Indomitable* which was working up in the West Indies – to the force, something we have been led to believe was only halted by *Indomitable* running aground and suffering damage that ruled her out. The decision to mobilize a force was finalized at a meeting of the War Cabinet scheduled for 12.30pm on Monday, 20 October, 1941. There were no representatives of the Army or the RAF at the meeting, only the Navy. What is clear is that Churchill, and probably Sir Anthony Eden and the Foreign Office, believed that the force would deter Japan from opening hostilities and that Malaya and Singapore were not directly threatened. There may also have been another driving force, discussed below, in the 'Secret Alliance' that was needed to ensure full military support and co-operation from the United States in the Far East.

What caught everybody out was the timing of the Japanese attack, unless one believes in some fairly extreme variants of conspiracy theory that Roosevelt actually concealed the likelihood of the attack from his commanders on the ground at Pearl Harbor in order to draw the United States into a war he deemed inevitable. It seems likely that the British Government was simply unaware of the ambition of Japanese war plans and of the speed and power with which they could execute them. Churchill was obsessed with the idea that *Prince of Wales* would do what the *Tirpitz* was doing in European waters – act as a distant threat and tie down huge resources guarding against it. Even though the KGV battleships were slower than the modern battleships built by other nations such as Italy, Germany and the USA, they were faster than their Japanese equivalent, at least until the massive *Yamato* was commissioned. *Repulse* had been built for speed at the expense of her armament and armour, but together the two ships could reasonably be seen as a fast raiding force. The Admiralty thought the removal of a KGV from northern waters might encourage *Tirpitz* to come out and argued in vain that the situation in the Far East was not comparable. But this was not Japan: the Royal Navy took orders from the Government, rather than issuing orders as the Government.

Britain was not ready for war with Japan in 1940. Many of the reasons lay at doors other than those of the Royal Navy. Yet whatever the detail of the arguments on the day, it seems clear that the Royal Navy in the 1930s itself underestimated the strength of the threat posed by Japan and did not take seriously enough the likelihood that Britain and Japan would go to war. Tom Phillips was one of the most influential senior naval officers in the late 1930s and must therefore take his share of the corporate responsibility for the fact that the Royal Navy in crucial areas was unprepared for war against Japan in 1941. He and the Navy in general could do little about the squeezing of their funding in the 1920s and 1930s, but they could have done more to integrate Intelligence input and access information about the capabilities of Japanese aircraft and ships. In a much earlier era, Queen Elizabeth I was starved for cash for any army or navy but found investment in Walsingham's spy network a very healthy compensation for the lack of cash to pay soldiers and sailors. Quite simply, the Royal Navy did not know enough about its enemy in 1941, down to the fact that one of its best brains, Tom Phillips, in all probability was simply unaware that he was within the range of the torpedo bombers that sank his two ships. Failure of Intelligence was also a failure of the naval establishment for which Phillips must take his share of the responsibility, and one he paid for by the loss of his life.

It is possible that Churchill's insistence on the deterrent effect of Force Z was in fact a cloak for his real motives in sending the ships out, which may have been as an act of good faith designed to draw the United States in to full military co-operation against the Japanese in the Far East. Fierce argument has raged over many aspects of Churchill's thinking before and during the war. It is at least a possible view that Churchill, as a realist, had long given up all hope that Britain could defend its empire in the Far East from within its own resources, and as a result was reliant on the active help of the United States. Deterrent to the Japanese or lure for the Americans came down to the same thing. Force Z was a military force sent on a diplomatic mission that should not have required it to fight, its job being either to deter the Japanese or to cement an alliance with America, or both. The government of the day and the Admiralty not only sent out a force that even by its own inadequate standards was ill-equipped for the job but was also designed to tackle what turned out to be the wrong job altogether. When that job changed its immediate reaction should have been to call the two capital ships back, or at least order them out of danger. As it was, it left them with no option but to take on a fight in which the odds were stacked against them.

Chapter 2

The Loss of *Prince of Wales* and *Repulse*
The Action: The Case Against Tom Phillips

It is a basic truth of human nature that the immediate reaction to a disaster is a massive closing of stable doors, the main feature of which is the overwhelming need to find a culprit or culprits. The racket caused by the stampede to find a scapegoat also helps to drown out the noise of those covering their backs. The sinking of *Prince of Wales* and *Repulse* has been the subject of, or covered in, numerous books. The sheer volume of comment has produced an orthodoxy summed up in what is probably the best – and certainly the most vivid – book about the engagement: '... the facts speak for themselves: two great ships and many good men were lost because one stubborn old sea-dog refused to acknowledge that he had been wrong.'[1]

To varying degrees most historians have tended to load the lion's share of blame for the disaster upon the shoulders of Admiral Sir Tom Phillips. To understand who actually was to blame one obviously has to know details of the action. These details are well publicized and documented and rank alongside the story of the sinking of the *Bismarck* in terms of the coverage they have received and the number of published books devoted to the action. In this chapter I have chosen to describe the events that led to the loss of the ships as briefly as possible and to combine in that account the majority of the negative comments and interpretations made by historians about Tom Phillips and his part in it. In fairness to post-war historians, no single book is as negative towards Phillips as what follows. Even some of those who condemned him most strongly for what happened list some things in his favour, one example being the recognition even by one of his fiercest critics that his calling off of the action was an act requiring considerable moral courage. However, if the charges laid against Tom Phillips are to receive a proper trial it is necessary to list all the charges against him so they can be re-examined, and concentrating the charges against him in one chapter is the most convenient way to do this. What follows is therefore wilfully unorthodox in that it expresses precisely the views that this book intends later to seek to demolish. My final two chapters give an account of the engagement that I believe tells it as it was. As this is a bare historical narrative I have not included here the vivid recollections of survivors from *Prince of Wales* and *Repulse*. I must also apologize that my chosen approach – to make a statement for the prosecution and then hear the case for the defence – does lead to some repetition.

The Preliminaries

Contrary to the Admiralty's wishes the force it was decided to send to Singapore as a deterrent to Japanese aggression did not consist of older 'R' class battleships, but of the new battleship *Prince of Wales*, the old but fast battle-cruiser *Repulse* and the newly-completed carrier *Indomitable*. Unfortunately the latter grounded outside Kingston Harbour on her working-up in the West Indies and was unable to join.

The appointment of fifty-three-year-old Sir Tom Phillips to command the new Eastern 'fleet' – in fact much more of a fast raiding force that could disrupt Japanese invasions – caused considerable consternation in the Navy. Commander in Chief, China, Vice-Admiral Sir Geoffrey Layton, was widely respected for his outstanding service as a submarine captain in the First World War, was an experienced flag officer and was already out in the Far East. Many thought him an obvious candidate for the post given to Phillips who had to be jumped up two ranks to Acting Admiral to give him seniority over Layton:

'Phillips was in many ways a strange choice. He had not seen action since 1917 and had not served at sea since the outbreak of war in 1939. Although he was a staff officer of proven ability, he had never been tested in battle as a fighting admiral and he had strong, if mistaken, views of the ability of a modern battleship to fend off attack by means of gunnery alone.'[2]

Phillips not only lacked relevant experience. He had the reputation as a difficult personality to work with and for being unwilling to listen to anyone who disagreed with him:

> 'Sir Tom Spencer Vaughan Phillips, KCB, aged fifty-three, had been behind a Whitehall desk since 1939 and he had last experienced action in 1917. A very small man – he needed to stand on a box when on the compass platform and was nicknamed "Tom Thumb" – he was notorious for his angry impatience and, more seriously, his strong conviction that aircraft were no match for properly handled warships, arguing that only greater resolution on the ships' commanding officers was needed to defeat the dive-bomber. He had always refused to listen to anyone who tried to persuade him that fighter protection was necessary for all ships operating within reach of enemy bombers.'[3]

Phillips, the son of an Army Colonel, had passed out as one of the top students in his year from the then training school HMS *Britannia*. He served on destroyers in the First World War and as well as staff work in the inter-war years commanded both a destroyer and a cruiser. In 1938 he commanded the destroyer flotillas of the Home Fleet. A collision between HMS *Encounter* and HMS *Furious* earned him a reputation as a bad seaman. At the time of his appointment to the Far East he was Vice Chief of Naval Staff and seen widely in the navy as a desk admiral.

Phillips was notorious for his belief that the well-handled capital ship was more than a match for aircraft: 'Yet it is probable that Phillips's views [on the vulnerability of surface ships to aircraft attack] were considerably more out of touch and mistaken than most of his contemporaries.'[4]

Phillips had acquired a reputation for believing that the well-handled surface vessel was capable of withstanding air attack, an impression confirmed by the Royal Navy's ability to do just that in early clashes with the Italian air force in the Mediterranean:

> 'The battles royal which raged between Tom Phillips and Arthur Harris ... were never-ending ... on one occasion ... Bert Harris exploded,

"One day, Tom, you will be standing on a box on your bridge … and your ship will be smashed to pieces by bombers and torpedo aircraft; as she sinks, your last words will be, 'that was a . . . great mine!'"[5]

Harris, otherwise known as 'Bomber' Harris, was a friend of Phillips and his comments need to be seen in that context rather than as coming from a rival or enemy.

Phillips's appointment over the head of others to command naval forces in the Far East may have had something to do with his friendship with Churchill, with whom he had stayed at Chequers. It was at Churchill's instigation that Phillips had been appointed Vice-Admiral in February 1940, probably in response to pressure from the First Sea Lord, Admiral Sir Dudley Pound, who had found Phillips's work as Vice Chief of Naval Staff invaluable.

Phillips's ships were initially designated Force G but changed to Force Z when they set sail on their final voyage from Singapore. It appears that the Admiralty intended *Prince of Wales* to halt its journey at Cape Town to allow for a review of the situation in the Far East. No document trail has been found that explains why this plan seems to have been dropped, and the ship steamed on to Singapore. The stop in South Africa allowed Phillips to meet Field Marshal Jan Smuts, Prime Minister of South Africa, who commented presciently to Churchill: 'If the Japanese are really nippy there is here an opening for a first-class disaster.'[6]

Phillips refused the chance to acquire a carrier, albeit a lesser one than the *Indomitable*:

'Yet on the very day that the *Prince of Wales* departed from South African waters the veteran carrier *Hermes* had arrived at Simonstown. She carried only fifteen aircraft and her maximum designed speed was a disappointing twenty-five knots. But she had the ability to provide a modicum of seaborne air support in the shape of Swordfish torpedo-bombers and reconnaissance machines. And even a little was better than none.'[7]

Phillips also refused further reinforcement, this time of an older 'R' class battleship that the Admiralty had wished to form the core of the Far Eastern fleet:

> 'For the second time in ten days Phillips had chosen not to strengthen his force with another major warship. *Revenge*, a vintage battleship dating back to 1916, had been berthed in Ceylon when Force G arrived but the Admiral was content to leave her behind when the other ships sailed for Singapore.'[8]

His ships sailed in to Singapore with much fuss being made of *Prince of Wales* and her name and presence released to the media in order to enhance the deterrent effect. To the intense annoyance of her crew, *Repulse* was not named, it being thought that silence on the number and nature of the other ships might serve to exaggerate their power to the Japanese. When news broke and it became clear that the Japanese were invading at points on the Peninsula, Phillips missed a golden opportunity to hit the Japanese invasion fleets when they were at their most vulnerable, and perhaps even change the course of the war:

> 'If the Eastern Fleet had been able to sail immediately the sighting reports were received and had successfully intercepted the Japanese invasion force at sea there is a good chance that the enemy might have been persuaded to turn back, for the stakes were high and the Japanese had not anticipated being discovered quite so early in the game.'[9]

Phillips was 'insufficiently alert to the pressing realities of the strategic situation in which he was involved.'[10] He had gone to Manila to talk to his opposite number Admiral Hart of the US Navy when the alarm was sounded and *Repulse* was on her way to Australia for a flag-waving visit. Phillips returned to Singapore by air and *Repulse* was called back, but the result was that the newly-designated Force Z set sail too late. Philips thus missed a major chance to disrupt the Japanese invasions by a lackadaisical response and failing to act at the start of the attacks when the Japanese were at their most vulnerable: 'During a vital period, neither Phillips nor his capital ships were ready for action.'[11]

8 December

Phillips is in no doubt that Britain is at war with Japan. The night before, his time, the Japanese had bombed Pearl Harbor and Singapore. He has four options: sail out to attach the Japanese invasion barges; retreat to Darwin in Australia; hide out in the islands and attempt to exert the same sense of menace that *Tirpitz* did so effectively in northern waters or stay in Singapore and risk bomb damage. He calls a conference on board his flagship and asks his commanders for their views. The silence is broken by Tennant, the Captain of *Repulse,* who says they have no option but to set sail in search of the enemy. There is no disagreement. An increasingly ill-looking Tom Phillips likens what they are doing to taking the Home Fleet into the Skagerrak without air cover, but says they have no option: 'Still, there is a point where a decision ceases to be courageous and becomes rash, and Phillips's decision came close to that point.'[12]

1735 hrs: Force Z slips its moorings at 1735. In company with the two capital ships are four destroyers – *Electra, Express* and First World War veterans, *Tenedos* and the Australian *Vampire.* Phillips asks for air reconnaissance ahead of his force on 9 December and reconnaissance and fighter cover off Singora on 10 December. As Force Z sails it is flashed a signal from the Changi signal station from Pulford saying, 'Regret fighter protection impossible' – at which Phillips is said to have shrugged his shoulders and said, 'Well, we must get on without it.' A later signal from Admiral Palliser in Singapore, left behind as Phillips's second-in-command to liaise with the other services, states, 'Fighter protection on Wednesday 10th will not, repeat not, be possible'.[13] On receiving the signal informing him that no air cover is available Phillips decides to head to Kota Bharu not Singora, which is 120 miles further north:

> '... although the information available to Phillips gave him no reason to foresee the full extent of the threat from Japanese aircraft, there was clearly *some* danger from air attack, and his decision to continue on

and to hazard two very valuable capital ships, rather than returning to Singapore or sailing elsewhere, was a very risky one.'[14]

'Early on 9 December Phillips was told by signal ... that the Royal Air Force would not be able to provide air cover, because all the airfields in northern Malaya were being evacuated. Nevertheless he elected to press on. Lack of experience, his belief, despite all the evidence of the past two years of war, in the invincibility to capital ships, and his own temperament led to this unwise decision.'[15]

The case against Phillips at this point is that once he knew air cover was not available he should have called off the operation.

9 December
0620hrs: A single lookout on *Vampire* spots a solitary aircraft. After Phillips calls for clarification, the report is disregarded. The plane does not seem to have been Japanese. Phillips is sometimes cited at this point as believing simply what he wanted to hear, choosing to disbelieve a lookout because he was the bearer of bad news: 'Phillips remained unconvinced and, adopting the attitude of an ostrich beset by danger, he metaphorically buried his head in the sand and shrugged off the warning.'[16]

1300hrs: An RAF Catalina appears and signals a Japanese landing at Singora. This is one of the few times that Force Z sees friendly aircraft.

1343hrs: The Japanese submarine *I-65* reports sighting Force Z. At 1550hrs it loses the ships in a squall, finds them again at 1652hrs but finally loses them when a Japanese float plane threatens to attack, and forces it to submerge.

1540hrs: The Japanese Admiral Ozawa receives the sighting report, and orders his cruisers to send out search planes. However, night is coming on.

1700hrs: The weather clears, and Force Z is sighted by a search plane from the cruiser *Kinu*, then by search planes from *Suzuya* and *Kumano*.

1710hrs: *I-65* signals that it has lost contact. Force Z steams on, unaware it has been spotted.

1835hrs: Force Z maintains radio silence, despite knowing it has been spotted. *Tenedos*, short of fuel, is detached and ordered to signal Singapore next day at 0800hrs that Phillips is breaking off the attack against Singora. At this point, Phillips knows that he has been spotted. There is no longer any reason to maintain radio silence, yet still he makes no signal of his intentions to Singapore.

1900hrs: Force Z swings west and increases speed to 26kt, giving the impression it is heading to Singora.

c.2000hrs: Japanese bombers mistake a force of Japanese cruisers and destroyers searching for Force Z for Force Z itself, and preparatory to attacking drop a flare over the cruiser *Chokai*. An attack is just averted. Force Z sees the flare, and immediately turns away.

2015hrs: Under cover of darkness Force Z turns south for the run to Singapore.

2238hrs: The moon rises, and the rain stops.

2302hrs: Palliser signals saying that enemy bombers are undisturbed and could attack Force Z five hours after sighting it. He also says the northern Malayan airfields are becoming untenable and hints that Air Chief Marshal Sir Robert Brooke-Popham may concentrate all air efforts on Singapore.

2335hrs: Palliser signals 'Enemy reported landing at Kuantan'. Kuantan is of vital strategic significance and is in effect on Force Z's way home to Singapore.

2352hrs: The Japanese submarine *I-58* sights Force Z. A faulty tube hatch delays the attack but eventually five torpedoes are launched at *Repulse*. All miss.

10 December

0052hrs: Force Z changes course south-west for Kuantan. No signal is sent to Singapore.

It is generally recognized that Phillips had little alternative other than to divert his passage home via Kuantan. Its capture would allow the Japanese to cut British communications in half and it was of supreme strategic importance. It was also further away from Japanese-held airfields. What is hotly disputed is the suggestion that Admiral Palliser in Singapore should have second-guessed Phillips's response to his signal about Kuantan and arranged for air cover. The official historian writes: 'One cannot but feel that Admiral Phillips's belief that air cover would meet him off Kuantan, when he had given Singapore no hint that he was proceeding there, demanded too high a degree of insight from the officers at the base.'[17]

0211hrs: The Japanese receive *I-58*'s sighting report and order the 22nd Air Flotilla to attack the ships later in the day, giving up on the idea of a surface attack.

0455hrs: Eleven search planes from 22nd Flotilla are dispatched.

0625, 0644, 0650, 0800hrs: Eighty-five Japanese bombers fly off from their land bases.

0630hrs: A solitary plane is sighted. It has been assumed to be Japanese, but there is no reason and no evidence to think it was.

0720hrs: *Prince of Wales* launches its Walrus aircraft to reconnoitre Kuantan. It is directed to land at Singapore, as is *Repulse*'s aircraft, launched later for anti-submarine reconnaissance.

0845hrs: The destroyer *Express* is sent ahead, and reports 'complete peace'. Some versions have it saying it is 'as quiet as a wet Sunday afternoon.'

Force Z dawdles whilst some barges and small craft are investigated. This action has received severe criticism, it being argued that it showed a complete lack of urgency and a failure to realize the seriousness of the situation Force Z found itself in.

0952hrs: Palliser signals reporting fifteen Japanese transports and an aircraft carrier off Singora '... further reinforcing the obvious, that no one in Singapore had expected Force Z to arrive off Kuantan that morning.'[18]

0952hrs: *Tenedos* is sighted and attacked by a Japanese reconnaissance plane searching for Force Z. It launches two bombs, both of which miss.

0955hrs: *Tenedos* reports the attack.

1015hrs: A Japanese Nell search plane piloted by Ensign Hoashi Masane, sights Force Z and sends a report. *Repulse* detects the plane on radar. The Japanese bomber and torpedo squadrons are low on fuel and about to reach their point of no return.

1020hrs: Force Z makes its first visual sighting of the enemy.

1030hrs: *Tenedos* skillfully avoids nine bombs, and sends off signals at 1005, 1020 and 1030hrs. It is unclear whether or not these were received in Singapore. The 0800hr signal, relaying Phillips's calling off of the Singora action, was received in Singapore, '... but there it was only inferred that the Admiral's plans had changed and that he could not have gone as far north as Singora.'[19]

1030hrs: Signal received from *Tenedos*. Phillips orders first-degree readiness for air attack, an increase of speed to twenty-five knots and a change of course for Singapore.

It is at this point that there is the most unity among commentators in condemning Phillips. It is frequently pointed out that had he sent a report to Singapore when he knew he had been spotted the squadron of Brewster Buffaloes reserved for covering Force Z could have been at the scene of the attack by the time the first torpedoes were launched:

'In Singapore, Admiral Palliser had still heard nothing from Admiral Phillips. At some point, perhaps after receiving the signals from the *Tenedos*, Palliser sent Phillips a signal informing him that he had two aircraft and asking for instructions on where to send them. Admiral Palliser received no reply and sent the aircraft off based on what he thought Phillips would do; unfortunately, his guess was not correct, and the aircraft went to the wrong location.'[20]

1115hrs: The Japanese aircraft have been sent out with over an hour and a half between the first and the last squadrons taking to the air, and have been in the air for several hours. The divided force attack as and when it spots the enemy. The first attack is by bombers on *Repulse*. One bomb hits. It detonates against deck armour she had gained in one of her many refits (the bomb, at 550lb, is a relatively light one, as all the available heavy armour-piercing bombs have been allocated to the Pearl Harbor attack), but appalling injuries are caused to some of the crew by burst steam pipes. In the cruel language unlikely to be appreciated by someone skinned alive by superheated steam, her fighting efficiency is not impaired.

Tom Phillips has been heavily criticized for his initial order for the two ships to manoeuvre together by flag signal, which totally confused both ships' fire control systems and masked their anti-aircraft fire. 'Admiral Phillips had made a fiasco out of his first handling of ships in action ...'[21]. He soon realized his mistake, and allowed the ships to operate independently.

1132hrs: Force Z is sighted by sixteen Nells of the Genzen Air Group with the first attack and by nine Nells of Lieutenant Ishihara's squadron, made on *Prince of Wales*. The *Express* signals, 'Planes approaching have torpedoes'. An officer on bridge of *Prince of Wales* says: 'I think they're going to do a torpedo attack.' Admiral Phillips is reported to hear the remark, turn round and say: 'No, they're not. There are no torpedo aircraft about'. Critics have jumped on these words with glee, seeing in them famous last words which sum up the truth about Tom Phillips.

1144hrs: One Nell is discomfited by *Prince of Wales* making a sharp turn to port and switches its attack to *Repulse*, but eight torpedoes are launched at

Prince of Wales. Survivors do not realize that the ship is hit at the stern by two torpedoes, as one hit produces a plume of water but the other is masked by the overhang of the stern. The effect on *Prince of Wales* is catastrophic. The bracket securing the port outboard propeller shaft to the hull shears and the unsecured shaft is allowed to continue revolving too long, tearing a gash in the hull along the length of the shaft. The ship takes on an immediate list of 11.5° to port. With only the two starboard shafts operating, speed drops from 25kt to 16kt. Flooding and shock damage disable much of the ship's electrics and render four of its eight 5.25 anti-aircraft turrets inoperable. The ship also loses her steering. The torpedo hits render *Prince of Wales* useless as a fighting vessel, but do not sink her. Even at this stage, when his ship could have been kept afloat, Phillips does not signal to Singapore for air support.

1145–1152hrs: *Repulse* manages to avoid seven torpedoes and six bombs, acting now as the focus of the Japanese attacks.

1158hrs: *Repulse* signals 'OEAB' (enemy aircraft bombing). In the brief lull that follows the last attacks on *Repulse*, Captain Tennant decides he should manoeuvre closer to *Prince of Wales* to see if he could offer assistance. He is horrified to be told that *Prince of Wales* has made no signal to Singapore, and immediately makes his own. Received in Singapore at 1204hrs, it results in the scrambling of eleven Buffalo fighters of 453 Squadron, at 1225hrs, under the command of Flight-Lieutenant Tim Vigors.

1210hrs: *Prince of Wales* hoists two black balls, the international signal for a ship not under control.

1218hrs: Twenty-six Bettys of the Kanoya Group, low on fuel, spot a seaplane (probably *Repulse*'s Walrus), and then spot Force Z.

1220hrs: *Prince of Wales* signals she has been hit, and asks Singapore to send destroyers. This signal has been seen by many commentators as showing Phillips's contempt for air cover: '… it is incredible that the Admiral should ask for destroyers rather than fighter aircraft.'[22]

1223hrs: A new Japanese attack has three planes break off from attaching *Prince of Wales* and turn on *Repulse* when she has already taken evasive action to comb the tracks of eight torpedoes launched at her from relatively long range. *Repulse* is hit by one torpedo on her torpedo bulge, and shrugs off the hit, continuing to steam at twenty-five knots. *Prince of Wales* is hit by four torpedoes evenly spaced along her hull. The last one on her stern is probably decisive, as it negates all damage control in that area.

c1223hrs: *Repulse*'s luck finally runs out. Caught in a pincer movement, she takes three torpedo hits on her starboard side, one to port. Her rudder is jammed, and she takes on a list of 30° to port.

1225hrs: Eleven Buffalo fighters are scrambled.

1233hrs: *Repulse* sinks.

1243hrs: The final attack takes place on *Prince of Wales.* A 1,100lb bomb hits the cinema flat, causing horrific injuries to the wounded gathered there in large numbers. The explosion also damages uptakes and downtakes to her last operating boiler room. The ship stops.

1252hrs: *Prince of Wales* signals an emergency, and asks Singapore to send tugs.

1305hrs: *Express* comes alongside *Prince of Wales* to take off survivors.

1318hrs: *Prince of Wales* rolls over and sinks. Two Buffaloes arrive, possibly sent by Admiral Palliser, followed by 453 Squadron. The death toll is twenty officers and 307 ratings from *Prince of Wales* and twenty-four officers and 486 ratings from *Repulse.* Neither Admiral Phillips nor Captain Leach of *Prince of Wales* survives, though the most recent commentator believes 'Admiral Phillips had not tried to 'go down with the ship'.'[23] One account has the last words Phillips was heard to utter as, 'I cannot survive this.'[24]

Though Phillips has had his defenders, including Dudley Pound, Phillips's son and a number of those who sailed with him on his last voyage, history has not been kind to Admiral Sir Tom Phillips. Many commentators have focused on his failure to comprehend the reality of air power:

> 'But, throughout the operation, Phillips continued to show a disregard, almost a contempt, for the dangers of any type of air attack. It is possible (and no more than possible, for there is no hard evidence) that Phillips had quarrelled with Brooke-Popham over the potential danger from the air. It is probable that he had made difficulties over co-operating with the RAF on 453 Squadron's provision of standing patrols.'[25]

Others have seen his failings as more concerned with his personality. 'Few [survivors] realized, however, that they had been let down, not by the RAF, but by the dogmatic obstinacy of their admiral.'[26]

Either way, majority opinion holds Phillips to have a very significant responsibility for the disaster:

> 'Apologists for Phillips have claimed that the admiral was upholding the fighting traditions of the Royal Navy by taking Force Z in to the South China Sea to look for Japanese shipping. If Phillips's foray had been well timed and executed that line of argument might have had some validity. But Force Z's final cruise was launched too late to be effective and was riddled with operational mistakes. Two capital ships and many lives were wasted.'[27]

Is it actually true, as stated in the most highly-regarded book written about the sinkings, that '... the facts speak for themselves: two great ships and many good men were lost because one stubborn old sea-dog refused to acknowledge that he had been wrong'[28]?

There is an alternative argument that of all the people involved directly and indirectly in the sinking of *Prince of Wales* and *Repulse*, Admiral Sir Tom Phillips and the crews of his ships were the least responsible of all for the tragedy.

Chapter 3

Admiral Sir Tom Phillips

Tom Spencer Vaughan Phillips was born in 1888, the son of a colonel and the grandson of an admiral. In this he was typical of a relatively small 'pool' of families who at that time supplied a significant number of the officer recruits to both services. He attended the training school *Britannia* (two wooden-hulled training ships moored in the River Dart) and was promoted to Lieutenant at the early age of twenty, largely as a result of his obvious intellectual brilliance. He had obtained the maximum possible number of five 'firsts' in his courses at *Britannia*. Tom Phillips was an extraordinarily intelligent man. Unlike the case in the great public schools of the day, candidates for *Britannia* had to pass demanding examinations in Mathematics (Arithmetic, Geometry and Algebra), English and a number of other subjects to qualify for a place. At the turn of the century of 240 Cadets nominated for entry, sixty failed the medical, 180 took the examination and sixty-three passed. Phillips has been accused of not suffering fools gladly, a feature he shares with most of the successful Admirals of the Second World War, but closer to the mark are probably those who report that he could retreat in to intense periods of concentration in which he blocked out other people, and thus appeared aloof, inconsiderate or rude. Phillips specialized in navigation, was present at the Dardanelles, but was 'marooned' on board HMS *Lancaster* for much of the war in the Far East and missed Jutland. In a varied and successful career he attended the first Royal Naval Staff College course after the war. He became Staff Officer to the notorious firebrand Admiral Sir Roger Keyes in the Mediterranean and proved his capacity to work with difficult people. He had two periods of roughly five years in all commanding destroyer flotillas and as captain of a cruiser, but Admiralty appointments were more common. When Phillips was promoted to Rear Admiral in January 1939 it was as Commodore commanding the Home Fleet Destroyer Flotillas. He was made Deputy Chief of Naval Staff on

1 June 1939 in succession to A.B. Cunningham, the post being renamed Vice Chief of Naval Staff in April 1940. It was from this post that he received a double promotion and became Commander in Chief of the Eastern Fleet, a rather grand name for a very small fleet indeed.

Phillips was no taller than 5ft 2in and most commentators state that he was known as 'Tom Thumb' in the Navy. In fact the name 'Titch' was both more commonly used, and a much more familiar tag in Royal Navy naming slang.

Much of the case against Phillips hinges on one opinion and one feature of his personality that have been repeated so often that they have become an almost unchallenged truth. The first is that he was a die-hard believer in the supremacy of the surface ship over the aircraft, and the second is that he was an arrogant, overbearing and short-tempered man convinced that only he was in the right. One particularly virulent writer sums this all up:

'It may have been to compensate for [his] lack of stature that he developed a rather pugnacious personality, a feature of which was his repeatedly putting forward his conviction that aircraft bombers were no serious opposition for a battleship. It was this haughty disdain for air power and his obsolete philosophy, together with arrogant self-confidence against an opponent that was "only Japanese" that was to lead to the disaster … in fact Phillips had never commanded any sea-going ship … For over twenty years the largest piece of naval equipment under his command had been an Admiralty desk ….'[1]

Phillips, of course, had held sea-going commands and there is no evidence that he dismissed the Japanese any more than the world in general at that time. There is conclusive evidence that by the time Force Z set sail Phillips had fully realized the dangers to surface ships posed by aircraft. A major element in what was undoubtedly a change of mind was the experience of the Royal Navy in the Norwegian Campaign in 1940, but also the experiences of Phillips's own son.

Prior to the lessons of the Norwegian campaign, Phillips was justified in thinking that aircraft did not pose a terminal threat to well-handled surface ships. In the 1920s Colonel 'Billy' Mitchell, head of the United States Air

Force, had sought to prove that battleships were vulnerable to air attack. The evidence for this was a series of staged bombing attacks on the captured First World War German battleship *Ostfriesland*. It took Mitchell's bombers an inordinate amount of time to sink *Ostfriesland*, which was not only an obsolete design with none of the deck armour needed to resist bombing attacks, but was also stationary and incapable of evasive manoeuvring, could put up no defensive fire and had no damage control to stem flooding. When the target eventually sank it was as the result of progressive flooding of precisely the kind that proper damage control should have been able to correct. Mitchell was not so much a loose cannon as a lighted match in a gunpowder store and Phillips was far too intelligent to be convinced by Mitchell's blatant propaganda. The experience of the Royal Navy in the Mediterranean at the start of the war, where ships were continually attacked by Italian aircraft, seemed to confirm that the air threat was containable.

It might be thought that the success of the Taranto raid in November 1940, in which three Italian battleships were sunk by Royal Navy Swordfish torpedo bombers, could have changed Phillips's mind. There was little reason for it to do so because yet again the targets were stationary. What did force a change of mind, or confirmed him in it, was the Norwegian Campaign, where for the first time the Royal Navy came up against the Luftwaffe, and the Stuka dive-bomber in particular. Stukas sank two destroyers, *Gurkha* and *Alfridi*, and the German air threat forced the Royal Navy to withdraw surface ships from the southern theatre of operations. In its turn the Royal Navy notched up the first sinking of a warship by aircraft when it sank the German light cruiser *Königsberg*. It is inconceivable that Phillips did not take on board the lessons of the campaign and his personal and operational closeness to the First Sea Lord, Dudley Pound, means he must have been involved in the decision to withdraw the British surface fleet in the face of the air threat. As a footnote, it is interesting what Phillips said to his fellow officers about leading Force Z out of Singapore: 'It was', he told the officers gathered in his day cabin, like 'taking the Home Fleet into the Skagerrak without air cover. Nevertheless, I feel we have to do something. So, gentlemen, we sail at 1500.'[2]

Skaggerak was the theatre of war over which the Germans had exercised air command in the Norwegian campaign. This is the language of someone with the lessons of the Norwegian campaign still strong in his mind. It is not the language of someone who dismisses the air threat.

Phillips talked about that threat to his son, by then himself serving in the Navy, and mentioned specifically to him the loss of HMS *Southampton* as a reason for his growing concern about the threat from the air. *Southampton* was sunk with the loss of eighty-one men by two bombs from German Stukas, on 11 January 1941. His son remembered his father linking the loss of *Southampton* with the mauling of the carrier *Illustrious* (the carrier from which the Taranto attack had been launched), again by Stukas, on 10 January 1941, but there is even more conclusive evidence to suggest that Phillips learnt in a very direct way of the reality of the threat from the air, evidence so far not noted by any other commentator.

Phillips married relatively late in life and his wife brought two children to their marriage. They had only one child themselves, Tom Vaughan Gerald Phillips (known as Gerald or 'Gerry') though family tradition relates that throughout his life Tom Phillips made no distinction between the three children in terms of his time and affection. Jack, the son of his wife by an earlier marriage, was something of a tearaway and tragically lost his life while an officer in the Sherwood Foresters, at about the time his step-father died. There is an extended series of letters in the family papers dealing with an incident in which Jack appears to have blown up someone's pond with a bomb with his step-father footing the compensation bill apparently without complaint. The letters that survive between father and the younger Gerry Phillips are warm and caring, unusually so in my experience at least of reading correspondence of the time. A typical letter, written as Phillips was on his way to Singapore, is addressed, 'My darling Gerald' and ends with, 'lots of love & I miss seeing you so much, Daddy'.[3] Phillips was not afraid of the 'l' word, and appears very much in touch with his emotions. The warmth and humanity of his letters to his son are touching. On his son's twenty-first birthday he finishes by writing, 'Mummy and I count ourselves very fortunate in you and thank God that you are as you are.'[4] The fact that Phillips wrote whilst actually in charge of Force Z and at the most demanding time of his life, is testimony to his sense of duty as a father and his love. Phillips took an intense interest in his son's naval career. Gerald, or Tom as he became known in later life, was posted to a 'J' class destroyer,

Jackal, which took part in the Crete Campaign and was in close company with the destroyers *Kelly* and *Kashmir* on 23 May 1941 when they were sunk by German aircraft. Phillips was given the most direct confirmation possible from his son that surface ships were vulnerable to air attack, even if (as seems most unlikely) he had not noted the fact from official reports to the Admiralty.

As a cruel footnote, *Jackal* was badly damaged by Italian torpedo-bombers in December 1941 at around the time their Japanese counterparts were killing Tom Phillips. Subsequently, in May 1942, German bombers hit *Jackal* so badly that she eventually had to be scuttled. Lady Phillips heard the news of the ship's loss before she heard that her son had been taken off her as a result of illness shortly before her last voyage, and for a period of time must have feared that her son had gone the same way as her husband.

The most convincing argument of all to suggest that Phillips was fully aware of the air threat was his continual emphasis on its necessity. As is shown below, it was none of his doing that deprived Force Z of its carrier. He was unrelenting in his quest for air cover, and made it absolutely clear to all those with whom he served what importance he placed on it. A note to the RAF to that effect was his last act before Force Z set sail and was delivered by hand from his private car:

> "I'm not sure", he told Captain Bell, his senior aide, "that Pulford realizes the importance I attach to fighter cover over Singora on the tenth. I'm going to write him a letter stressing the point, and asking him to let me know for certain what he can do."[5]

Phillips left his subordinates in no doubt as to the importance he attached to fighter cover: '..the Admiral most certainly did not believe that ships should be subjected to heavy air attack in 1941–2 without the assistance of fighter defence.'[6]

Phillips made one of his most telling comments to the American Admiral Hart in Manila shortly before sailing with Force Z: 'With the Navy what it really comes down to when you are within range, if you have the fighters you can do your job. And if you haven't it is, as at Crete – none too good.'[7]

In May 1941 off Crete the Royal Navy lost three cruisers and six destroyers to air attack, including the two witnessed by his son.

There is therefore no evidence to suggest that, as one commentator has said, '... the most likely explanation for the decision not to break radio silence is that Tom Phillips 'was confident his ships could defend themselves ...'[8]

Even Captain Stephen Roskill, the official naval historian and no supporter of Phillips, admitted privately (though not as far as I know in print) to a leading historian and to Phillips's son that Phillips had changed his mind: 'I have no doubt at all that your father changed his views – certainly by 1941, and perhaps earlier ... By the time your father got to Singapore I am sure he was fully alive to the realities of the air threat.'[9]

One of the most authoritative commenters on the war in the Far East wrote:

'The Tom Phillips of the autumn of 1941 was therefore not the Tom Phillips who had made light of the air danger in the Norwegian campaign a year and a half earlier. He was certainly alive to the threat imposed by dive-bombers and torpedo-bombers in particular. The legend, nevertheless, persists, as legends will, that Phillips had undergone no change in his views on the threat from the air.'[10]

It is therefore simply not true that Phillips believed in December 1941 that surface ships did not need air cover. He probably had believed this at one stage in his career, but his mistake was to leave a legacy of comments from this period that historians intent on a good story simply could not resist. It is time this accusation against Phillips was permanently laid to rest.

There may be a hidden agenda here. It is documented that Phillips disagreed with both 'Bomber' Harris and Churchill about the bombing of Germany. Phillips was not the type of man to disclose the reasons for his disagreement with the country's wartime leader and one of its most powerful military leaders; to do so would have been against every code of conduct he followed, and be deemed disloyal. It has been assumed that the arguments over the bombing of civilian targets were largely to do with Phillips's dismissal of air power, and possibly even a rather territorial feeling that the resources expended on Bomber Command should have been more properly expended on the Royal Navy. It is more likely that Phillips realized that victory against the U-boats, arguably the major concern of his boss and confidante, Dudley Pound, and Pound's greatest victory, could have been achieved far more quickly if the RAF's long-range bombers had their course reversed and were sent out over the Atlantic. To defeat the submarine menace a bomber did not have to drop a bomb on a U-boat. It merely had to force it to submerge, where the Type 1XB boat, the most successful in the war, had a top speed of 7.3 knots and a range of less than seventy miles at four knots underwater. Criticism of the civilian bombing campaign has centred on its morality and its strategic effectiveness. It should more properly focus on whether or not that campaign was the most horrendous example of misuse of military resources in the war, and Phillips's brain was exactly the kind that would focus on a truth such as this. Churchill and Harris survived the war to fight their corner. Phillips has never had the chance to tell us what his corner was. We do know that he was a brilliant and perceptive man who was quite capable of seeing the wood for the trees. He argued for the sending of modern fighters, and tanks, to Singapore and had he been listened to the defence of Singapore would have turned out to be a very different story. He predicted the useless carnage of the Royal Navy's involvement in the campaign for Crete and Greece.

As for Phillips's abrasive personality, a close examination of the historical record shows a very different picture of him from the one often presented. Certainly he did not suffer fools gladly, could have a sharp tongue and be short-tempered: 'As VCNS his great qualities were rather marred by ill health, which combined with the strain and anxiety of his office, made him over domineering and intolerant, and increased the strain under which we all worked.'[11]

What has not to my knowledge been published before is that Phillips suffered from a hereditary bone disease, Multiple Epiphysial Dysplasia, which was almost certainly responsible for his stature. Something of a cross between rickets and chronic arthritis, it arrests bone growth in what would normally be its last spurt in teenage years and can cause the sufferer constant discomfort and occasional sharp pain. The illness may well have contributed to a lack of patience and some short temperedness from Phillips, but there is no evidence that it ever affected his judgment or intelligence.

Furthermore, obstinacy and even obduracy need to be placed in context. Successful military leaders do not achieve what they do by being nice. British Admirals of the Second World War were frequently 'strong-willed'. Certainly, there were Admirals such as Robert Burnett who had been a PE instructor and used to slap his bottom saying that was where his brains were. The hail-fellow-well-met approach could and did work in certain circumstances and with certain people. Unfortunately, and in private, rather a lot of those he served with tended to agree with Burnett about where his brains were. More typical was Admiral Sir Bertram Home Ramsay. His obstinacy and unwillingness to back down when he thought he was right led to him being placed on the retired list before the war. Only brought off it because of the chronic manpower shortage at all levels in the Royal Navy in 1939, it was Ramsay who master-minded the Dunkirk evacuation, saving countless lives by arguing almost as a lone voice that beaching craft on the sands of Dunkirk so as to allow them to evacuate troops who would never have made it beyond the shallows would not break the ships' backs. He then went on to plan, brilliantly, the whole naval side of the D-Day landings. Even his ever-loyal widow penciled in to some of the family papers the comment: 'Reflection 1967. Maybe BHR [Bertram Home Ramsay] was too intolerant and opinionated at times!'[12]

Arguably the most famous Admiral of the war, A.B. Cunningham, was a charismatic and heroic leader at sea who drove his staff mad on shore and dismissed any request that cost money as 'Too velvet-arsed and Rolls Royce for me!' As part of research for an earlier book I talked to Admiral Vian's driver, who if he had given permission for what he knew to be published would have been responsible for posterity taking a rather different view of Vian. He said to me, in admittedly admiring tones: 'Now that Vian … if his mother'd been standing in front of the car stopping 'im from doin' what 'e wanted 'e'd have run her over no problem.' Willingness to be knocked over easily was not a recipe for success at the top of the Royal Navy in the Second World War, and doing so to one's mother apparently acceptable to at least one Admiral and a cause of some admiration from his driver.

A number of those who have written on Phillips's personality would possibly see this as a description of him: 'Always serious-minded and a hard taskmaster – a dedicated "slave driver" as one of his officers described him – he did not tolerate fools gladly and his wrath when roused was truly devastating. He was a man of steel, who did not bend easily.'[13]

In fact it described Admiral Sir Roger Backhouse, a brilliant officer who was preferred above Pound for the post of First Sea Lord in 1938. Like Pound, Backhouse in effect worked himself to death though, like Pound, his official cause of death in 1939 was a brain tumour. If one looks at his contemporaries, on a Richter scale of pugnacity Phillips sits only about halfway down. Armed forces can forgive their leaders many things: weakness and inability to fight one's corner are not among them.

It also needs to be remembered who Phillips worked alongside. Admiral Dudley Pound, First Sea Lord for the first four years of the war, took over after Backhouse's death. He was a comparatively mild-mannered man and it is uncertain how long he was growing the brain tumour that was to kill him, along with two strokes, in 1943. Dudley Pound's temperament allowed him to duck and weave in the face of some of Churchill's wilder moments and still salvage something for the Navy. It also had its weaknesses. His opposition to the sending out of *Prince of Wales* and *Repulse* did not alter Churchill's decision. Phillips's more acerbic and assertive personality may have been a very necessary counterbalance to his superior at the time, even something of a successful double act, though it would not recommend him to those who thought they had got their way with Pound and then ran up against Phillips.

Yet with all this, Phillips's personality as it is often described bears little or no resemblance to the person described by many of his contemporaries. This applies from the top downwards. A.V. Alexander, the Labour First Lord of the Admiralty, wrote of him:

'I cannot put into words my sense of the loss sustained by the Royal Navy, the nation, and all of us here who counted your distinguished husband as loyal colleague and personal friend. I always, through difficult days last year, found in him a constant support and encouragement, not only because of his knowledge and resource [sic] but the impression one always got of complete reliability.'[14] …

'The First Lord, Alexander, considered him "a great leader, a great Christian, a man of perhaps as high a standard of conduct as it would be possible to find anywhere in society."'[15]

Pound was equally unstinting in his praise: 'He had such a wonderful combination of brilliance, soundness of judgment and drive and he was head and shoulders above his contemporaries .... His friends are legion, both in and out of the Service ...'[16]

Phillips had a capacity to get on with people in other navies and other nations, and win their respect:

> '...The years he had spent in the corridors of power had made Tom Phillips very much aware of ... political considerations and was, indeed, one of the more cogent reasons why he had been picked to command the Eastern Fleet.'[17]

> '...Phillips had a knack of getting along well with others outside the Navy: the Services, civil servants, diplomats, and particularly Foreign Naval officers.'[18]

It certainly worked. General Smuts was no easy person to win over. His response to his meeting with Phillips was: 'Admiral Tom Phillips has been here for most useful talks ... He has much impressed me and appears admirable choice for most important position.'[19]

He seems to have impressed the American Admiral Hart every bit as much. Hart said he was, 'as good an Englishman to work with as I have had for some time.'[20] Hart wrote in his diary for 5 December 1941:

> '...I had pictured a big, burly personable magnetic sort. He's a bare 5ft. two and decidedly the intellectual type – good stuff, all right, and has a first-class brain ... We were quite frank with each other, laid our cards down, and wore no gloves ... Well I acquired considerable respect for Phillips...'[21]

Even more importantly, he persuaded Admiral Hart to station four destroyers in Singapore, which were actually on their way there when Force Z was sunk. There was more than military good sense in these reinforcements. Had they been in Singapore and the Japanese attacked (and of course while Phillips was negotiating the deal no one knew about the impending attack on

Pearl Harbor), their presence might have drawn the United States into the war without an attack on America's main base. This and the concept of the 'Secret Alliance' are discussed below, but in any event politics played a major part in the decision to send Phillips and Force Z to Singapore, and politics would have inevitably played a large part in the success of their mission had the Japanese not decided to start the war when they did. Phillips was no wheeler-dealer politician, but he was an extraordinarily intelligent and perceptive naval officer who could deeply impress those who were.

His reputation as a desk Admiral rather than a fighting one also seems to be unsound. Certainly he had not had the seagoing experience in 1941 of some of his contemporaries, but those who criticize him often overlook that he took Force Z out in enemy-infested waters, evaded the minefields the Japanese had laid to trap him, dodged submarines and used prevailing bad weather so skillfully that it was only at the last minute, and when his assailants were at their last gasp, that he was spotted. It ended in disaster but right until the last minute the voyage of Force Z was handled in the best fighting traditions of the Royal Navy and with considerable tactical skill.

It was not merely the good and the grand who thought highly of Phillips. There are too many letters on this theme to do justice to in the Phillips papers. A sampling would include:

'To me the Admiral was the very embodiment of the great English leader. I loved and admired him more than I can ever explain on paper.'[22]

Phillips was capable of inspiring the greatest loyalty, as the widow of one of those officers lost with him shows: 'My husband was serving as Flag Lieutenant to your husband, and I had two letters from him this week posted in Cape Town, saying that he had never had respect and admiration for anyone as he had for "his Admiral" and that he was a really great man. My husband did not give his heart freely and I feel much comforted to feel that he lost his life serving such a man. It seems the only spark of brightness in what is a very sad time to me.'[23]

Another contemporary wrote: 'Of all the naval officers with whom I have had the honour of being associated in the last twenty years, there is none who has commanded a higher share of my regard for his character his professional brilliance and the great charm of his personality ...'[24]

Others comment on his 'kindness and thoughtfulness'[25] and 'lovable personality'[26]. In one of the best epitaphs an officer could ever receive, a correspondent writes, 'I have never served under a better officer.'[27] His Flag Lieutenant in HMS *Aurora* wrote of Phillips's 'infinite kindness and patience.'[28]

Phillips also commanded great loyalty from those far junior to him. A Lieutenant wrote to Churchill after his 'magnificent defence' of 'this great little man', the letter marked in an unknown hand, 'Prime Minister to see':

'Our first meeting was not a happy one. New to the Admiralty and its working, and warned against the admission of unauthorized intruders, my first night watch alone in your old War Room was disturbed in the early hours of the morning by a diminutive figure in pyjamas. I asked who it was. VCNS [Vice Chief Naval Staff] was the answer. "That means nothing to me. Have you a Basement Pass?" persisted I in my ignorance. A silence that could be felt, followed by and [sic] explosive but none the less amused "Good God" made me realize how greatly I had blundered. Later contacts outside the War Room were happier, for we discovered a mutual interest in old prints, and I came to know him well. I shall always remember his unbounded loyalty to yourself and the First Sea Lord, his quiet authority and unsparing sense of duty, his rare quality as a leader, his utter devotion to the Service.'[29]

One of the letters Phillips wrote to a friend on his way to Singapore tells of him noting a Midshipman reading a John Buchan novel, one of the friend's favourite authors. It is a throwaway line, but interesting to note that an Admiral with a newly-acquired and burdensome command had the time to note what a Midshipman was reading.

One of the officers who was there at the death, and one of the last to see Phillips alive, wrote to his widow: 'All of us who have been with him for so many years felt like spaniels who had lost their master.'[30]

The Phillips papers are full of tributes. A former Petty Officer writes in pencil:

'Will you please accept your Ladyship our heartfelt sympathy you have sustained by the loss in action of your husband. The Navy has lost a good Father as the lads always named him who served in and under his Command. Rose and my son joins with me in this sincerity in this sudden bereavement.'[31]

Of all the tributes paid to Phillips, two stand out to me. Captain Tennant of *Repulse*, who has been as universally praised for his actions as Phillips has been damned for his, might be expected if anyone did to have a low opinion of Phillips. In a very telling letter to Lady Phillips, he wrote:

'I saw your husband several times before 10 December. It was very good to see him again and he was very charming & good to work with. I so entirely agreed with his plans for operations and told him so. Please accept my deepest sympathy.'[32]

'Charming and good to work with?' Why is it that so many historians have chosen to blot comments such as this out of the record? There is no mention in the many books that comment on Phillips of the man who arranged for a copious supply of make-up to be left in his day cabin when it was used on board ship as the Ladies Withdrawing Room for social functions, as female guests often failed to realize how hot it became on a warship and the consequent effects on their make-up.[33] Nor is Phillips seen as the type of man whose widow received a letter of condolence from a small boy who worshipped Phillips ever since the man had taken the trouble to show him round his ship: 'I am sorry that Admiral Sir Tom Philips [sic] went down on the *Prince of Wales* I can remember the time when he took me over the *Aurora*. I came home from school yesterday.'[34]

There is also in the Phillips papers a letter from, of all people, the owner of Young's Motor Stores, Tooting Bec Road, London. Phillips loved tinkering with cars. He was the proud owner of registration number A 74, which the family kept until after the war, and when appointed Commander in Chief he wrote: 'This chapter is going to be very difficult for my personal life, because as C in C I am so much in the limelight I can't go and play about with bits of cars & all the other wrong things I like to do.'[35]

Clearly he was not only known as a customer at Young's Motor Stores, but well remembered. The owner wrote: 'I shall remember him as a Gentleman with a strong yet charming personality, with eyes that twinkled but spoke volumes, who could find great pleasure in the simplest things of life – in brief – a Very Gallant English Gentleman. Would it be asking too much of you to let me have some very small memento of his, say a button off his Uniform? If granted, I would greatly treasure it as a remembrance.'[36]

Whatever else he may have been, Phillips was not the bullying martinet he has sometimes been portrayed as. Perhaps one answer as to why this vision of him has persisted is given by this comment: 'His manner of being completely absorbed in a thought or matter, as he had a great power of concentration, at times gave the impression of not caring for others, and this was sometimes misconstrued as being rude, or indifferent to his subordinates.'[37]

Admiral Sir Tom Phillips was a brilliant, dedicated and ferociously hard-working Naval officer with a capacity to see the truth, however unpopular that was, and say so. If he occasionally criticized junior officers, he was prepared to do the same to Churchill. He was also a far richer, warmer and more interesting personality than many historians have been willing to admit. It is often said that history is written by the victors. So it is, but perhaps for only a hundred years or so after the victory. The days are gone when any book on the naval history of the Second World War was incomplete without the approval of Lord Cunningham of Hyndhope, and it was treason to criticize Churchill. It suited many of those who survived the debacle of the loss of *Prince of Wales* and *Repulse* to see the commander of Force Z as a personality equally as flawed as the mission in which he lost his life.

As a footnote, occasional references to Phillips's health, his pale complexion and the fact that he kept picking at his desk drawer and popping whatever he took out of it into his mouth have linked this to a suggestion that he took amphetamines or other drugs. In fact if he had an addiction at all it was to 'Peter's' chocolate, which after his death was found in large quantities both in his desk and even his safe. Reportedly his fondness of chocolate was something he was reluctant to admit in case it was seen as making him seem weak in the macho world in which he lived and worked.

There is one final question that has not yet been answered. Did Tom Phillips choose to 'go down with the ship'? We know that he remained in a relatively dangerous part of the vessel as it was about to sink, despite taking the time to order his staff to safety. There are survivors' comments that have Phillips and Leach, the Captain of *Prince of Wales*, walking down the side of the ship as it capsized. His last words were reported as, 'I cannot survive this.' Leach's body was found face down in the water, floating by virtue of a half-inflated life jacket, and when it was turned over in a vain hope of finding life it was noted he showed the signs of someone who had been dragged underwater and drowned before he could make the surface. A survivor recollects seeing Phillips face down in the water, whereupon he started to swim towards him in order to take off a signet ring or similar from the body to give to the family, but gave up the idea as being too macabre. The likelihood is that Phillips was dragged down by the sinking hull and drowned before his life jacket could bring him to the surface. However, this raises the question as to how hard Phillips fought to regain the surface. My own, entirely personal, conclusion is that Tom Phillips chose neither to live nor die, but rather as a man whose judgment of himself would be far harsher even than that of history, did not choose to fight death when it came.

Phillips was a man of honour who in his own mind could probably not have survived the gambler's loss that he had sustained, despite the fact that all war is a gamble and this one, the sailing of Force Z, was actually less of a risk than has often been supposed, and where the principle quality Phillips lacked was the one most prized by Napoleon in his Generals – luck. Yet his worst bad fortune was to die and so be prevented from giving his version of events as a counter to all those who were so willing to do so in order to cover their backs. Admiral Sir Tom Phillips lost his reputation in part because so many of those who survived him were so assiduous in protecting their own.

Chapter 4

Singapore and Signals

Singapore

The majority of books written about the sinking of *Prince of Wales* and *Repulse* acknowledge that the loss of the two ships was part of the wider defeat of British power and influence in the Far East, culminating in the loss of Singapore itself. The fact that Force Z was always seen and constituted as a separate command, with the navy working independently of the control of both the Army and the RAF in Singapore, has tended to mean that the loss of Force Z is talked and written about in many respects as a stand-alone incident, a harbinger of the defeat that was to come to Singapore but not linked by umbilical cord to Singapore itself. It is an easy mistake to make. A battleship at sea looks like the classic island unto itself, a self-contained world operating independently from the land. The truth is that any warship functions only whilst it is being stored, fuelled, maintained and repaired from shore. The nuclear submarine is the first and only warship able to function effectively and healthily for long periods without calling in to a port. A further truth about *Prince of Wales* and *Repulse* is that their survival hinged on two vital inputs from Singapore – intelligence reports and communications. It was to play a major role in the sinking of the two ships in that both these areas were not being managed to the necessary level of efficiency in Singapore's command structure. Of course the two ships were 'independent' in the sense that, subject to orders and the range of his ships, Tom Phillips could take them wherever he wished. Yet at the same time they were acting as one of the major arms of the military effort Singapore could exert against a Japanese attack. If they were not the only such arm, the weakness of the RAF in Singapore made them almost such. Inevitably, these two arms were not immune from the illness affecting the main body back at Singapore.

The Admiralty did not seek to deny the possibility of war against Japan in the inter-war years, though it underestimated the probability. It took a decision to a question to which there was no perfect answer in stating that there were too many potential threats facing Britain to allow the Royal Navy to station capital ships in Singapore in peacetime. The plan was for such vessels to be rushed there in the event of war – the so-called idea of a 'main fleet to Singapore' – in the meantime trusting to its land defences and air cover. The time for which Singapore would have to defend itself alone varied, with ninety days the most likely option. This was the theory. In practice there never was going to be the money available in 1930s Britain to make Singapore anything like the impregnable fortress Britain wished its own and other people to think it was, nor was the Royal Navy ever likely to have enough ships at its disposal to send a significant fleet so far away from the home theatre of operations, where the very survival of England as an independent nation would be at stake. The 'main fleet' idea was little more than spin to calm down Australia in particular or to attract the United States to using Singapore as a main base. It was thought, not without reason, that it would help deter Japanese aggression if Britain knowingly talked up the 'impregnable fortress' concept of Singapore. Such puffing of reality cost nothing. Unfortunately, it was a bluff that the loss of confidential papers sent for Singapore on the steamship *Automedon* blew apart, and a bluff that as a result the Japanese felt able to call.

Ironically, the great British naval base at Singapore commenced in 1921 but not finally completed until 1938, exacerbated tensions. Seen as defensive by the British, it was violently objected to as an offensive weapon by the Japanese and seen as a sword pointed at the Japanese heart. If so, it was a remarkably blunt one. Threat evaluations had suggested the risk to Singapore came from sea-based bombardment and assault, and that its back door of thick Malay jungle was impassable to any significant number of land forces. It is a common misconception that most of its heavy guns pointed only out to sea. This was not true. What was true, and crucial in Singapore's inability to defend itself, is that the available ammunition for these guns were armour-piercing shells designed for use against ships but hopeless for use against ground troops, where high-explosive shells were essential. Armour-piercing rounds simply buried themselves in the ground which then contained much of the explosion. In 1937 Major-General Dobbie, in overall command in Malaya, realized how vulnerable Singapore was, but it was too late, and only paltry sums were spent on reinforcing the northern perimeter, or the east where landings might take place. Similarly, the Singapore Defence Conference held in 1940 recognized that with Japanese expansion into Indo-China the main threat to Singapore was possibly to come from the north and ground troops, and asked for 582 modern aircraft to act as Singapore's main defence until the Royal Navy arrived. The majority of these were never sent. Something that did happen was a new command structure – after all, it was a cheap option and might make those involved feel that at least something was being done. The importance being placed on air cover as Singapore's main defence until naval reinforcement could arrive is illustrated by the appointment of Air Chief Marshal Sir Robert Brooke-Popham as overall Commander in Chief of Far East Forces. He was due for routine replacement when hostilities broke out. His appointment should not be seen as a belated realization on the part of the powers that be that air power was now the dominant force. Rather, it was the only option left after it had been accepted that the dominant force, sea power, would be late in coming.

We now know that Singapore was a disaster waiting to happen. One area was a lack of clarity over what would actually be defended in the event of hostilities – the Malayan Peninsula or parts of it, or just Singapore itself. Operation Matador was a plan for a pre-emptive invasion of southern Thailand, produced by the military in part because they knew the real weaknesses of Singapore's defences. In the event it was never initiated as the result of a cocktail of fear of breaching Thai neutrality, lack of resources and the speed of the Japanese advance overwhelming the decision-making process.

Another serious weakness was air defence. British aircraft:

'... operated from the airfields recently carved out of the Malayan jungle – Alor Star, Kota Bharu, Gong Kedah, Kuantan and the others – with much difficulty. Although the C in C Far East, Brooke-Popham, had lain down that defence of the airfields was to take precedence over everything else except the naval base itself, Pulford had received few weapons for this purpose, and the anti-aircraft and ground defences of all the airfields were quite inadequate to meet determined attack. The real facts of the air situation in Singapore ... were far worse even than Phillips had judged from the figures he had been shown before his departure. In the event of serious attack, Malaya possessed no measurable air defence at all.'[1]

Phillips quite rightly distrusted the Brewster Buffalo fighters that were the stalwart of Singapore's air defence (*see Chapter 8*) and had argued to the Chiefs of Staff on 25 April 1941 for both Hurricane fighters and tanks to be sent to Singapore, further testimony that this 'desk' Admiral was alive to the demands and reality of actual combat. Both tanks and fighters were available but were sent instead to Russia. It is doubtful that they had a major impact on the military fortunes of the Russians, but beyond doubt that they could have had a major impact on the battle for Singapore. The failure to equip Singapore stretched even to the supply of the Boys Anti-Tank Rifle. A British design that came into service in 1937, it was ineffective against the thickness of armour found in most German tanks and was superseded by the bazooka, but would have been effective against the Japanese light tanks used in the assault on Singapore, which had armour of 16mm thickness against the 20mm the Boys Rifle was designed to penetrate. Two hundred were sent to Russia before the Japanese invaded, none to Singapore.

However, it is only selected parts of the military provision for the defence of Singapore that relate to the sinking of Force Z. Air cover is so important a part of this that it is dealt with below in a separate chapter. It is perhaps worth stating that Phillips was aware of the chaos that was Singapore – he wished to go out there in the summer of 1941 to try and sort some of that chaos out – but he was overruled.[2] He was not, of course, in any way responsible for the lamentable state of its defences. The fact that as a result of the sinking of the merchant ship *Automedon* the Japanese knew of Singapore's weakness is also dealt with in a later chapter.

Recent research has focused on an area that may have contributed significantly to the loss of the ships. Inter-service rivalry was intense at Singapore, co-operation between the Army, Navy and RAF notable by its absence. It was to take a very long while indeed for Britain to learn how to manage combined operations, and it had certainly not done so by the time hostilities hit Singapore. In some respects Tom Phillips was to prove as much a victim of the petty rivalries, jealousies and failure to talk to each other that beset the Army, Navy and RAF in Singapore, as he was a victim of the Japanese. We have already seen how the RAF ignored the views of the Army in positioning its airfields. Partly as an attempt to solve some of these problems, and prior to the opening of hostilities, a new underground command building was being opened, known as the 'Battlebox'. 'Thus the defences of Malaya were split between the naval base and Sime Road, with the Battlebox becoming a third command centre to take charge of the Singapore aspect of the operations.'[3]

Despite the existence of separate command centres, initially they could only communicate out through the domestic telephone system. The problem was not limited to an actual geographical separation of the command bases, or a situation that leads one to wonder sometimes if the various services did not see each other, and not the Japanese, as the enemy. It had further ramifications:

'In practice, however, the lack of skilled manpower to run two almost identical war rooms and insufficient clarity among field commanders and officers in Malaya meant that many operational calls and signals were still being routed to Fort Canning which then had to be re-routed to Sime Road. As a result, the decentralized war rooms created greater confusion and down time as it took ages for ground intelligence and reports to filter up and be represented on duplicate situation charts...'[4]

The picture that emerges is one of chaos, and chaos in particular linked to ineffective communication. This becomes historically significant because signals, or the lack of them, are at the heart of the story of the sinking of the two ships. To understand why signals failures may have made a major contribution to the disaster one needs to understand also that Signals Intelligence was a relatively new phenomenon for the Singapore military. The Far East Combined Bureau (FECB) or Centre for Operational Intelligence and Signals (COIS) was housed at the naval base, but intended to serve all three services, and intercepted much Japanese traffic. They were helped by the Japanese tendency to chatter over the radio, and to send messages in 'clear' rather than in code. However, FECB and COIS suffered from insufficient manpower, and were not accepted by the top brass: '… the military commanders in Southeast Asia had little faith in these new forms of intelligence gathering and disregarded much of the contents of the daily situation reports.'[5]

In one of the more bizarre episodes in this story, staff at FECB could see *Prince of Wales* and *Repulse* out of their office window. Yet the only information they received about the sailing of Force Z was from their own eyes, when they came in to work and saw the empty berths. It was the reports of landings that came from FECB that had caused the ships to be scrambled, yet no-one thought to tell the originators of the mission that it was happening.

It appears that FECB intercepted Japanese signals stating that British capital ships had been sighted off Kuantan. One can only agree with the historian of military Singapore when he writes:

'Not keeping the FECB informed about ongoing operations meant that the signal intelligence officers were not overly concerned about a Japanese report in P/L (plain language) on 10 December, which said British capital ships were sighted at a specific position off Kuantan. Although Malaya Command and the Admiralty were informed immediately, no one at these headquarters had pieced the two together and realized that Japanese fighters had obviously spotted Force Z and were now planning to destroy it. Had the FECB been kept in the loop, it is highly likely that defensive air cover would have been sent sooner to aid the capital ships, rather than only after receiving distress calls from the floundering vessels.'[6]

In other words, British High Command in Singapore knew Force Z had been sighted off Kuantan *in time for such fighter cover as there was to be sent out to cover the ships* but no action was taken. If this is true – and the fact of so many records being lost when Singapore fell means that some issues can never be fully proven to the most exacting historical standards – it was an act of criminal negligence.

This also relates to the suggestion examined in more detail below that Singapore or the Admiralty actually knew of the existence of Japanese torpedo-bombers, this providing an explanation as to why the First Sea Lord sent a signal to Phillips shortly before Force Z was sunk warning him to be on his guard against a Taranto-like attack on his ships in Singapore.

Signals procedures at Singapore raise another issue. It is sometimes argued that Admiral Palliser in Singapore had no reason to think Force Z would head for Kuantan following his signal of landings there. What is overlooked is that *Tenedos*, detached by Phillips because of its lack of endurance, did send the signal Phillips had given it confirming his return to Singapore and asking for additional destroyers to screen Force Z against Japanese submarines on the run-in to Singapore. It is inconceivable that Palliser did not have enough information to allow him to know at least roughly where Force Z was, or at the very least to arrange air cover as a contingency plan.

> 'On the night before *Prince of Wales* was sunk, Phillips told me categorically, however, that he was quite convinced that in the event, fighter cover would be provided, and that his Chief of Staff, whom he had left behind on shore at Singapore, would arrange this… It seemed incredible to him that his Chief of Staff would not appreciate that he had gone to Kuantan in answer to the signal reporting the landings.'[7]

However, of equal interest are the signals *Tenedos* sent out saying she was under attack from Japanese aircraft. These do not appear to have been received in Singapore.

One conclusion, and the one most widely adopted by historians, is that the signals were indeed not received. Technologically such a thing is possible, even though they were picked up by *Prince of Wales*, and as far away as the Indian Ocean. If the signals had been received, air cover would surely have been sent over Kuantan. Phillips had no reason to think that the *Tenedos* signal had not been received in Singapore, and in the belief that it had, saw no need to break radio silence and give away his exact position, on the basis that Singapore had all the information it needed. A further factor which historians have tended to ignore is that if, as he had been told, a major landing was taking place at Kuantan, it would be reasonable to suppose that every available aircraft in Singapore would have been scrambled to be there.

Given the chaos that was Singapore's command structure, it has to be a possibility that the *Tenedos* signal was in fact received but either not communicated upwards or not acted on when it was. The latter appears to have been the case with the intercept revealing Force Z had been sighted. Yet the finger of suspicion has to point at Admiral Palliser. He had been left behind in Singapore to act as Tom Phillips's eyes and ears and to act as the liaison officer for Force Z. Even on the undeniable evidence, history has let him off lightly. He sent a signal to Phillips stating categorically that air cover would not be available, and repeating the word 'not' so that there could be no misunderstanding, yet failed to either cancel this earlier message or tell Phillips that air cover was in fact available. He sent a further signal which clearly implied that such fighters as there were, were being held back for the defence of Singapore. From a host of reports of Japanese activity he chose to send a signal stating clearly that the Japanese were landing at Kuantan which happened to be a completely false report. It is sometimes said that Palliser might have been unaware of the fact that the report was false. It might equally be said that there is no record of him trying to find out either way. He apparently failed to realize that his signal would leave Phillips with no option but to head for Kuantan, and failed to organize air cover for that eventuality.

If one believes Air Vice-Marshal Pulford, no one told him and the RAF where Force Z was; unfortunately, Pulford was ordered to leave Singapore shortly before it fell in a launch that was sunk by Japanese forces. Pulford died of starvation on the island on which he was stranded. Historians have universally assumed that Tom Phillips was to blame for the fact that Pulford claimed not to know the whereabouts of Force Z. It may well be that the brunt of the blame lay with Pulford's own pilots.

As we have seen above, one of the staunchest defenders of Phillips, Commander Michael Goodenough, blamed Palliser for the disaster and carried a campaign for blame thus to be apportioned to the writer of the official naval history of the war: 'I am sure that Phillips's attitude was that he believed his Chief of Staff would arrange the provision of a fighter defence.

It seemed incredible to him that his Chief of Staff would not appreciate that he had gone to Kuantan in answer to the signal reporting the landing.'[8]

Goodenough also referred to the 'muddle' in Singapore, a clear swipe at Palliser.

It seems incredible to me too. Palliser died in 1956 and seems to have been almost totally silent on the loss of the two ships from which his career certainly did not suffer. In 1944, Palliser was made Fourth Sea Lord and Chief of Supplies and Transport. He was made a Knight Commander of the Bath in 1945, and a full Admiral in 1947, retiring in 1948. He did write a letter of condolence to Lady Phillips, but among so many outpourings of emotion it seems cold, formal and clipped. Any criticism of Palliser has tended to be over his failure to second-guess Phillips and the decision to divert Force Z to Kuantan. This is unfortunate, as it puts a smoke screen over an area of equal culpability, which is why Palliser appeared to keep the voyage of Force Z as secret from the RAF as from the Japanese. Why did Palliser not ensure that FECB knew about Force Z? Why did he not plug in to them as a vital source of intelligence? Why did he not countermand his earlier signal saying fighter protection was not available? If he was at all troubled by the whereabouts of Force Z, why did he not send it a signal stating where he thought it was, leaving it to Phillips to break radio silence and reply if he deemed it necessary? In summary, Phillips's Chief of Staff in Singapore signalled information to Force Z that was either misleading or plain wrong and failed to liaise either with the RAF or intelligence and intercept forces in Singapore. One is left wondering what he did actually do on the day Force Z died.

There is also the mystery, reported on in only one book, of the two Buffaloes apparently sent out by Palliser:

'At some point, perhaps after receiving the signals from the *Tenedos*, Palliser sent Phillips a signal informing him that he had two aircraft and asking for instructions on where to send them. Admiral Palliser received no reply, and sent the aircraft off based on what he thought Phillips would do; unfortunately, his guess was not correct, and the aircraft went to the wrong location.'[9]

At the time of writing I am trying to track down this signal. Assuming it exists, it is clear that it carries no time, and it begs the question of where on earth Palliser felt Force Z was going if not to intercept the invasion he had told them about. I can find no comment from any survivor suggesting receipt of a signal from Palliser, which would surely have been a major talking point on the bridge and been received by *Repulse* as well. Perhaps the mysterious signal was not received by either ship or simply not reported in the frantic activity of the moment. As is discussed below, there were clear problems with *Prince of Wales*'s signalling capacity once the engagement started: 'Meanwhile (1240) *Prince of Wales*'s radio had apparently gained power – or, more probably, Phillips was flashing messages to his destroyers to be relayed on.'[10]

The same author points out that the first signal from *Prince of Wales* 'had clearly been composed earlier and was delayed in transmission, either because of the necessity of passing it on to a destroyer, or because of atmospheric conditions.'[11]

Historians have assumed too easily that *Prince of Wales* was able to send signals with immediate effect.

What is interesting on two counts, is that the RAF *did* send aircraft to Kuantan early in the morning of the day of the sinkings – three Hudsons and six Vildebeest bombers, as well as two Buffaloes. They saw nothing and were not seen by Force Z. Firstly, it argues for very badly trained aircrew if aircraft are sent out to attack an invasion force and cannot even spot a battleship, a battle-cruiser and three destroyers at the very place they are sent to. Secondly, it proves Phillips was right in thinking an invasion report for Kuantan would provoke air cover. He was undeniably correct because it did just that. The RAF did not cover itself in glory that day. Their aircraft abandoned Kuantan aerodrome which was followed by a near-mutiny from ground staff. Their errors, and the errors of those who took reports in Singapore, were compounded by a Blenheim bomber that took off from Kuantan that morning and reported that it had seen a battleship or aircraft carrier at 0649. As the result of radio failure, its report was not actually made until 1013. No one seems to have thought this might be Force Z. This may have been the solitary aircraft seen from *Repulse* at around 0630. The RAF had two opportunities to identify that Force Z was at Kuantan, and failed on both occasions.

The conclusion is inescapable. Regardless of any mistakes that may have been made by Phillips, British forces had several opportunities to identify the presence of Force Z at a danger point, from intercepted signals to sightings made or not made from their own aircraft, which identification must have provoked a combat air patrol. The link was not made and the patrol was not sent. Tom Phillips should not have needed to call for air cover; it should already have been sent.

All this relates to the three strongest charges against Phillips, all of which concern the failure to send signals. The first charge is that he failed to call for fighter cover, the second that he failed to tell Singapore he was diverting to Kuantan, and the third that he failed to notify Singapore when Force Z was attacked.

The first charge is the easiest both to dismiss and to explain. The saga of the perceived failure to call for fighter cover is in itself an interesting insight in to how history works, or sometimes fails to work. We now know that a handful of Brewster Buffalo fighters were available to Force Z when it was attacked. Armed with that knowledge, it is clear Phillips should have called for fighter cover. *Yet Phillips had no reason to believe that cover was available, and every reason to believe it was not.* Hindsight has meant that historians have lost sight of the view from the bridge of *Prince of Wales*. He knew RAF bases were falling like ninepins. He had been told categorically that fighters were not available and that information had not been rescinded in several subsequent signals. It had been suggested to him by signal from Palliser that if any air cover did become available it would be held back for the defence of Singapore. It is difficult to think of anything that might have led Phillips to believe the cover he had pleaded for was in fact available. Only an idiot asks for something they know is not there, and whatever else Tom Phillips might have been, he was not an idiot.

There is one key fact that no commentator has noted that validates Phillips's decision not to send out a call for fighters. Captain Tennant of *Repulse* has been widely praised for his actions during the engagement, and for realizing that no signal had gone out from *Prince of Wales* telling Singapore Force Z was under attack. Yet when Tennant did signal, at 1158, he made no request for fighter cover, but for destroyers and, later, tugs. It was not just Phillips who believed no such cover was available. Nor was it even just Phillips and Tennant. Phillips was surrounded by experienced officers on the bridge of *Prince of Wales*. Never once since the sinking has there been any evidence that any of those officers believed air cover was available.

The second and third charges are basically that Phillips kept radio silence when he should have reported he was changing course to Kuantan and when Japanese aircraft first engaged him. The two issues need to be treated separately.

Commander Goodenough was not the only person who believed Phillips was entirely justified in assuming Palliser would know that the only possible course of action for Force Z was to divert to Kuantan on receipt of the signal that landings were taking place there. Had they intercepted a landing, *Prince of Wales* and *Repulse* could have wreaked carnage among the invasion barges and might quite literally have altered the course of the war. However, such an operation was only possible if Force Z could surprise the Japanese, surprise that could all too easily be lost if Force Z signalled its intention to proceed to Kuantan. Palliser cannot seriously have assumed that Phillips would telegraph his intentions to all and sundry, thereby giving up surprise, the one thing he had on his side.

One of the most compelling writers on the sinking of Force Z, Arthur Nicholson, argues in his book *Hostages to Fortune* that the absolute imperative in Admiralty standing orders against breaking radio silence might have strongly influenced Phillips: 'W/T silence should not be broken to report a single enemy aircraft unless the Commanding Officer considers its presence is a first indication that there are enemy surface forces in the area, of which the Admiral is not already aware.'[12]

These instructions would certainly have influenced Phillips, though not necessarily as a result of a slavish obedience to orders. He knew of the bitter rivalries at the Admiralty, and that commanders who were perceived to fail were subject to witch-hunts. Captain Leach of *Prince of Wales* was nearly brought to a court martial for breaking off the action against *Bismarck* until other senior officers rallied round. Phillips would have known of the move by Churchill to court-martial Admiral James Somerville for lack of offensive spirit at the Battle of Spartivento in November 1940, when Somerville had actually handled the action well. As well as being aware of the vultures at the Admiralty, Phillips was also well aware of the major part played in the sinking of the *Bismarck* by an ill-advised signal to his base sent by the German Admiral which revealed *Bismarck*'s position. However, while both these may have been contributory factors, they are unlikely to have been decisive. More likely is the simple fact that as far as Phillips was concerned there was nothing Singapore could do for him. He did not believe, and had no reason to believe, that it could offer fighter cover. Such vessels as he had left behind might have been useful as an anti-submarine screen on the approach to Singapore, where the Japanese might have been expected to concentrate their forces, but were little more than a liability in an action that Phillips quite reasonably believed would centre on bombing. Calling for reinforcements from Singapore would be little more than asking lambs to join the slaughter. What reason did Phillips have for signalling Singapore? Is it an accident that Tennant's signal at 1158 giving his position and the message 'Enemy aircraft bombing' was to 'Any British Man-of-War', not to Singapore?

The facts are that Tom Phillips and Force Z were alone on the morning of 10 December. Sent on a wild-goose chase based on faulty intelligence, the reinforcements of surface vessels they could call on were a joke, and as far as they knew there was no air cover. They were the only effective naval force available from Singapore and their intelligence was that the RAF and their airfields were collapsing like dominoes in a row. Force Z should never have been sent in the first place, was hopelessly outclassed and should have been either called home or ordered in to hiding before honour and duty forced it to engage in a battle it could not win. The Phillips papers contain a story that suggests Phillips correctly predicted the scenario that saw him lose his life. Prior to the war, Phillips confided to Captain S.E. Norfolk that 'correct course' in the event of a deterrent force being sent to Singapore would be withdrawal from Singapore, but said that 'the decision to carry it out could not be left to the man on the spot as it would look like cowardice ...' He little knew that when the time came he would be the man-on-the-spot and that the order would not be given by the man responsible.[13]

There is one other possible explanation for *Prince of Wales*'s radio silence. Evidence that the ship could transmit radio signals throughout the action seems to be, when it comes down to it, based on the comments of one survivor, a senior rating in charge of one of the two transmitting stations inside the ship's armoured citadel, quoting in the hugely influential book by Martin Middlebrook and Patrick Mahoney, *Battleship*.[14] The fact remains that it is known that *Prince of Wales*'s radio aerials were affected by the shock of the first torpedo hits and that the flagship appears to have sent no signals by radio until 1220. It is clear also that she was having trouble communicating, failing to respond to *Repulse* before the latter was sunk:

'Tennant was beginning to feel disquiet about the state of his flagship's communications. Signals inquiring about the *Repulse*'s damage and describing her own were being transmitted only by Aldis lamp, and even these were disjointed and uncertain. It was clear that the internal damage to the *Prince of Wales* was serious and that she was no longer able to report progress of the battle to Singapore by wireless, and that this duty was now Tennant's.'[15]

In other words, Tennant's signal was not prompted by concern about his Admiral's judgment in not signalling Singapore, but rather by concern that he lacked the capacity to do so.

There is an explanation as to why a signal reporting the first attack on *Prince of Wales* might not have been sent:

'The first torpedo … that struck the *Prince of Wales* is known to have flooded the wireless cypher office, where all signals were being handled. In the ensuing hurried evacuation of this office it would have been easy for even an important signal to fall by the wayside. That the need for such a signal (under attack) cannot have entered the mind of the Admiral at all is improbable. There were various officers with him …'[16]

The failure to send an 'under attack' signal may be as simple as something lost in the hurried evacuation of a communications centre, or something that each individual involved felt someone else had been tasked with. Were this to be so, it would be far less culpable than the failure of Singapore to act on the news that the Japanese had sighted Force Z.

An objective assessment of the known facts suggests that Admiral Sir Tom Phillips had no reason to think air cover was available to Force Z and every reason to think that, if it were, it would be sent to Kuantan – as indeed it was. Singapore, on the other hand, had every reason to send that cover, but failed to do so. On the day, British pilots, the British military based at Singapore and Phillips's own Chief of Staff were simply not good enough.

Chapter 5

Churchill and 'The Secret Alliance'

Few wartime leaders have aroused such controversy as Winston Churchill. For many, his charismatic leadership and indomitable will to win were the difference between defeat and victory for Britain in the Second World War. For others, his inveterate meddling, particularly in naval matters, mercurial temperament and some of the undoubted mistakes he made undid much of the good he did. There were hugely contradictory elements to his character: 'A.V. Alexander noted in his diary … "Yesterday Pound remarked to me 'At times you could kiss his [Churchill's] feet – at others you feel you could kill him.""[1]

Churchill achieved many things for the Royal Navy. He was made First Lord of the Admiralty in 1911, though is probably still best remembered for the debacle that was the Dardanelles campaign of 1915 which was largely responsible for him losing his job. As an idea – in effect, the opening of a second front with a view to ending the carnage and stalemate of the western front, a killing ground that Churchill had the prescience to predict – it had merit. Its problem was that it did not make sufficient allowance for the flat trajectory of naval shells being as ineffective as they were against forts on land and it faced a lethal combination of command incompetence and inexperience of both combined operations and amphibious landings. Churchill was probably more personally culpable for the disastrous Battle of Coronel in which a hopelessly outclassed British force was outgunned and outfought by German cruisers acting as surface raiders. Back at the Admiralty in 1939, and subsequently as Prime Minister, he maintained a close involvement with naval affairs at all times. If it is true that what the good men do is oft interred with their bones while the bad lives on, some of Churchill's major achievements, such as the easing of conditions for lower ranks and support for convoys are forgotten whilst his meddling in the Norwegian campaign is not.

The sinking of *Prince of Wales* and *Repulse* is in many ways a miniature version of the whole debate over Churchill revealing both sides of the man and the leader.

There are a number of commentators who hold Churchill responsible for the loss of the two ships. When Admiral Sir Tom Phillips said to his senior officers, 'We have to do something', one survivor responded: 'My own thoughts were "Yes, indeed you have got to do something but this is quite against your own reasoning and the position in which you find yourself must be laid at Churchill's feet."'[2]

The survivor was not alone:

'He [Churchill], and he alone, had been finally responsible for sending the battle fleet to Singapore at this dangerous time, and against the strong pleas of those whose task it was to manage Britain's maritime affairs. He had selected the ships, and even the Commander in Chief. If direct blame for the catastrophe has to be attached to one man, then Winston Churchill must accept it.'[3]

Yet as we have seen there are many who blame Tom Phillips far more than Churchill: 'Phillips, and only Phillips, was responsible for the ships being where they were ...'[4]

One of Churchill's' strongest defenders has written: 'A different commander might not have endangered his ships on such a reckless mission ... Force Z was destroyed in circumstances that could have been avoided, and in pursuit of objectives that neither the Admiralty nor Churchill had explicitly approved.'[5]

The Case Against Churchill

It is comparatively easy to draw up a case against Churchill, not only for the loss of *Prince of Wales* and *Repulse*, but for the loss of Singapore as well. As Chancellor in the inter-war period he had been a player in the denial of resources to building up the defences of Singapore. Churchill was told on a number of occasions that Singapore was vulnerable, and that it should be given an even higher priority in defence terms than Egypt.[6] In effect, and to summarize much research, Churchill believed that Japan was unlikely to declare war on Britain, that if it did America would immediately join with Britain and declare war on Japan, and that if hostilities did commence Singapore was unlikely to be a primary target. He scornfully told Baldwin: 'A war with Japan! But why should there be a war with Japan? I do not believe there is the slightest chance of it in our lifetime.'[7]

It also seems likely that the Admiralty did not dismiss the threat from Japan as a military force nearly as much as Churchill did:

> 'There is firm evidence, however, that the Admiralty did *not* underestimate its potential enemy and it is on the record that as late as September, 1941, Churchill was grumbling to Alexander, the First Lord: 'The NID [Naval Intelligence Division] are much inclined to exaggerate Japanese strength and efficiency.' In point of fact the NID had got it right. It was Churchill's persistent and personal under-estimation of Japan over a long period of years which proved to be the culprit when disaster engulfed the Royal Navy in the months that lay ahead.'[8]

The above is important, as historians who are opposed to Phillips can imply that he had in large measure the same dismissive attitude towards the Japanese as effective fighters as Churchill was perceived to have. He may have been party to the error of judgment that believed war with Japan was unlikely; there is no evidence that he dismissed its capacity to fight effectively if war did break out. Some contemporary comment about the Japanese was simply the expression of what we would now categorize as appalling racist superiority. There is no evidence that Phillips had these opinions, any more than there is that he shared Churchill's dangerous tendency to underestimate Japanese fighting efficiency.

The outbreak of war in Europe in 1939 did nothing to change Churchill's priorities. Indeed, when Germany declared war on Russia in 1941, Singapore became even less of a priority. Once he had reassured himself that the Soviets could survive longer than a year at war with the Germans, Churchill focused even more on the war in Europe, if needs be to the exclusion of other campaigns: 'Churchill and the War Cabinet accepted the necessity of providing military aid to the Soviets on the largest possible scale, even at the expense of Britain's own military operations.'[9]

Having knowingly starved Singapore of resources and reinforcement, when a crisis loomed with Japan Churchill overruled the Admiralty and insisted on sending a new battleship to Singapore, a 'fast raiding force', though possibly envisaged in the first instance as being accompanied by a modern carrier. The debate over this is well documented, even exhaustively so. The Admiralty did not wish to lose one of its few modern battleships to the Far East, wishing to retain the two in service as a counter to any breakout by the German *Tirpitz*. Instead, the Admiralty wished to send a force consisting of old 'R' class battleships.

The 'R' class are the only Royal Navy battleships subject to confusion over their name. Official and unofficial sources refer to them variously as the 'Revenge' or the 'Royal Sovereign' class. One modern historian refers to them as the 'Ramillies-class'.[10] A First World War design, they marked a backwards step from the preceding Queen Elizabeth class. They were the last Royal Navy ships to be designed to burn both oil and coal, with the oil-fired Queen Elizabeth class giving rise to fears that Britain's navy would depend on a fuel it could only get from overseas, as distinct from relying on coal, of which it had its own more than adequate supplies. Designed to be cheaper than the Queen Elizabeths, they were very slow, with a top speed of twenty-one knots, and had armour largely designed round the expectation that the most likely action they would be involved in was relatively close-range surface conflict, the result being inadequate deck armour such as defended against air attack. Their secondary armament of 6-inch guns had no anti-aircraft capability, and proved too heavy to be effective as quick-firing defence against the large destroyers being planned by other navies at the time. They were almost impossible to modernize, and even what could be done was estimated to need eighteen months per ship. Where they could still have a role was in shore bombardment (*Ramillies* was used in the Normandy landings for this purpose), and in convoy escort. Their slow speed did not matter nearly as much in this context, and their eight 15-inch guns could see off almost any threat to a convoy from surface raiders. The strongest argument for deploying them to the Far East was that they were the vessels the Royal Navy could most easily spare from the European theatre, but the proposal was not entirely cynical. If supported by a carrier, as was the plan, they would have air defence. Their reinforcement by the slow battleships *Rodney* and *Nelson*, better armoured and even more heavily-gunned, as was also planned, would provide a balanced force which, if it were to be overwhelmed, would require a very large concentration of Japanese forces.

However, it was Churchill who overrode the Admiralty, and insisted on sending out a modern KGV battleship, the *Prince of Wales*. Ironically, the ship to accompany her, *Repulse*, had originally been planned as an 'R' class battleship, with her and her sister ship *Renown* subsequently changed to a battle-cruiser design. Churchill wanted a fast, deterrent force, but one suspects that the choice of *Prince of Wales* was a political choice more than a military one. Quite simply, Churchill gambled that by sending out one of Britain's finest and best ships a point about British intentions and commitment to the Far East would be made both to Australia and the colonies, and to the Japanese. Churchill can thus be accused of sealing the fate of Force Z firstly by sending out a 'fleet' that was no such thing and was far too small, and secondly by allowing it to proceed into danger even when it became clear that it would not be accompanied by a carrier – though whether or not a carrier *was* actually ever intended to accompany Force Z is no longer certain, and is discussed in a later chapter. It should be noted that Tom Phillips was opposed to Churchill's proposal and argued strongly against it, as spokesman for Dudley Pound who he represented, at the meeting on 17 October 1941.

Churchill can be blamed in two associated areas. Firstly, his idea of sending Force Z was ineffective as a deterrent – as if the dispatch of one new battleship and one old battle-cruiser would defer the monster that was the Imperial Japanese Navy. Secondly, it may have had the opposite effect to deterrence. Its effect seems to have been to provoke the Japanese in to redeploying two battle-cruisers and part of the Kanoya Air Group from Formosa to Saigon, these being the aircraft which eventually sank *Prince of Wales* and *Repulse*. Churchill may actually have been the agent whereby the only weapons likely to sink *Prince of Wales* were placed on the scene and enabled to do so.

A very telling criticism of Churchill, and one that arguably pins more blame on him for the sinkings than any other, is what appears to be a classic case of non-joined up thinking. One can argue that it was perfectly reasonable to send out a deterrent force, but that Churchill failed to realize that his deterrent force had changed through circumstances beyond his control in to a fighting force. As such, Force Z was clearly neither balanced nor strong enough, and should have either been called home by Churchill, or ordered in to hiding at Pearl Harbor or an Australian port such as Darwin.

What Churchill wrote and said he did could be very different from what he actually did. For example, in the First World War he claimed to be actively against investment in airships, but in fact argued strongly for them.[11] Initially, he defended the actions of Tom Phillips: 'Admiral Phillips was undertaking a thoroughly sound, well-considered offensive operation, not indeed free from risk, but not different in principle from many similar operations we have repeatedly carried out in the North Sea and the Mediterranean.'[12]

An even more telling admission is to be found in a minute he dictated to his Chiefs of Staff on 7 December:

'...I agree with the President [of the United States] that 'we should obviously attack Japanese transports' in conditions prescribed ... Attack is therefore solely one of naval opportunity and expediency ...'[13]

He later sought to backtrack, as in a letter he wrote to the official naval historian for the war, increasingly implying that Phillips's plan was his own and Churchill's advice was either to hide in islands or join the US fleet: 'The last thing in the world that the Defence Committee wished was that anything like the movement which Admiral Phillips thought it right to make to intercept a Japanese invasion force should have been made by his two vessels without even air cover.'[14]

This is disingenuous. Phillips had signalled his intention to seek out and attack Japanese invasion forces on 8 December. It is an accepted convention in the Royal Navy that if a commander stated his intention to do something, it is to be assumed he has permission and authority to do it unless he is specifically told the contrary:

'Now every British naval officer of those days was familiar with the convention whereby the originator of a signal using the word "Intend" neither demanded nor expected an answer *unless the addressee disapproved of the intention expressed.*'[15]

Regardless of whether or not Phillips in reality had any option other than to seek out the enemy (something discussed below), it is beyond any reasonable doubt that Churchill had the time and the ability had he so wished it to countermand Phillips, and that in the absence of any reply Phillips could only have assumed that was he was doing had the full approval of his superiors. Churchill's attempt to shift responsibility off himself and onto Phillips does him no credit. It has also left the field more open to the detractors of Phillips and deprived a dead man of a champion his reputation sorely needed. As one historian has commented: '... Even now his treatment of some officers, and his invariable search for scapegoats when anything went wrong, leaves an impression almost amounting to vindictiveness ...'[16]

Churchill's memoirs refer to a meeting – 'mostly Admiralty' – that was convened in the Cabinet war room to consider the naval situation in the Far East on the evening of 9 December. Churchill tried to argue that this meeting reached the conclusion that the best thing for *Prince of Wales* and *Repulse* to do was to make an appearance at Singapore, and then vanish and hide in the islands or join the American fleet, the former allowing them to act as a threat to Japanese ambitions without putting themselves in undue danger. The problem is that generations of historians have been unable to find a shred of contemporary documentary evidence supporting Churchill's account of 'the disappearing strategy'.

This leads on to the issue of whether or not Churchill can be let off the hook of blame by arguing that Phillips himself should have adopted the disappearing strategy:

'A clear distinction should therefore be drawn between Churchill's decision to place two capital ships at Singapore on the eve of war, and the subsequent decision, taken thousands of miles away, that resulted in these ships being caught in the open and without air cover off the coast of Malaya on the morning of 10 December 1941.'[17]

In other words, Churchill put the ships in Singapore. He did not make them leave it to attack the Japanese: only Phillips could make them do that.

It is a feeble argument, akin to saying that Churchill pointed a gun at someone and pulled the trigger, but they could always have moved out of the way. To all intents and purposes Tom Phillips had no option other than to use Force Z to try and disrupt Japanese invasion plans. True, he had received two signals suggesting he might withdraw his ships, but the 'prodding' signal he received on 7 December sent from Pound but undoubtedly backed by Churchill, that asked what action it would be possible to take with naval or air forces seemed to make it clear that the Admiralty wanted action. Phillips had, as discussed above, signalled his intention to attack and not had that challenged. He undoubtedly had a chance to do serious damage to Japanese invasion plans, believed he was out of range of Japanese torpedo-bombers and would undoubtedly have been accused of cowardice had he retreated, as Captain Leach of *Prince of Wales* had so nearly had done to him, not to mention Admiral James Somerville after Cape Spartivento. The impact on the morale of Singapore of the two ships running away would have been disastrous, the boost to the Japanese tremendous. Ironically, the fuss that the Government and Churchill insisted on making about the dispatch of *Prince of Wales* made it far harder for the force to do nothing. That same fuss provoked the Japanese to transfer within range the very aircraft that sank the ship, so making the fuss in the first place was not one of Churchill's most triumphantly successful ideas. And, of course, the two Royal Navy ships were not just the major but perhaps, given the weakness of the RAF, the only means Singapore had of striking a blow against Japanese aggression, and not to use them would not just have been cowardice, but a rank admission of defeat.

Churchill's own relationship with Phillips has tended not to do the latter any favours. A man perceived as having political patronage does not always recommend himself to other senior officers who may not feel they have that same access to corridors of power, and many of whom distrust politicians anyway. Churchill clearly thought highly of Phillips who spent weekends at Chequers, the Prime Minister's country retreat, and the admiration was, most of the time at least, mutual. Writing to a family friend after he met with General Smuts, and despite his falling out with Churchill, it is Churchill's opinion of Smuts that Phillips uses to validate his own: '... there is no doubt that Winston's description of him as the greatest man alive today is fully justified.'[18]

The letter Churchill wrote when Phillips was appointed a Vice-Admiral has clear warmth:

'My Dear Phillips,

It gives me great pleasure to tell you that we have all agreed that the importance of your work and the part you play at the heart of the Naval War requires your immediate promotion to the rank of acting Vice-Admiral. The official intimation will reach you during the day, but let me take this occasion of offering my cordial congratulations.'[19]

Phillips is sometimes assumed to have achieved his promotions simply through the influence of Churchill. In fact, Dudley Pound was Phillips's greatest supporter and arguably played a more prominent role in his advancement. It is clear that Pound found Phillips invaluable.

However, it is beyond doubt that there were significant differences of opinion between Churchill and Phillips and that their relationship cooled dramatically as a result. The latter objected to the mass bombing of German cities, and the campaigns for Greece and Crete. It is difficult to believe Phillips was not right on both counts. Had the RAF's long-range bombers been sent out under the banner of Coastal Command with the radar necessary to detect U-boats the whole course of the war could have been changed, the war shortened and thousands of lives – particularly those of merchant seamen – been saved. As for Crete and Greece, Admiral A.B. Cunningham eventually acquiesced to Greece[20] and produced the famous comment to the effect that it took a few years for the Royal Navy to build a warship but a lifetime to build a reputation. It was a good speech, but bad tactics. Cunningham's strapline ignored the fact that the ships sunk in the Greece and Crete campaigns were not only vital to the war effort, but in many cases took down to the bottom of the sea with them men whose training had taken many years, and whose experience was invaluable in a navy strained to the very limit in finding the men to man its ships.

Churchill did not like objections to his ideas:

'The clash of powerful wills, that had once worked in sympathetic harmony, destroyed all confidence between these two self-assertive men. Churchill ... determined to be rid of Tom Phillips as soon as he could without causing a crisis at the Admiralty.'[21]

A friend of Phillips's wrote after the war that Phillips stood up to Churchill, albeit reluctantly, and without losing respect for him:

'He had the greatest respect for the P.M. but did not always agree with him and was outspoken enough to say so... I remember his saying that he did not think the P.M. liked being opposed, but he had to do it.'[22]

It is not as clear that the respect was mutual. In the First World War Churchill, as First Lord of the Admiralty, had packed off Sir Doveton Sturdee to chase down German raiders in the Falkland Isles following a disagreement, and it may well be that sending Tom Phillips off to the Far East was a repetition of this trait on Churchill's part. If so, it is a further charge against Churchill, namely that he chose a commander for Force Z for reasons that had little or nothing to do with his military suitability.

It is therefore quite easy to cast Churchill as the villain of the piece in the loss of *Prince of Wales* and *Repulse*. Churchill misjudged the likelihood of Japan declaring war against Britain and consistently underestimated the threat to Singapore. He was partly responsible for the parlous state of Singapore's defences. He sent crucial supplies to Russia rather than Singapore. He should never have sent the ships out there in the first place. He chose Force Z's commander for the wrong reasons. Force Z was a diplomatic mission suddenly required to fight but unsuited to do so. He put his voice behind giving the despatch of the force a high public profile, believing it would increase the deterrent effect, but in practice both ensuring crucial Japanese reinforcements and that the ships would have to sail to attack against all the odds. Once war was declared he should have pulled the ships back either into hiding, or ordered them to join the American fleet, and his 'prodding' signal and failure to order Phillips to withdraw were an effective death sentence for the ships. He tried to cover for his own failings, after an initial defence of Phillips, by blaming Phillips for the disaster.

However, it is possible to take another view.

The Case for Churchill

It is very hard to forgive Churchill for his shameless backtracking following the sinkings, whereby he sought to claim he had always intended Force Z to retreat from Singapore. He did not and lied to cover his back. This was an act of moral cowardice and distasteful on a personal level. But just as Admirals do not have to be liked, so with great leaders. Machiavelli would have willingly allowed his leaders a measure of hypocrisy and falsehood if the result had been that Machiavelli was spared torture. The same instinct for survival that saw his attempt to wriggle out of responsibility for the sinkings also drove his wider instinct for the survival of Great Britain. On this wider canvas, it is clearly true that Churchill did not have the defence of Singapore as a top priority. It is possible to argue that in this he was correct. The war in Europe threatened the very continued existence of Britain. The loss of Singapore threatened its income and its influence. It was not that Churchill thought Singapore unimportant, merely that he ranked it as less important than the survival of the country. There is actually nothing unsound in his suggestion that Australia could just as easily be defended by ships based in Darwin. Even Roskill, one of Churchill's fiercest critics, can only find to say about this idea that Churchill did not seem to consider where the ships for this defence might come from. One might equally as well ask where the ships for the defence of Singapore would come from.

In effect, Churchill and Phillips were linked by more than their former friendship. Both took a gamble. In Phillips's case, the gamble was that a surprise attack under cover of monsoon bad weather might significantly delay or stop the Japanese invasion of the Malayan Peninsula. It was not an unreasonable gamble, given what Phillips had been told, and what he thought he knew.

Churchill's gamble was on an altogether larger canvas, though not without its own justification. He gambled that the Japanese would not wish to take on Imperial Britain, that if they did so America would come in on Britain's side and that in the event of hostilities it would take months to wear down Singapore, not so much by its military strength but more by reason of its distance from Japan's starting point. He gambled that Japanese involvement in Indo-China would continue to occupy them. Perhaps most of all, Churchill knew that a Britain near bankrupt after the First World War could not afford on its own the war on two fronts that crippled Germany in two world wars. What might have saved Singapore was a sizeable portion of the American fleet based there, not to mention the American air force. Churchill's gamble failed, in no small measure because the Japanese acted more speedily and more effectively than anyone had expected. If one was a serviceman sent to Singapore as a raw recruit, without tanks or modern aircraft, was taken prisoner at Singapore and subsequently became the victim of appalling Japanese cruelty, one can be excused for seeing Churchill in a most unflattering light. The same goes for the family and friends of those who died on *Prince of Wales* and *Repulse,* who could quite reasonably have blamed Churchill and a number of others before they blamed Tom Phillips. But if that gamble had succeeded, and Britain held on to Singapore, it could and would have been a very different story.

So what is the truth? Churchill's role in the sinking of *Prince of Wales* and *Repulse* was crucial. It was the wrong force for the threat it was destined to meet, and Churchill, who has so often been criticised for interfering in naval matters, for once failed to intervene when it might have done some good and order the two ships in to hiding. That he bears a very significant responsibility for 'Britain's greatest naval defeat' cannot be denied. He gambled with these two ships as his chips. His bluff was called, he lost his bet and many men died. When push came to shove, he was probably the only man who could have issued orders that would have saved two ships, nearly a thousand lives and British prestige in the Far East, the latter perhaps for only a short while. Years on from the event, we can argue from our armchairs that Tom Phillips could have ordered his force away from the sound of the guns, and in so doing denied the very life blood of the service he served so well. For the only British force capable of offensive action in a theatre of war where Britain was facing its greatest-ever defeat simply to run and hide was never going to happen, and the subsequent fate of other Royal Navy vessels in the same theatre of war when Japanese carriers arrived suggests it would only have delayed rather than stopped the inevitable. Admiral James Somerville's Far Eastern Fleet, a 'forgotten fleet' to match the 'forgotten army', played hide and seek with the Japanese, achieved very little and came near to disaster on several occasions. Churchill, on the other hand, could have issued the order for the ships to 'disappear', and at least deferred a tragedy. His mistake was the one single action most responsible for the loss of the ships. For every action Tom Phillips took there was a clear reason. There was no clear reason for Churchill not removing from Force Z the obligation to mount an offensive operation.

Why did Churchill not order the two ships out of danger? The most likely reason is that he was constitutionally incapable of seeing attack as anything other than the only form of defence and may well have believed that offensive action on the part of the two ships might actually have made a difference to the British defence of their Far Eastern countries and interests.

There may be another lesser, almost pathetic reason. Churchill worked into the small hours when others were at their least effective, and had a strict instruction that he should not be woken before 8.00am except in the event of Britain being invaded. His peculiar regime did not only play havoc with the biological time clocks of those who served with him. It meant that his availability frequently did not match that of those same people. Following a typical late-night meeting in the Cabinet war room it may simply be that Churchill's own work regime meant he was out of action during the only time when, after reasonable thought, he could have given Phillips an acceptable reason to call off the proposed action. By the time he woke up and was back in action himself, the events that were to put two fine ships permanently out of action were irrevocable.

Perhaps the fairest summary is to say that Churchill did not sink *Prince of Wales* and *Repulse* by his actions, but by his inaction. By his failure to act, he did not sink them: he simply failed to keep them afloat.

However, there is a third explanation as to why he sent out Force Z in the first place, and why he was reluctant to send it into hiding.

'The Secret Alliance'

In the section below I am deeply indebted to the work of Alan Matthews, whose exhaustive research and use of original sources reflect the best traditions of historical scholarship.[23]

There are two questions surrounding the whole issue of the defence of Singapore that have not been satisfactorily answered. The first is why Churchill, belligerent to the core and always unwilling to cede ground, should have knowingly diverted resources from Singapore over a long period. The second is why Tom Phillips was chosen to command the force. It is not only that he lacked recent combat or sea-going experience. After many years of peace few Admirals at the time had this, and some of those had raised doubts about their ability by their conduct in the actions in which they were involved. The promotion to senior rank of one who had seen victorious combat – Harwood, the victor of the Battle of the River Plate fought against the German pocket battleship *Graf Spee* – had not been a success. Furthermore, Phillips's position at the Admiralty meant that he was among the best informed of all senior officers as to what had been learnt so far in the war at sea. What makes his posting extraordinary is that he was widely recognized as the most brilliant staff officer in the Royal Navy and was heavily relied on by the First Sea Lord, Dudley Pound, who it is clear would sorely miss his support. So if, as is commonly argued, Force Z was simply a deterrent force that would have failed in its job if it had to fight, why did Pound and Churchill consent to their most brilliant staff officer exchanging a place at the heart of Britain's maritime war for a seat on the Admiral's bridge of *Prince of Wales*? This is not to say that Phillips manifested any just cause or reason for thinking that he would be as effective in a fight as any British Admiral.

The answer may lie in the consequences of the secret staff talks President Roosevelt allowed to take place in Washington in early 1941, the so-called American-British Conferences (ABC). These were held in the crucial context of two viewpoints. Firstly, it was not only Churchill who believed that on its own Britain could not defend Malaya. In October 1940 the British Chiefs of Staff warned of the strength that Japan could bring to a southward drive, not least of all in the form of the Imperial Japanese Navy:

'In the absence of United States support, we could take no effective military action in the present circumstances to prevent Japanese penetration of Indo-China and Thailand. The greatest deterrent to Japanese aggression is the threat of American naval action on their lines of communication, and it goes without saying that we should use every endeavour to secure American co-operation in intimidating Japan.'[24]

It seems likely that in Churchill they were preaching to the converted. Secondly, it was not only the British who would face overstretch in the event of a war against Germany and Japan. The American Navy, big as it was, had to cope with the vast expanse of the Pacific as well as the Atlantic Oceans, and recognized that in the Philippines they had a potentially indefensible asset. In the light of this the Chief of US Naval Operations, Admiral Stark, had produced the Plan D Memorandum.[25] In this it was stated that in the event of the United States becoming involved in the war America would prioritize the European theatre, with it playing a subordinate defensive role to the British in the Far East, alongside Dutch naval forces. As part of this strategy American naval forces would be sent in to the Atlantic, thus allowing the Royal Navy to reinforce its Far Eastern fleet. The British delegation hoped to persuade the Americans to adopt Singapore as a major base of their Far Eastern fleet. Admiral Stark rejected this, on the grounds that it would not provide for an effective defence of US interests. Yet given other opinion at the time and given the decision to make the Atlantic the primary area of operations, there was a sense that the Americans at this time might be prepared to accept the loss of the Philippines and base their main fleet at Singapore. Other points of disagreement were British reluctance to reinforce Hong Kong as a submarine base and let it be used by the Americans, and issues related to Brooke-Popham controlling allied forces. However, the major concern seems to have been the Royal Navy's failure to provide an initial force of ships in the Far East. Churchill was content to leave the Singapore issue, having gained the crucial point that the US would join in the war. A low point as regards the ABC agreement was reached when the Americans advised the War Cabinet that:

'Until such time as a plan is evolved whereby British Naval forces take a predominant part in the defence of the British position in the Far East Area, they [the US] will be constrained to withdraw their agreement to permit the United States Asiatic fleet to operate under British strategic direction in that area.'[26]

Following this message, a series of steps were taken or planned. Churchill agreed, contrary to his earlier approach but in line with what the Americans wanted, to reinforce Hong Kong. Brooke-Popham was informed of his impending replacement by Lieutenant General Sir Henry Pownall. The Americans were told that *Prince of Wales* was being sent to Singapore, along with the news that: '*Repulse* and *Revenge* are now in the Indian Ocean... with the battleships *Royal Sovereign* and *Ramillies* [leaving] during November and *Resolution* in December.'[27]

Thus American demands for a force capable of operating north of the Malay barrier, as asked for by the Americans, were being met, and as if to emphasize the point it was suggested that a further meeting was held with Admiral Phillips who was en route to Singapore in *Prince of Wales*. We know that Phillips's first action in the Far East was to seek and have a meeting with the US Admiral Hart. Whatever plans were laid, they were rendered redundant by the attack on Pearl Harbor, something not envisaged in any of the meetings around a joint waging of the war in the Far East.

It is possible that both sides would have considered that they had gained the better deal if the reinforced British fleet had ever docked in Singapore. The Americans did not have enough forces at their disposal to defend the Philippines, and the proposed alliance may have been their best way of doing so. The Americans also admitted that Manila and naval facilities in the Philippines were only suitable for use as advanced operational bases which implies an outcome for the British they would welcome: a main base for the British and Americans at Singapore, and operating bases in the Philippines. Such an arrangement might well have been seen as the best defence for both Singapore and the Philippines.

It is by no means an accepted view among historians that Churchill was dominated in his thinking on Far East strategy by the hope of a military alliance that would in effect use America to retain British power and influence in the Far East, and have the British and American 'main fleets' using Singapore as their base. There is considerable evidence to suggest that Churchill had realized this was a practical impossibility, and that the Americans had never seen it as an idea that had enough in it for them.

However, there is an alternative scenario which envisages Churchill having an exaggerated vision of American power and strength, having a long-term ambition for Singapore to house both fleets and seeing a last-gasp chance to bring this plan to fruition with growing tension in the Far East, and having a private understanding with Roosevelt that this was a desired end. Any such understanding would, by definition not be documented. Roosevelt faced a massive block of opinion in his own country that was irreconcilably isolationist to its core, and to give any assistance to Britain's war effort had had to adopt an element of subterfuge. In this theory, Churchill's apparent willingness to accept the reluctance of the American naval negotiators to contemplate a move to Singapore, and tell his own team to back off, was simply because Churchill considered that if a deal was to be done it would be agreed at an altogether higher level than joint naval talks. Forcing the issue at this level would simply stir up opposition and make it even harder to quell in the event of Roosevelt being willing to take an executive decision.

There are snippets of information, which give strength to the idea that the concept of a joint naval base at Singapore was not dead. It was at the behest of the Americans that there were further naval conversations in the spring of 1939. The delegate representing the Admiralty, Commander T.C. Hampton, had to travel incognito ostensibly as a land agent called 'Mr Hampton'. A highly secret conference was held with Admiral William D. Leahy and others at Leahy's home. In the course of this conversation Leahy expressed as purely personal opinion that in the event of war the US fleet should move to Singapore, but that this would depend on the British sending out 'an adequate token force' to Singapore.[28] The travelling incognito and the meeting at home illustrate just how fearful Roosevelt was of those in his own country who wanted nothing to do with a war by European countries. The token force was deemed necessary to placate wider American public opinion. Though nothing concrete emerged from the discussions, or at least nothing on paper[29], they lead the Admiralty to conclude that a token fleet of two or three battleships would suffice to satisfy American public opinion.

However, proponents of the 'secret alliance' theory suffer firstly because if it existed at all it would have to be well and truly secret, and because if it existed at all it was much more in the way of a secret understanding than an alliance. The attraction of the idea is that it ticks so many boxes in terms of the unanswered questions surrounding Force Z. It explains:

1. Why Churchill was so willing to divert military resources away from Singapore, and deny it additional expenditure, even though he knew and

had been told that his impregnable fortress was no such thing: Churchill believed the extra resources Singapore and the Far East required would come from the USA.

2. His enthusiasm for a new KGV battleship to be sent: it was not only to deter the Japanese, but perhaps even more to impress the Americans with his seriousness of intent, as Admiral Leahy had suggested was necessary.

3. The choice of Admiral Tom Phillips to command Force Z, a man who could only be spared from the Admiralty for the most pressing of causes. There is overwhelming evidence that he was the best brain working on the naval staff at the time, and an invaluable aide to Pound. To offset the need to keep him where he was, what more pressing cause was there, other than defence of the homeland, than the defence of British interests in the Far East? Tom Phillips was a highly intelligent man who proved his skills as a diplomat by the warm responses he obtained from General Smuts and the US Admiral Hart. When Admirals Cunningham and Somerville complained that someone with more combat experience should have been sent, they missed the point; what the Far East command needed was not a knight in ironclad armour but a diplomat. There was no reason to think that Phillips would perform as a fighting Admiral any less well than his peers; there was every reason to know that he was a better and more convincing envoy than most of his peers.

4. Why the former commander in the Far East, Admiral Layton, was not given command in the Far East. As discussed in a later chapter, Layton was a fighting admiral, but the man who could call a person he was working with a 'black bastard' was clearly not a diplomat.

5. Why Phillips's first priority in the Far East was to visit the American Admiral Hart; negotiating a working military alliance was Phillips's mission, not a vain assault on overwhelmingly superior Japanese forces.

6. That if it is true as suggested below that there never really was intent to reinforce Force Z with a carrier, the fact of this being a diplomatic mission rather than a military one explains what would otherwise be an extraordinary omission.

7. Phillips's call for 'R' class battleships to be sent to him urgently. They would have little use as fast raiders against Japanese invasion forces, but would be a firm declaration of intent to the Americans. Phillips's request

suggested that he saw his main mission being to meet the conditions set by the Americans at the ABC Conference, which insisted on a significant number of British ships being sent to Singapore.

8. Why Churchill failed to order Force Z into hiding. It would have been a perfectly reasonable thing to do if Force Z's mission had simply been to deter the Japanese. It would have been a very bad thing to order the only major British ships in Singapore to leave it if Churchill's object remained the hope that Singapore would act as the joint base for British and American forces. We know now the speed and relative ease with which Singapore would be taken. Churchill did not, and seen from his viewpoint it was perfectly feasible that Singapore might hold out for long enough to host a part of the American fleet, and benefit from its long-range bombers and air force. What would have been disastrous would be to have ordered the Royal Navy to leave Singapore whilst trying to persuade the American Navy to join it. That alone would have killed the idea. The Americans could hardly be asked to send their ships to Singapore if Britain was sending its ships away from it. Churchill may well have seen the presence of American warships, and the long-range bomber cover they would bring with them, as the only way to ensure the survival of Singapore. After all, a brief visit by Tom Phillips to Admiral Hart had resulted in four US destroyers being despatched to Singapore.

9. Secret support from Roosevelt for a joint base at Singapore answers one of the questions posed by the distinguished historian Arthur Marder: 'The persistence of the British in pushing for an American naval presence at Singapore is a puzzle.'[30]

It is less of a puzzle if one believes that it had the secret support of the President of the United States.

If this is what happened, it shows Tom Phillips in a different light. For a man who had to transform himself overnight from ambassador and diplomat to frontline fighter, he showed remarkable courage and got more things right that he did wrong in the battle which followed. For Churchill, it suggests that he made two mistakes in his assessment of the situation in the Far East. We know he underestimated Japanese strength and capability. Did he also exaggerate and place too much faith in the power of the United States?

There is a modern point to all this, if one believes that history can contain warnings for the future. The warnings are not to trust too much to a special relationship, not to overestimate the power and reach of American military might and not to place responsibility for one's own defence in the hands of the United States.

Chapter 6

The Ships: *Prince of Wales*

'*... the weakest battleships completed by any nation during the Second World War era...*'[1]

Prince of Wales was a new King George V class battleship, of which five were to be completed. It was the second unit to be commissioned in 1941, *King George V* having completed on 1 October 1940. From the outset they were seen as being outclassed by the bigger German *Bismarck* and *Tirpitz*. Churchill complained that the fact of three KGVs being needed to offset *Tirpitz* was, '... a serious reflection upon the design of our latest ships, which through being undergunned and weakened by hangars in the middle of their citadels, are evidently judged unfit to fight their opposite number in a single ship action.'[2]

This was slightly unfair – only by having three ships available could two be guaranteed to be available to fight at any one time because of the requirement for refit and repair – but not by much. *Tirpitz* had more weight of armour, better watertight subdivision, a heavier main armament that could out-range the King George Vs by 3,000 yards, a faster rate of fire, a two-knot speed advantage and a vastly superior endurance and range. The reason, of course, was that *Prince of Wales* was built to conform to treaty limitations of the 1920s and 1930s, which Germany ignored. Churchill was right to complain: 'Once again we alone are injured by treaties.'[3]

The existing accounts of the sinking of *Prince of Wales* make little or no mention of the fact that Tom Phillips's state of the art or even 'unsinkable' flagship was a disaster waiting to happen, and a vessel with serious design flaws. There are a number of reasons why this element of the disaster has featured so little in writing about it. Ship design is a highly technical area and few historians are technically qualified in it. It is also a highly specialist area, restricted largely to books intended to appeal to a very small number of people and, dare I say it, terminally boring to those outside this narrow circle. Information about weaknesses in the design of any weapon of war tends to have 'Top Secret' slapped on it at the time, for the very good reason that one does not want the enemy to know one's weaknesses; such labels tend to stick long after the actual need for the information to be kept secret has lapsed from a mixture of pressure from those responsible to cover their backs, obsessive secrecy and institutional lethargy. It is also easy to sell the equivalent of a pup in warship design to the general public, particularly if it is a beautiful ship: HMS *Hood* is an example.

However, *Prince of Wales* also illustrates a cycle in the design of warships which has been active over the past hundred years. In time of war the absolute priority is to win. In time of peace that priority has to compete with others, most often the need to save money or adhere to political rather than fighting imperatives. As an example, in 1982 the Royal Navy found itself in a shooting war for the first time in many years. HMS *Sheffield*, at the time a thoroughly modern vessel, was first put out of action with tragic loss of life and subsequently sank as the result of being hit by an Exocet missile whose warhead in all probability did not explode. Bad ventilation helped sink *Sheffield*, as did the failure of electrical systems. The requirements of protection against nuclear, chemical and biological warfare meant a priority in keeping a sealed atmosphere within the hull, whereas when large quantities of rocket fuel are burning off in a ship's guts, survival can depend on the ability to vent smoke and fumes to the outside world. There were far too few breathing masks on board and issue clothing whose artificial fibres melted in to the flesh of wounded men. *Sheffield* was a classic example of a warship designed to the priorities of peacetime and without due attention to the likelihood of it being hit. Forty-one years earlier, the designers of *Prince of Wales* had been forced to design Britain's new generation of capital ships to what was essentially a political agenda. As with *Sheffield*, lessons were learnt. The tragedy in both cases is that so many men had to die to re-learn lessons that should never have been forgotten. It would also be far too easy to blame those who actually designed the ships. They merely try to make sense out of the brief they have been given or limited to, by others.

Also in time of war ships are hit and damaged, and lessons learnt in how to keep them afloat and moving. These lessons seem the first to be forgotten in time of peace. Damage control is rarely a fashionable specialization in peacetime, but it is crucial to a ship's survival. Poor damage control was a factor in the sinking of *Ark Royal* in 1941, as it was in the sinking of *Prince of Wales*. It is thought to have been a weakness of the Imperial Japanese Navy as well.

The Sinking

Much more is known now about the body-blow torpedo hits that sank *Prince of Wales* as the result of informed dives on the wreck. Before discussing the design weaknesses of the class, there is one feature of the sinking that has to be recognized above all. In the first torpedo attack, a Japanese torpedo struck the ship under the stern at a point where the hull was almost concave. A few feet to one side and the torpedo would have missed. The resultant blast was so concentrated under the hull that survivors saw no great plume of water as they did with other hits. The ship was lifted bodily out of the water, the upward thrust of the explosion being countered at this point by the massive weight of the aft quadruple 14-inch gun turret. The impact snapped off the 'A' bracket that secured the propeller shaft to the hull, and what happened then is graphically described in one of the earlier accounts of the sinking:

> 'A massive hole had been torn in the hull but, much more seriously, the 240-foot shaft of the port outer propeller had been distorted and, still churning viciously, had fractured bulkheads, riveting and fuel-piping along its entire length before it could be stopped. Within minutes flooding had disabled several engine-, boiler- and machine rooms. Diesel and turbo dynamos failed, depriving salvage pumps of electrical power. Lighting, communications and ventilation failed, the steering-motors were dead and four of the eight AA turrets were inoperative. *Prince of Wales* ... was crippled, with a 10° degree list, wallowing at 15 knots and with her quarterdeck only two feet above sea-level.'[4]

This one hit effectively killed *Prince of Wales*, its catastrophic effect not sinking it, but leaving it totally vulnerable to the subsequent attacks that did. Was it, as has sometimes been said, a 'lucky' hit? It was not luck that trained the crack Japanese pilots, or saw Japan invest so heavily in aircraft and torpedoes that significantly out-matched those of the Allies. It was rather the fortunes of war, and illustration that in war protagonists sometimes get the luck they work for.

Human Error

It was at one stage fashionable to blame the loss on poor damage control, and in particular on failure to switch off power to the damaged shaft fast enough. Defence against this claim has been helped by the fact that one of *Prince of Wales*'s leading damage control officers survived the sinking. In fact it seems unlikely that failure to withdraw power from the shaft was a significant factor. The vast port outer-shaft was revolving at 204 revolutions a minute, and once forced out of alignment it took only seconds for the shaft to destroy far more than had been destroyed by the actual explosion.

There were damage control issues that did not help. Too much time was taken trying to lay power-lines to affected areas instead of using the ship's other ring main to remedy the problems, the same issue which had been a factor in the sinking of *Ark Royal*. Some watertight doors were left open by crewmen rushing to escape the flooding. Perhaps more crucially, a Commissioned Warrant Officer lost his head and flooded the after magazines, being stopped only when he was in the process of repeating the action for the forward magazines.[5] No one likes to record these incidents, which do not typify a crew who showed great bravery and devotion to duty. Perhaps all that can be said about the inevitable, understandable and occasional human failures shown after the ship was hit was that they did not sink *Prince of Wales*, but they certainly did not help keep her afloat.

Origins of the King George V Class Battleships

When the Department of Naval Construction was asked in 1935 to submit draft proposals for a new class of battleship it was seventeen years and a world economic depression away from the last war, nineteen years away from Jutland and the last time British battleships had faced sustained enemy fire. More importantly, it was working to almost impossible restrictions placed on it by the Washington Naval Treaty, and in particular a limitation of 35,000 tons and a main armament of no more than 14-inch guns, subsequently ignored by all other navies. The first two ships (*King George V* and *Prince of Wales*) were ordered on 29 July 1936.

The most authoritative guide to British battleship design states that these vessels were, 'probably the best 35,000-tonne limited displacement battleship ever produced.'[6] The American 'South Dakota' class appear to prove this wrong, and were superior to the KGVs in nearly every regard. The sacrifices made to meet Treaty restrictions, and other weaknesses, were to contribute significantly to the relative ease with which *Prince of Wales* was sunk by the Japanese. Mere size in a battleship did not guarantee survivability, as the 18-inch-gunned Japanese *Yamato* proved, but the most effective battleships of the Second World War, from *Bismarck* to the USS *New Jersey*, were significantly larger than *Prince of Wales*.

General Design Features

There were some notable good features in the KGV design, particularly as regards armour protection, and they scored a number of creditable firsts in having a dual-purpose secondary armament, being completed with radar and designed to carry aircraft. It is difficult to see how the designers could have done better working under the treaty limitations, but what to a designer appears as a necessary compromise can be a death sentence to those who have to fight the ship.

Among many weaknesses, there were design faults that had no bearing on the action in which *Prince of Wales* was lost. *Prince of Wales* was never called on to fire her ten 14-inch guns in her final action. It was probably a good thing. By the time the ships had been ordered, other nations had refused to ratify the 14-inch limitation on main armament. It was decided that the year needed for a new design was too long to wait, and the existing 15-inch turrets were too heavy for the new design. As it was, the proposal for three quadruple turrets proved too heavy, and a twin turret was mounted in place of one of the quadruple turrets, to further design furore – not, as is often supposed, because of the weight of the turret but rather because of the weight of the extra magazine protection it was now deemed the two additional guns would require. There were major problems operating the new quadruple turrets, which had nearly 3,000 working parts, and which suffered badly from problems with a complex series of safety interlocks and insufficient clearances. In the *Bismarck* action the main armament on both *Prince of Wales* and *King George V* was at times only twenty to fifty per cent effective. It is often claimed that these teething troubles were solved, with the destruction of the German battle-cruiser *Scharnhorst* in 1943 by *Duke of York* cited as the example. *Duke of York*'s radar-directed fire was extraordinarily accurate, but this has cloaked the fact that *Duke of York* should have fired around 800 14-inch shells during the engagement, but managed only 446. However, when *Prince of Wales* was sunk there were no heavy seas, no large surface opponents and her main armament was not called into action.

The class had a flush deck, in answer to an Admiralty demand for 'A' turret to fire directly forward at zero elevation. This helped make *Prince of Wales* a very wet ship in a heavy sea, and in the action against *Bismarck* heavy spray coming over the low forecastle seriously affected the rangefinders for 'A' and 'B' turrets, greatly reducing the effectiveness of the main armament. It has been suggested that this problem was solved in later vessels by fairing, a streamlined refuse chute and breakwaters.[7] Perhaps it was so, but when in the 1980s I talked to men who had served on board both *Duke of York* and *Howe* many repeated the story that in a heavy sea the cry went round, 'Seals in the shell room!'

The KGVs were also fuel-hungry, consuming twice the fuel at twenty knots of comparable American battleships, with a serious effect on their range and capacity to stay at seas, something that nearly stopped *King George V* from engaging *Bismarck*, and was instrumental in *Prince of Wales* ceasing to trail her.

However, other weaknesses were to impact on the loss.

Superstition and Bomb Damage

Prince of Wales was seen by the rest of the Navy as a jinxed or 'Jonah' ship. There was a bomb near-miss while she was building. Fleeing from the threat of further German bombs in Liverpool, she ran aground on her way to Rosyth while under tow. An accidental discharge of a pom–pom injured a dockyard worker, and she suffered from three small fires, as well as injuries when men suffered bad falls. However, it was the *Bismarck* action that did the most damage to her reputation. *Prince of Wales* actually did rather well in this action. She was far from fully worked-up and her machinery was malfunctioning, and particularly her main armament. She correctly identified *Bismarck*, took seven hits which killed thirteen people and wiped out most of the bridge personnel and landed two hits on *Bismarck*, one of which left her down by the head and was to force her to end her sorties as a result of disruption to her fuel supply. Interestingly, she managed this even though her gunnery radar was inoperative, malfunctioning radar being a persistent problem that was still around when she left Singapore on her last voyage. She was ordered to break off the action by the senior officer left after *Hood* blew up, largely because the problems with her main armament meant she was like a man fighting with at least one hand tied behind his back, and because Britain could not afford to lose two battleships on the same day. As regards her crew, one author sums the situation up admirably: '... there is some evidence that the morale of her crew was not all it might be. The lack of time allowed to work up the ship peacefully, the trauma of seeing the *Hood* blown to pieces, the recurring mechanical defects for which time for proper rectification was never allowed, few opportunities for leave – all these had impaired the settling down of the crew.'[8]

Added to these were the problems of a navy having to cope with a vast influx of 'hostilities only' ratings. There has been much debate over the morale and efficiency of the crew: all that can be said with any certainty is that Tom Phillips's flagship was not manned to a peak of efficiency that best fitted it to sail into extreme hostilities. Of crucial significance was the inability to give proper training in anti-aircraft gunnery, if only through the lack of trial targets. Captain Tennant of *Repulse* wrote in his official report:

'*Prince of Wales* and *Repulse* had both been without serious anti-aircraft practice for some months and I am afraid the shooting was not good – torpedoes were mostly fired outside pom-pom range at about 2,500 yards.'[9]

Yet a much more alarming episode that could have played a major part in her sinking took place before she was finished. On 31 August 1940, while in the fitting-out basin at Cammell Lairds, a low-level German attack dropped a bomb that landed between the basin wall and the hull. Quite serious damage was caused. It has been suggested that whilst obvious damage was repaired, the impact of the bomb may have sheared off or weakened bolts and rivets beyond the area of obvious damage that appeared whole, but which subsequently contributed to the opening up of the hull under Japanese bomb attack. There is no record of remedial work being undertaken or examinations carried out beyond the area of immediate damage, which was towards the stern. Examination of the USS *Pennsylvania*, which suffered a similar torpedo hit to *Prince of Wales* but survived to be examined, suggested that the hidden, unsuspected damage inflicted by such as shock could extend a significant way beyond the point of impact. It is possible that the explosion and downward pressure of the quadruple turret ripped a line out along the hull, effectively following a fault line caused by the dockyard hit.[10]

Armament

Prince of Wales should have been the best-ever British battleship in terms of its anti-aircraft armament. The 5.25in dual-purpose secondary armament, housing in eight twin-turrets, was a good idea in theory. Most battleships, including *Bismarck*, had a four tier arrangement of main armament, anti-destroyer armament, heavy and light anti-aircraft armament. Guns that could be dual purpose, and throw a heavy enough shell to cripple a destroyer but still have a high enough rate of fire to be used against aircraft, saved weight that could be transferred to the other eternal two points of the designers' triangle, propulsion and armour. The problem was that the twin 5.25in turrets did not work well enough: 'There is little doubt that these guns (or perhaps more accurately their fire-control systems) were still not combat efficient.'[11]

The turrets were cramped, and the guns were too heavy and slow to track to fulfill their anti-aircraft role. Designed for ten to twelve rounds per minute, seven to eight was more normal and all that could be attained. The lack of a fully-mechanized ammunition supply was a serious drag on rate of fire, crew having to transfer 80lb shells and their cordite charge manually from hoists to loading trays. Perhaps more importantly, the four directors that controlled the guns had major weaknesses. They were not tachometric (fully stabilized) and '… did little better than guess at the location of the aircraft they targeted.'[12]

No gun is better than its director. The 14-in gun that sank *Scharnhorst* in 1943 was a defective weapons system of relatively light caliber that nevertheless benefited from highly accurate gunnery radar directing fire. It is a pity that the Admiralty's decision to buy the outstanding foreign 40mm Bofors gun for anti-aircraft defence in 1939 came too late for more than one of them to be mounted on *Prince of Wales* (on her stern), or that the sacrifice of buying foreign was not extended to the outstanding American 5-inch dual-purpose gun, sometimes known as the 5in/38.

It is often stated that the crews had no time to work up, anti-aircraft fire in particular needing practice targets that were simply not available on the way to Singapore. This is certainly true, and the aim of *Prince of Wales*'s gunners does not seem to have been good, but when push came to shove, the much-vaunted secondary armament proved not fit for purpose. In fairness to the designers the loss of electrical power rendered half the turrets useless for much of the action.

Nor were the multi-barrelled 'pom-poms' an antidote to Japanese air power. Essentially short-range weapons, they all too often took effect on a target after it had launched its load of munitions. Captain Tennant of *Repulse*, quoted in the following chapter, believed the weapons consistently shot behind their target – an ironic comment if true, as it was exactly the criticism made against *Bismarck*'s anti-aircraft fire. The pom-pom's ammunition also took badly to the tropical climate, which caused the round to separate from the casing before it could be fired. Bad ventilation on board the ship caused many problems, as discussed below, including an inability to store ammunition at temperate and humidity-levels that kept it serviceable.

Power Supply

The loss of electrical power played a crucial role in the sinking of *Prince of Wales*. Electrical power was provided by six turbine-driven dynamos and two diesel-driven generators for emergency power. It was realized too late to save *Prince of Wales* that turbine-driven generators in particular were very susceptible to battle damage. The loss of electrical power resulting from the first torpedo hits on the ship took out of action half of its main defence against aircraft, the 5.25in dual-purpose turrets, but the effect was even more serious than this. It seriously restricted internal communications, with an appalling impact on the ability of those in charge to muster damage control resources where they were needed, and communicate with those doing the job when they were there. *Prince of Wales* was a modern ship, and as such electricity was the life-blood that powered through its veins and arteries. The minute that blood supply stopped, the body started to die.

There has been a tendency to cite the fact that the crew of *Prince of Wales* never had time to work up as a contributory factor to the ship's loss. Of course it would have been better for the ship if more of its complement had been trained for longer, but the best damage control officers in the world still need to know where and what the crucial damage is, and the best men in the world need to be able to be told where to go, see it when they arrive, and, if needs be, coordinate what they are doing with other damage control parties. Loss of electrical power also crucially reduced the ship's capacity to pump water out, and made existing serious ventilation problems even worse. The breakdown of much of the ship's electrical generating capacity appears to be the result of both the shock of the crucial torpedo hit on the stern and flooding. In any event, the shock seemed to have knocked out a significant portion of the ship's electrical generating capacity, perhaps because machinery was not secured to the hull by shock-proof mountings.[13]

There is also the unexplained failure to use the ring breaker system to switch power to vital areas. Instead, time and energy were taken up running cables to areas which had lost power. It is tempting to blame the lack of working-up time for this failure. It is more likely that the crew of *Prince of Wales* were the first in the war to have to deal with such a situation (though it may have played a part in the loss of *Ark Royal*), and the lessons to be learnt could only be acquired through hard and bitter experience.

Anti-flooding Measures

If *Prince of Wales* found herself in a situation where she could not pump out the water that was coming in, her design added to the problems flooding caused when the water was inside the hull. The KGVs as originally designed had an Achilles heel that at one time it was believed resulted in her capsizing. The most recent research on the wreck suggests otherwise, but does not lessen the seriousness of the design flaw.

The whole midships section of *Prince of Wales* between her funnels was dominated by the hangar and catapult for her Walrus aircraft. Aircraft were removed from British battleships from 1942 onwards. A Japanese bomb pierced the catapult deck, bursting in the cinema flat below and blowing out a large section of the side of the hull, with resultant large-scale flooding. The cinema flat extended right across the hull, and the flooding that collected in it played a clear role in her capsizing. Modifications to the other vessels relocated and eliminated this space, and with hindsight extra tanks for watertight integrity were also added.

Rarely commented on is the fact that *Prince of Wales* was also designed with what are known as centreline machinery space bulkheads. These are in effect watertight subdivisions designed to increase a ship's survivability, but war experience showed they severely restricted a ship's ability to counter flood, and so reduce a list, if a ship was hit on one side. The only other major navy to adopt these was the Japanese navy, and of seventeen cruisers heavily damaged on the one side of the hull, all bar one capsized. The system only worked in larger ships, and has been described as a 'serious design flaw'.[14]

Added to this might be the fact that there were significant gaps round the trunking and cables that ran through the hull, as they passed through supposedly watertight bulkheads, compromising watertight integrity, and weak bulkheads that collapsed under water pressure. All in all, *Prince of Wales* had design flaws which gave her a significantly increased risk of capsizing, particularly in a situation where she took most of her hits on one side. It is ironic that the design brief for the ship stipulated that it should be able to survive six torpedo hits on one side of the ship, more than it actually received.[15]

Ventilation

Whereas the Admiralty were in all probability not aware of the increased risk of capsizing inherent in the design, there were other weaknesses they were aware of. In fairness, they did raise these as reasons why KGVs should not be sent to the Far East. Admiral of the Home Fleet Sir John Tovey cited the ships' ventilation systems as a reason why they should not be sent to the Far East, along with the fact that their evaporators were not designed to cope with long periods at sea and fears that a crucial gearing mechanical element of the main 14-inch gun turrets would not work effectively in very hot climates.[16] A ventilation system can seem to an outsider as a convenience rather than a necessity for fighting a ship. In fact it is vital, in three ways. The possible negative effect on ammunition has already been mentioned. In addition, unless controlled, the temperature inside a metal hull can rise to levels, particularly in engineering spaces, in which humans simply cannot work, and will quite literally collapse. Temperatures on board *Prince of Wales* on her journey out reached 136° Fahrenheit in boiler rooms, 122° in engine rooms and a staggering 150° degrees in machinery rooms where the machines were run for more than four hours, and these temperatures were reached with all electrical ventilation systems working. Even before the temperature reached a level where men simply cease to function it could make a savage cut to efficiency of working. Finally, an efficient ventilation system clears a hull of smoke and fumes from battle damage.

One would imagine that a blue-water navy created in part to service a world-wide empire would design ships that could cope in the tropics. In fact, the KGVs seem to have been designed for service in the north Atlantic. One problem faced by British designers was the compromise between the need for ships on long overseas cruises to have relatively large spaces to house the crew and make life bearable for them, and the clash between this design requirement and the need for smaller and smaller watertight subdivision to guard against sinking. The German Navy in two world wars sacrificed habitability for watertight subdivision, assuming that for much of a ship's life its crew would be housed on shore in barracks. However, this does not excuse the failure to install an efficient forced ventilation system, a different matter entirely. The KGVs, and most British battleships, could not cope with tropical climates, at least at the start of the war. Bad ventilation cannot be said to have sunk *Prince of Wales*. It can be said to have significantly reduced her fighting capacity.

Turning Radius

There is one other failing of the KGV class that was the fault of its designers. The turning circle of a vessel – how far it takes to make a turn – is a crucial factor in its ability to manoeuvre and dodge both bombs and torpedoes; it is, in effect, how nimble the ship is. The KGVs compared badly with some other British and American ships as regards their turning circle. Under the same speed and helm, the USS *Washington* had a turning radius of 575 yards. The equivalent for *King George V* was 930 yards, ironically much the same as for *Repulse*'s sister ship *Renown*, but with both comparing badly to the 625 yards of the older battleship *Nelson*. The reason *Repulse* dodged her first onslaught of torpedoes so much better than *Prince of Wales* was not so much that she was brilliantly handled, though she was, but rather that her earlier attacks were concentrated on one side. Nevertheless, the poor turning ability of *Prince of Wales*, probably the result of the decision to give her only one rudder, meant that in another area Britain's newest battleship lagged behind in the features she would most need to survive: 'To sum up, while the Japanese torpedo-bombers had already given Captain Leach an extremely difficult problem, the *Prince of Wales*'s poor turning radius may have made his job impossible.'[17]

We now know that she was only a few feet away from avoiding the hit that in effect sank her.

Armour and Other Protection

Defence against torpedo attack was not so much by armour as by a Side Protection System, or 'SPS'. This was based on the idea of using space to dissipate the force of an explosion, whereby twenty-five empty, energy-absorbing compartments were placed along the ship's side. *Prince of Wales* was built to fit the Royal Navy dry-docking facilities at Portsmouth and Rosyth, limiting their beam to 103ft and the maximum depth of the SPS compartments to 13.5in. Events proved this not to be enough. The situation was not helped by the fact that Captain Leach had had to order several compartments to be flooded, to correct the ship's list, but even the loss of shock-absorbency this brought the compartments is not the reason the ship's basic torpedo defence system was overwhelmed:

'The attack by Japanese torpedo-bombers against *Prince of Wales* during December 1941 proved this dimension to be inadequate as shock-absorbency and the integrity of the bulkheads was destroyed.'[18]

Prince of Wales could not and did not survive multiple torpedo hits on one side, and was never going to do so.

Conclusion

By April 1942 a number of stable doors had been bolted in the remaining ships of the class, largely as a result of the loss of *Prince of Wales*. Alterations and additions included much additional watertight subdivision and 'blanking' of doors and openings, significantly more pumping capacity, shock-proof mountings for machinery and fittings, duplicate power-leads for the 5.25in mountings and significant improvements to generating capacity.[19]

Prince of Wales was almost certainly one of a class of battleship that was the best of those designed in response to inter-war treaty limitations. It did mark an advance in design terms, taking more torpedo hits than ill-fated, First World War designs such as the Royal Sovereign class battleship *Royal Oak*, still lying on the seabed at Scapa Flow where it was famously sunk by *U47*, or the Queen Elizabeth class *Barham*, sunk by torpedo in the Mediterranean in 1941. Yet the fact is that this supposedly 'unsinkable' battleship had serious design flaws that were exposed in action. Tom Phillips set out with a flagship that was unable to mete out the punishment it was designed to inflict, and unable to stay afloat when it in turn was punished. His flagship was not fit for purpose.

Tom Phillips was also sailing to a meeting with crack Japanese pilots who were probably the only unit in the world trained to a high level in delivering bomb and torpedo attacks against surface vessels, and had been posted to the area as a result of any secrecy surrounding the dispatch of Force Z. Opposed to them were a crew who were barely trained at all to meet such a threat. The Royal Navy had insisted on eight months as the absolute minimum to work up a ship to full fighting efficiency. The Admiralty had allowed *Prince of Wales* to sail to fight a far more powerful opponent after only seven weeks.

The inbuilt inability of *Prince of Wales* to withstand battle damage also renders irrelevant and inapplicable any criticism of Phillips as a seaman. The best seaman in the Royal Navy would have made no difference to the outcome of the battle once early damage rendered *Prince of Wales* a sitting duck.

Phillips was sailing to war in a ship that was shown in the most dramatic manner not to be unsinkable, as the media had claimed, but all too sinkable, with systemic weaknesses that made it unacceptably vulnerable to precisely the type of attack to which it was subjected. It was not only the physical weakness of his flagship that made Force Z such a hollow threat. It was human weakness as well, and Tom Phillips was responsible for neither the physical nor the human deficiencies in his force. He was not only let down by the Admiralty. He was let down by his flagship, and by the honesty of Great Britain in adhering to treaty limitations in the 1920s and 1930s.

Chapter 7

The Ships: *Repulse* and Escorts

HMS *Repulse*

HMS *Repulse* was launched in January 1916. Originally intended as an 'R' class battleship, the decision was taken to remove guns and armour in exchange for a speed of over thirty knots, and turn *Repulse* and the similar vessel *Renown* into battle-cruisers. As a point of comparison, figures for 1917 show that *Hood,* whose fate is well known, had 6,500 tons of armour and 7,500 tons of plating; *Repulse* 2,440 tons of armour, 3,300 tons of plating.[1] With only six 15-inch guns in three double turrets, there was considerable concern among gunnery experts that this unusually small number of guns would make spotting fall of shot and hence accurate gunnery very difficult, and that it left the ship seriously under-gunned. In fact six guns were decided on in three turrets for no better reason than that this was the maximum number than could be made available if the ships were to be built in the fifteen months demanded by Admiral John Fisher. If ever there was a self-inflicted wound this was it, and Fisher's actions were tantamount to culpable negligence. As originally built the ships appeared to be too lightly constructed, earning the nicknames in the Navy 'Refit' and 'Repair'.

In one of the many ironies that mark the loss of these ships, *Repulse* was a pioneer in the development of naval aviation, when on 1 October 1917 she flew off for the first time at sea a fighter plane from a platform secured over two of her main guns.

The blowing up of three British battle-cruisers at the Battle of Jutland has given the type of ship a bad name, but this is not wholly justified. There is some evidence that the battle-cruisers blew up because flash-proof shielding had been removed in order to speed up rate of fire. There was certainly a school of thought current at the time that rate of fire was going to be crucial in any fleet engagement. Safety precautions, such as flash-proof scuttles between the turrets and the magazines, can slow down the rate of fire, and it is not unheard of for sailors on the spot to make unauthorized modifications – unauthorized, that is, by the Admiralty – to machinery. If this was one of the causes of the blowing-up of three battle-cruisers at the Battle of Jutland, it was certainly not the only cause. The instability and tendency of British cordite to blow up was at least as damaging and dangerous. In any event, the lesson was that a heavy main armament did not justify putting a ship in the heart of an engagement against similarly-gunned vessels; for that, a corresponding weight or armour protection was needed. The battle-cruiser was ideal for hunting down raiders, or as a scout for the main fleet. Its high speed also made it able to provide big-gun escort for carriers, whose ability to launch aircraft was greatly aided by a high speed airflow over the deck and were therefore designed to be capable of speeds over thirty knots. *Repulse* was therefore an interesting medley. She was under-gunned and under-armoured even for a battle-cruiser, but used in the right way was a useful vessel.

In any event, *Repulse* and others had more armour slapped on them in the aftermath of Jutland, one piece of which saved her from incapacitating damage in the early stages of the Japanese attack, but unlike *Renown* she was never fully modernized nor re-engined in the inter-war years, being capable of only twenty-nine knots when she was sunk as distinct from her design thirty-two knots. Her ventilation was significantly better than *Prince of Wales*. However, her biggest weakness was a lack of deck armour to resist bomb attacks, and what was generally recognized as a seriously inadequate anti-aircraft armament consisting of six antiquated, hand-operated 4-inch guns and three eight-barrelled two-pounder 'pom-pom' short range anti-aircraft mountings. Captain Tennant of *Repulse* wrote in his official report on the loss of the ship: 'I believe that 90% of short range stuff that is being fired at any aircraft goes behind them.'[2] One comment on her anti-aircraft fit was: 'But her AA armament was juvenile to a degree. She was, in Admiral Hayes's words, 'armed with not much more than an umbrella to push at the enemy like an old lady'... the *Repulse* was indeed the worst-armed from the AA aspect of all the Royal Navy's capital ships.'[3]

Neither was *Repulse* privy in any serious way to one of the Royal Navy's greatest advances in the inter-war years, the development of radar. She carried only a Type 284 surface set, which had been fitted on her way out to the Cape. It was not integrated into the gunnery control system, which was still controlled by voice messages. To add insult to injury, the radar was wedged on to 'B' turret, which had to sweep round for the radar to be effective, to the detriment of its machinery.

The battle-cruiser was based on a perfectly sound idea, namely that of a ship which would combine the firepower of a battleship with the speed of a cruiser. As noted above, such vessels were ideally suited to act as the hunters of commerce raiders. They served best as scouts for the main fleet, heavily-gunned enough to take on anything smaller than a battleship and fast enough to clear off when the battleships appeared – which raises the question as to why on earth *Repulse* was chosen to sail with *Prince of Wales*. Never mind that she was singularly unsuited to meet the threat that eventually sank her, by virtue both of her lack of armour and lack of effective anti-aircraft weaponry, or that there was no fleet as such for her to scout for – she was barely a knot faster than *Prince of Wales*. She was equally unsuited to taking on the Japanese battleships that seemed at the outset her most likely opponents. Yet *Repulse* was an extremely happy and efficient ship, with none of the problems besetting *Prince of Wales*, something achieved in no small measure by the fact that around two-thirds of her complement were pre-war regulars who had served some time with the ship. What she was not was a vessel fit for the mission on which she was sent. In the film *Zulu*, the nervous young soldier awaiting the onslaught asks, 'Why us?' The Sergeant Major answers to the effect, 'Because we're 'ere, lad, because we're 'ere.' It is tempting to think *Repulse*, finely manned and captained though she was, sailed with Force Z because she was there, and because she was a ship no-one could find another use for.

The warships that accompanied *Prince of Wales* and *Repulse* as escorts were woefully few in number and half were obsolete. The two destroyers *Electra* and *Express* were modern, 1930s built. Sailors are superstitious, and *Electra* was seen as bringing bad luck because she had been with *Prince of Wales* when *Hood* blew up and sank. It was *Electra* that had picked up the only three survivors from *Hood*. However, as individual ships these were undoubtedly fit for purpose. Both had received high-angle 4.7-inch gun mountings capable of elevating to 40° as distinct from her 30° of earlier classes, giving them a useful anti-aircraft role. *Electra* put this to good use when she shot down a German bomber in April 1940. *Electra* at least was retro-fitted, after a collision, with a 3-inch anti-aircraft gun and a 20mm Oerlikon mounting. *Electra* survived to be sunk in the Battle of the Java Sea on 27 February 1942, that battle suggesting strongly the fate that awaited any Allied naval force that did not at least have numerical and qualitative parity with the Japanese.

Express was one of the last vessels to leave Dunkirk, having played a crucial part in the evacuation of British troops. She was eventually transferred to the Royal Canadian Navy as the *Gatineau*, and ended her days safely but ingloriously as part of a breakwater in Royston, British Columbia.

Of the other two escorts, HMS *Tenedos* had been launched in 1918, and was obsolete, hampered not least of all by a very limited range. She was sunk by Japanese carrier-borne aircraft on 5 April 1942, in an engagement that also saw the losses of the carrier HMS *Hermes*, and the cruisers *Dorchester* and *Cornwall*.

The same engagement saw the loss of Force Z's fourth escort, HMAS *Vampire*, which was sent to the bottom by a second strike of Japanese aircraft after the one that sank *Hermes*. *Vampire* was launched in 1917, and though useful enough to shoot down at least one Japanese aircraft prior to her sinking, was also obsolete.

At least two other destroyers should have accompanied Force Z. Admiral A.B. Cunningham was ordered to send two destroyers to join Force Z. One of them, *Jupiter*, was described by Phillips as a 'notorious crock'. She had spent an unusual amount of time in refit and repair, even for a class with known hull weaknesses, and it appeared that she suffered from faulty riveting during her construction. The other gift from Cunningham was HMS *Encounter* which had to go into dock immediately on arrival at Singapore for renewal of her stern bushes. Cunningham had sent one ship that had faulty fuel tanks and took on a 10° list when full of fuel, and another with a corrugated bottom which meant that with the helm amidships she could not steer in a straight line.[4]

Cunningham has never properly been called to task for the dirty trick he played on Force Z. He cannot have failed to know that when asked to send reinforcements to a body of ships about to face action under the most demanding of circumstances, he chose to respond by using the request to rid himself of two liabilities.

The decision is made even less praiseworthy by the fact that Cunningham undertook serious sniping at Tom Phillips for his lack of combat experience. Cunningham had no such excuse: he had combat experience, and must have known how useless these ships were for combat, and he of all people was in a position to realize the crucial importance of a decent escort for Force Z. History has tended to focus on the air threat to the ships, because with hindsight we know this is what sank them. The paucity of the escort available to Phillips posed a serious threat to his ships in two other areas. Force Z was sighted in the first instance by a Japanese submarine and had had a salvo of torpedoes, all of which missed, launched at it. The submarine threat to Force Z was a serious one and the only antidote was a decent screen of escorts. The reason for this need is sometimes misunderstood. Surface vessels do not need to spot a submarine or even to attack it to reduce seriously its effectiveness as a weapon of war. Submarines hunted on the surface, at least before the final German U-Boat designs and nuclear submarines, submerging only to kill. With a tiny speed submerged, and low endurance, a submarine forced to submerge either by surface vessels or aircraft could be rendered impotent, in an ideal world unable either to catch up with a target or position itself to make a successful attack. To work this trick, the commander of a surface force needs both to throw out a screen of escorts around his capital ships, and keep some close so their sonar can hope to detect any that have broken through the screen. Furthermore, if a submarine's conning tower is detected on radar, there need to be a number of escorts sufficient to allow for one to be sent to force the submarine under, without denuding the main force of cover. Chasing the *Bismarck*, the Admiral commanding the hunting force could signal his destroyers to break off if they could not keep up, because foul weather, poor visibility and high seas reduced the submarine threat. This did not apply in the calmer water off Kuantan, and that Phillips was clearly aware of the threat is evidenced by his request for additional vessels to screen his hoped-for return to Singapore, and the comment he made early on the morning of 8 December: 'I certainly can't go to sea until I have more destroyers.'[5] Certainly four destroyers was the minimum deemed necessary to escort capital ships at the time in the Royal Navy.

A further threat against which Force Z was under-defended was the mine. Mines pose a very serious threat to capital ships. The only damage inflicted on the German battle-cruisers *Scharnhorst* and *Gneisenau* in the infamous Channel Dash of February 1942, was by mine, and only one of Force Z's escorts had proper minesweeping capacity. A common image of the mine is the single, floating horned monster lying waiting in the middle of the ocean for a ship to run over it. A classic example is the equivalent of a mine in the film *The African Queen,* in which the German warship conveniently heads to the one spot in the lake where a warhead awaits it. This, of course, is not how it works. The random sowing of mines is a useless act. The mine comes in to its own when it is known that surface ships will have to traverse or gather in a given, limited area. The British knew in 1942 exactly the path *Scharnhorst* and *Gneisenau* would have to take to make it home, and were able to lay mines accordingly. The entrances to Singapore were an obvious area, and one of which the Japanese made full use.

Phillips was also short of another type of ship that would normally have been de rigeur for a force of his type. The cruiser is a fast scouting vessel, large enough to see off any surface ship short of a battleship and nimble enough to get out of its way if it does come across any such. Cruisers would have been invaluable to Phillips to act as his eyes and ears, both for Japanese invasion points and any threatening force of surface ships. Again, he made clear his concern in a signal to the Admiralty, saying: 'Need for further modern cruisers is great.'[6] A few more days and he might have had a force containing five modern cruisers. However, the Japanese proved unwilling to postpone their invasions to allow the British to build up a suitable number of vessels.

So did Phillips act rashly in taking Force Z out without adequate escort? The answer is no. He has been criticized for his decision-making and for rashness in taking out Force Z, but in the case of his escorts he certainly took a gamble, but one that was justified. As regards submarines, he saw them (quite reasonably on the basis of the information given to him) as more of a threat than bombers. An officer close to Phillips wrote: 'Admiral Phillips was very conscious of the danger from Japanese S/Ms; our own S/M screen was quite (through lack of recent training) inefficient. He certainly rated the danger from S/M attack as greater than that from high-level bombing attack.'[7]

Asdic was relatively inefficient and unable to give a depth reading (a crucial issue as depth charges had to be set to explode at a given depth), and likely also to be confused by the different temperature layers found in tropical waters. Yet a fast capital ship moving at over twenty knots and zigzagging is an extremely hard target, and the one thing Phillips's ships had on their side was speed. As for mines, Phillips ordered Force Z to steer east and away from the Japanese minefield off the eastern entrance to Singapore Strait (it is not known whether this was by accident or design), and steered clear of a further Japanese minefield by the Anambas islands. His destroyers were relatively untrained in anti-submarine work, and only one was equipped for minesweeping. Yet in both cases, submarines and mines, Phillips's judgment that the risk was justified was born out by events, something for which a man accused of being an armchair admiral has not received enough credit. One is left to wonder if with even one of Cunningham's 'crocks' available to him the submarine that spotted Force Z might not have been differently dealt with.

As with so many commanders before and since, Phillips had to act with what he had been given. He did actively seek destroyer reinforcement, both from the US fleet and by ordering two 'S' class destroyers from Hong Kong, as well as asking for the cruisers *Exeter* and *Achilles* to join him in Singapore.[8] He had also earlier asked for the four 'R' class battleships to join him.[9]

What does seem inexcusable is Cunningham's action in sending two 'crocks' to reinforce Force Z. What is slightly sickening is the excuse that was offered as to why *Encounter* and *Jupiter* were chosen by Cunningham. They were recent arrivals, it was argued, so their departure would do less to break up the team, and most of the destroyers in the Mediterranean were 'F' class ships, so it made sense in terms of maintenance, repairs and spares to detach an 'E' and a 'J' class. It was nonsense, of course, and pure duplicity. The Mediterranean used the request as an excuse to clear out its trash bin.

There appears to have been some confusion on the part of historians between what is an understandable act on Cunningham's part – no beleaguered wartime commander wants to lose his best ships – and what is excusable: 'Having been asked to detach two ships, the Commander-in-Chief, Mediterranean, not unnaturally detached the two oldest vessels under his command.'[10]

Cunningham shared with Churchill charismatic powers of leadership and the capacity to inspire those who served with him. Yet as we shall see in a later chapter, his was a flawed personality, as was Churchill's. Another similarity with Churchill was Cunningham's willingness to blame others for what was his fault. It does not reflect well on him that he felt justified in blaming Phillips for the loss of *Prince of Wales* and *Repulse*, but failed to acknowledge that when called on for support he had paid the due of loyalty all servicemen owe to each other in false coinage.

The closer one looks at the ships that made up Force Z the more one is forced to conclude that this was a diplomatic show force rather than a fighting force. Its most powerful component, regardless of chronic design weaknesses, was never fully-worked up, and, as a comparator, would not have been allowed to sea as a result by the German Navy. Its second capital ship, that needed to be flung about the sea like a destroyer to avoid bombs and torpedoes, had steering engines so venerable that its crew felt they were not up to the strain and had been told to 'go easy' on them. Two of its four escorts were ships designed for an earlier war and not equipped to meet the threats of the new one. Tom Phillips did the best he could with what he had. He proved his credentials as a fighting Admiral by seeking additions to his force at every opportunity. He may have been a diplomat; he was also a fighter. Yet what he had to fight with, despite his best endeavours, was not good enough. The blame for that is not Tom Phillips's, but goes home to Churchill, the Admiralty and Admiral A.B. Cunningham. It was the result of their actions that the force that set out from Singapore earned this description from one of the most highly-regarded historians of the period:

'So it was a puny force of six ships – puny compared to the forces available to the Japanese in the South China Sea – that sailed off into the bright, red sunset at 1735 on 8 December.'[11]

Chapter 8

Intelligence, SS *Automedon* and 'Matador'

There has long been a theory that the British knew more about Japanese intentions in the Malayan Peninsula in 1941 than was admitted at the time. There is the story, reported above, that Singapore intercepted Japanese sighting reports of Force Z. There is also a story which cannot now be verified because the source of it, an officer who survived the sinking of *Prince of Wales*, died before his account could be checked:

> 'There is also hearsay evidence that the Intelligence on Admiral Phillips's staff found, on his return to Singapore after the sinkings, that the naval staff ashore had known of the presence of Japanese torpedo-bombers in Indo-China while Force Z had been at sea but had not thought it necessary to send a warning signal.'[1]

Another historian claims that the British had a limited ability to read Japanese naval signals, and that the British knew four hours in advance an attack would be launched against Force Z. Unfortunately, the source for this allegation is not made clear.[2]

As we have seen, there was confusion in many levels of communication, including between the signals Intelligence division and the army and RAF. It is at least possible that vital intelligence was not passed on to both commanders in Singapore and to Force Z. This matters because had Phillips been more clearly informed he would have been extremely unlikely to stay around Kuantan as he did, but chosen instead to make maximum speed back to Singapore. It also needs to be remembered that the delay off Kuantan was at the behest of Captain Tennant of *Repulse*, and did not originate with Phillips.

What is clear beyond reasonable doubt is that Phillips was woefully ill-informed about the range and power of Japanese aircraft. This is dealt with more fully in a chapter below, but in essence the Royal Navy based its assessment of Japanese capabilities round its carrier-based biplane, the 'Stringbag' or Fairey Swordfish, and the land-based Beaufort. Both had significantly shorter range than their Japanese counterparts. British experience pointed to 200 miles as the standard reach of torpedo bombers, and that the risk from them at 400 miles or over was negligible. The British had no idea that Japanese aircraft were capable of at least twice that range, and could launch torpedoes at twice the height and twice the speed of their Fleet Air Arm equivalents. It is interesting that this failure to recognize the strength of Japanese *materiel* did not extend to Japanese submarines, which were regarded as a potent and effective threat. As for surface ships, the last ship built for Japan in Britain was the battle-cruiser *Kongo* in 1910. Ironically, it was this vessel the crews of Force Z were told they were most likely to face if they met any Japanese surface forces, and the men were understandably optimistic about the outcome of a duel between Britain's most modern battleship and a battle-cruiser, albeit modernized, that pre-dated the First World War.

Thus though dismissal of Japanese *materiel* was not universal and across the board, what does seem to have infected service culture, and spread to the ranks, was an arrogant, colonial, racist and above all plain wrong judgment on the fighting prowess of the Japanese:

'In lectures troops were told that the Japanese were small, myopic and technically backward ... The British military attaché at the Tokyo embassy complained after a visit to Malaya: 'our chaps place the Japs somewhere between the Italians and the Afghans' ... Japan's failure to defeat China had not impressed European soldiers.'[3]

The publicity given to the arrival of *Prince of Wales* in Singapore and other vessels (a failure to name that rankled with survivors of *Repulse* until their dying day) was also quite a gross intelligence failure. Intended to inflate Force Z as a deterrent, it arguably failed entirely in that aim and gave the Japanese significant operational intelligence. It also created a level of public expectation that in effect made it impossible for the two ships to sneak out and hide in the islands or retreat. As the Admiralty sowed, so Force Z reaped.

One question that remains unanswered despite the vast amount of print expended on the story of Force Z is whether or not the Admiralty actually knew that the Japanese had long-range torpedo bombers within range of the British force. One reason for thinking they did is the unsubstantiated report credited to a now-dead survivor of *Prince of Wales*: 'After I got back to Singapore, Tom's Staff Officer (Intelligence), who also survived the sinking, told me that he had discovered since his return that intelligence about these torpedo bombers had been available in Singapore.'[4]

A further piece of evidence is the otherwise inexplicable signal timed at 2210 on 9 December, when Force Z was en route to Kuantan, from the Admiralty, warning Phillips about the danger of a Taranto-style attack on Singapore. Such a signal only makes sense if the Admiralty had been told the Japanese had torpedo-bombers capable of reaching Singapore:

'Tom asked if I knew what the First Sea Lord was getting at. I said I knew what he was referring to but that I couldn't see any relevance since there was, so far as I knew, no possibility of torpedo attack in the Johor Strait until either the Japanese had carriers in the area or had established shore-based aircraft in Malaya. He said that was what he felt too.'[5]

If it was indeed known by the Admiralty or even at Singapore, it is clear that it was not known to Phillips, or to any of his staff.

The sinking of the two ships was unusual in that more people survived than were killed. We have testimony from a wide range of people, including senior people who were with Phillips until the last minute. This was not like the sinking of the *Bismarck*, where the most senior survivor was a relatively junior officer whose vision of what was going on was limited to what could be seen from a gunnery director tower. Unfortunately the deaths of people most closely concerned with this issue has meant that it is likely forever to remain a premise rather than ever be proven a certainty. It would, however, be typical of the dysfunctional organization that was Singapore if vital intelligence had not been passed on to the person for whom it was

most vital. The story of *Prince of Wales* and *Repulse* is full of ifs and buts
– if the weather had not lifted, if Force Z had not lingered off Kuantan,
if the Brewster Buffaloes had arrived in time… To this list must be added
another topic: if Phillips had known there were torpedo-bombers in range
of his force, would he have acted differently? It can never be proven beyond
reasonable doubt, but I believe the balance of probability is that a man of
Phillips's proven intelligence would have at the least addressed the return
of his ships to Singapore with a degree more urgency. As ever in this most
imponderable of disasters, even then Force Z might not have avoided its fate.
Was Force Z sunk by the failure to pass on vital intelligence information?

Operation Matador

It is frequently said that the military at Singapore were unprepared for war
with Japan. This is not true. A disaster had been predicted in the mid-1930s
and was reinforced by further reports after the outbreak of European war.
The problem was that, with one exception, precious little had been done
to bolster the known weakness of Singapore's defences, particularly as
regards a land invasion. This arose not because of an under-estimate of the
weakness of Singapore, but more a belief – or perhaps just a hope – that
actual war would never happen. One thing that was done was planning for
Operation Matador, a pre-emptive invasion of southern Thailand to prevent
a Japanese occupation. In the event, the British imposed double jeopardy
on themselves with the plan. Planning for Matador took time and resources
away from reinforcing the Jitra Line, sometimes described as Singapore's
Maginot Line, time and resources which were not justified when Matador –
which had actually been sufficiently viable for the Commander-in-Chief to
be given permission on 5 December to launch it on his own initiative in the
event of invasion – was called off: '… preparations for Operation Matador
had been allowed to distract attention from quite basic safeguards at Jitra.'[6]

No one can know now whether or not Matador might have worked. Its
basic concept was sound, and had it succeeded even in part it would have
helped keep control of vital airfields in RAF hands, with a subsequent knock-
on effect on the RAF's ability to provide cover for Force Z. It was bedeviled
from the outset by an almost obsessive fear on the part of the Government of

breaching Thai neutrality before the Japanese had given at least equal cause for complaint to the Thai Government. However, what really killed it was failure to act on and delayed intelligence, which allowed for indecisiveness on the part of the military command. This failure to pass on or make proper use of intelligence could be seen as strengthening the case for arguing that other, vital information was not passed on to Force Z. On 6 December a Hudson bomber spotted the Japanese invasion force of about twenty transports, with naval escort, but Brooke-Popham in Singapore persuaded himself in Singapore that he could not be sure of the convoy's destination, and even wondered if it was part of a ruse to get Britain to violate Thai neutrality before Japan did. Bad weather closed in, and though the RAF sighted the invasion force again on the afternoon of 7 December, for some reason the information did not reach Singapore HQ until 9.00pm that night, when the convoy had split up to mount various landings. Brooke-Popham postponed a decision on Matador. By 8 December it became clear that the Japanese had won the race to Singora: Matador, a pre-emptive strike, made no sense after the event.

The failure to launch Matador had in it the seeds of destruction both for Singapore and *Prince of Wales* and *Repulse*. As regards the former, Matador meant that vital supplies of things as basic as barbed wire and signaling cable were stored ready for transport, rather than being available to defend against the Japanese. As for the latter, the collapse of air bases along the length of the Peninsula was a major factor in denuding Force Z of air cover. Had Matador been launched, it would no doubt have been as chaotic as the rest of the defence of Singapore. The difference would have been that it would have shared some of the chaos in unsettling the invaders, instead of concentrating the chaos on the defenders alone.

SS *Automedon*

Another incident related to Intelligence that has caused considerable controversy, is the sinking of the steamer *Automedon* on 11 November 1940 by the German surface raider *Atlantis*. For some reason the ship had been entrusted to deliver to the Commander-in-Chief in Singapore a package containing Top Secret documents which gave the gloomiest possible assessment of the strength of British forces in Singapore, stated that a fleet would not be available anywhere near immediately to be based in Singapore, that Hong Kong was indefensible and that Britain would not declare war on Japan if it invaded Indo-China. In effect, the documents displayed extraordinary weaknesses in Britain's ability to defend its Far East territories, and suggested in the event of war Japan would face far less resistance than might otherwise have been expected. It remains a mystery why such important and secret documentation was given to a lowly steamer to deliver. Brooke-Popham, who had finished his journey to his new command by seaplane, could even at a pinch have taken it himself. The material was contained in the type of small, green weighted bag, with holes in it that allowed sensitive documentation to be thrown overboard if it looked like the material would be captured or compromised. Unfortunately, in opening fire on *Automedon* the first shells from *Atlantis* destroyed the bridge and killed the personnel who would normally have disposed of the bag. An enterprising German officer leading the boarding party recognized from its appearance what value the bag might hold. *Atlantis*'s Captain transferred the bag to a ship he had captured earlier, which delivered it safely to the German Embassy in Tokyo and thence to Berlin, but not before a copy had been given to the Japanese. There was some initial suspicion from the Japanese, who suspected a forgery designed to draw Japan in to war with Britain. It now seems certain that the report on the military preparedness of Singapore may have played a significant part in Japan's willingness to contemplate all-out war, though it is doubtful that the leaking of the document caused war. Certainly it is reported that the Captain of the *Atlantis* received an ornate Samurai sword, of which the only other two awarded were to Goering and Rommel.

In effect the captured paper said that in the event of war, or the threat of war, Britain would play for time to allow forces to be built up, and would not be in a position to offer military resolve for some months. Whilst such information might not in itself have caused war to break out, it is conceivable that it might have influenced the nature of that campaign. The Japanese took an extraordinary gamble in the speed of their assault, and indeed in taking on Singapore itself. Their armour-piercing bombs had all gone on the attack on Pearl Harbor. There were no spare torpedoes after the initial attacks on

Force Z. Japanese naval forces were stretched to the extreme, as is witnessed by the fact that the nearest carrier when Force Z was attacked was nearly 2,000 miles away and the heavy escort for the invasions was supplied by a venerable battle-cruiser that had been launched before the First World War. We know now how short the Japanese were of essential supplies when Singapore surrendered. Is it possible that the realization that Britain saw time as its greatest asset in the capture of Singapore was the most potent reason behind the Japanese launching a campaign that denied this commodity to Britain above all others?

If this is the case then the *Automedon* did play a part in the sinking of Force Z. Tom Phillips left Singapore with a 'puny' force, the possibility of air support was thrown into chaos as was, possibly, communication between his ships and Singapore because the speed of the Japanese advance meant that the British, Indian and Australian forces opposing them were permanently on the back foot.

In what might seem an odd link, there is a connection here between the sinking of *Prince of Wales* and *Repulse,* and the British failure to sink the German battle-cruisers *Scharnhorst* and *Gneisenau* and the heavy cruiser *Prince Eugen* in the Channel Dash of February 1942. Operation Cerberus, as it was codenamed by the Germans, involved the three ships and their escorts sailing straight past England's front door to reach their home ports. Hitler gambled that the British would simply not be quick enough on their feet to cope, and a master stroke was to have the ships leave at night, when the Admiralty – who knew a great deal about the operation not least of all because they had a French naval officer feeding them information – had decided that the ships would use the darkness to traverse the narrowest and hence most dangerous part of the Channel. A series of mechanical and human errors meant that the ships were not spotted for twelve hours, and when they were it was a question of too little, too late. The confusion and even chaos surrounding the attacks on the German ships by aircraft and light surface ships is chillingly reminiscent of some of the action taken against the Japanese at Singapore. Perhaps no army, navy or air force responds well to surprises, but British armed forces in the Second World War did seem to have a weakness in this area, particularly if the operation in question required co-operation between Army, Navy and RAF.

Chapter 9

Aircraft

ircraft dominate any discussion of the sinking of Force Z. One area that has not commanded much discussion is what has hitherto been the accepted fact that the new carrier *Indomitable* was intended to accompany Force Z. In November 1941 *Indomitable* carried twelve Fulmar aircraft, twenty-four Albacores and nine Sea Hurricanes, but ran aground whilst working up in the West Indies. Repairs in Norfolk, Virginia, took only twelve days, but this was too late for the ship to join Force Z. Discussion has tended to focus on the difference *Indomitable* might have made to Force Z.

The Fairey Fulmar, designed for carrier work, carried a crew of two because it was envisaged that it would be involved in long oversea flights. It was not expected to meet fighter opposition, so it prioritized long range and heavy armament over manoeuvrability and speed. It would certainly have been a useful addition to Force Z's defences, as there were no fighters accompanying the aircraft that bombed Force Z. In many respects Force Z faced exactly the threats the slow and rather cumbersome Fulmar had been designed to cope with. The Sea Hurricane's performance suffered somewhat from the design changes needed to render it fit for flying from carriers, but was a useful fighter. The Fairey Albacore, more usually known as the 'Applecore', was an improved Swordfish with an enclosed cockpit and a design that allowed it to act as a dive bomber. It would have had no obvious role in defending in the attacks launched against *Prince of Wales* and *Repulse*.

Indomitable herself was a very useful design. Essentially an improved *Illustrious* class, the improvement centred on remedying one of the major defects of British carriers with their armoured flight decks, namely the small number of aircraft they were able to carry. *Indomitable* carried an extra half hangar, achieved by reducing the thickness of her side armour, and hence carried significantly more aircraft than *Illustrious*, though accurate figures are very difficult to give. To state the obvious, some aircraft are bigger than others. Figures for aircraft carried are significantly affected by whether the aircraft have folding wings, whether or not fire curtains are down and whether or not the navy in question is using 'deck parks' for aircraft. Thus one source gives aircraft number for *Illustrious* as thirty-three in 1940, but fifty-seven in 1944. It is probably safe to use as a comparator forty-five aircraft as the number *Indomitable* could comfortably launch, as distinct from thirty-three for the *Illustrious*. She was also designed with a heavy anti-aircraft barrage of her own, though it is not clear how much of this was fitted by November 1941. Her armoured flight deck allowed her to survive a direct hit from a Stuka and Kamikaze attacks later in the war, and though a tough nut to crack there is no reason to think she was capable of surviving the concentrated Japanese air attack on Force Z, particularly as one assumes she would have been the priority target. Her defensive strength was in the armoured flight deck that protected her from bombs. Her hull was vulnerable still to torpedoes, more so than *Prince of Wales* and *Repulse.*

However, theoretical war-games played years after the event cannot distinguish between the notional power of an air group and its effectiveness in battle. Firstly, the effective operation of a CAP (Combat Air Patrol) requires considerable skill from the controllers. It was fighters chasing after low-level US torpedo bombers and hence ignoring incoming high-altitude dive bombers that were partly responsible for the Japanese losing three carriers as the Battle of Midway, and there were no more experienced practitioners in carrier warfare than the Japanese. Inasmuch as one can judge, any CAP from *Indomitable* would have gone after the bombers which launched the first attack, rather than the torpedo bombers which caused the crucial damage. Secondly, it requires considerable training for surface ships to exercise the self-discipline not to blast its own aircraft out of the sky when those aircraft are offering close support. As with any carrier engagement, success or failure for *Indomitable's* aircraft would have depended on the ship's ability to launch enough aircraft of the right type to meet in time the incoming threat, and to direct those aircraft on to the right targets. But yet again we would have had the *Prince of Wales* scenario, of a ship given an inadequate time to work up to full efficiency because of the exigencies of wartime, with even less experience of a shooting war than *Prince of Wales*, inexperienced pilots and no training as part of an integrated battle group. Most commentators believe that had *Indomitable* joined Force Z it would simply have joined them at the bottom of the sea, and in this instance most commentators are right.

But the question of whether or not *Indomitable* would have made a difference may be even more academic than that. One of the few things that up until now has been a more or less accepted truth about the sinking of Force Z is that it was planned that *Indomitable* should join it. The carrier was working up in the West Indies, it is usually said, and was only stopped from joining Force Z because it ran aground on 3 November and had to sail to the USA to have a new bow fitted. It has taken a good many years for a historian to spot that there is no actual record of this decision having been taken: 'The *Prince of Wales* and *Repulse* were simply not going to have an aircraft carrier at any time in the near future, but they were sent on to Singapore anyway.'[1]

The situation at the time regarding carriers was dire. *Victorious* was needed for the Home Fleet. *Ark Royal* was sunk on 14 November. *Illustrious* and *Formidable* were under repair in USA until 12 December. *Eagle* and *Furious* started long refits in October. It is easy to see why sending Britain's most modern carrier to a deterrent mission in the Far East, particularly when she was not fully worked-up, might have seemed a less than brilliant idea. There may have been an intention or understanding that *Indomitable* would be sent, but there seems no contemporary record of it as a certainty, and Nicholson argues that the idea was dropped almost immediately.[2]

I have been unable to trace any order to *Indomitable* to proceed to join with Force Z prior to the ship grounding on 3 November, and even if she had been ordered to Singapore then it would have been virtually impossible for her to get there in time. Churchill and the Admiralty appear to have been covering their backs in suggesting, publically and vociferously after the event, that it had always been intended to provide Tom Phillips with a fleet carrier, something that shows how much the living can influence the stories around the dead. Certainly on 3 November when she grounded, *Indomitable* was proceeding from Bermuda to Jamaica, with none of the signs of what one might expect for a new ship ordered to a combat zone, such as increased training or the fairly frantic resupply of ammunition and stores that precedes a long cruise. It does seem that what, post-event, was trumpeted as a certainty was in fact nothing more than an intention which never materialized other than as a form of post-mortem justification. One piece of evidence that suggests Phillips at least never did believe he was going to get *Indomitable* is his complete silence on the issue. Given the fuss he made over the need for air cover before Force Z sailed surely there would be some form of protest from Phillips about its absence from his force if he had ever expected it to be there? On the surface the only reasonable explanation as to why Phillips never complained about the loss of *Indomitable* is that he never expected to have it in the first place and, of course, that he did not really expect his ships to have to fight.

If one follows the issue of aircraft and the loss of *Prince of Wales* and *Repulse* chronologically, there is the issue of why *Hermes* was left in Simonstown when Force Z virtually passed it on its way to Singapore. *Hermes* was the first ship to be designed and built as an aircraft carrier, though not the first to be commissioned. Actually begun during the First World War, she was not commissioned until 1927, partly because of a series of design changes ordered in the light of experience with the existing ships that had been converted to carriers. By 1938 she had been placed in reserve and was used as a training ship, and was called out of retirement for the war. Slow (her maximum speed when new was twenty-five knots), lightly armed and armoured and carrying only a handful of aircraft (a design maximum of twenty that realistically was nearer fifteen), she could neither have kept up with *Prince of Wales* and *Repulse*, nor defended them. In any event her capabilities were irrelevant. She was in Simonstown with condenser problems, and was in no fit state to travel. What was in effect a refit was to last from November 1941 to February 1942. *Hermes* would have been a complete liability for Force Z, would have robbed it of the speed that was one of its few advantages and in any event was mechanically disqualified. *Hermes* was never going to replace *Indomitable* or indeed any modern fleet carrier.

The next issue was the ability of the RAF in Singapore to do its job. Discussion has tended to focus on the quality of the aircraft the RAF had in Singapore, and the failure – bitterly resented by Tom Phillips among others – to send modern fighters to Singapore. Yet the RAF's problems in Singapore went deeper than issues of *materiel*. Long before the arrival of Force Z there were problems of plain bull-headedness:

'All of the new Malayan airfields were vulnerable to attack by a force landing on the sandy beaches dotted along the east coast, yet the Air Force had insisted on these sites – despite objections from the Army whose job was to protect them … This was the origin of a serious rift between the two services.'[3]

One questions whether this was the origin of a rift or merely a symbol. In effect, the RAF chose to go its own way because it wanted the increased range the siting of its airfields would give, and be damned to whether or not they were defensible. There was no coordinated air defence policy for Singapore, and the defence of the city when it was first raided by Japanese aircraft was left to searchlights and guns. If these decisions suggest failings on the part of the leadership of the RAF, events lower down the food chain suggest there were problems there too.

The first landings at Kota Bharu airfield preceded Pearl Harbor by seventy minutes. They were not the RAF's finest hour. RAF personnel, disheartened by Japanese strafing and land attacks, set fire to buildings and lorries, and then abandoned base by truck despite no orders having been given to do so. Similarly, when Kuantan Air Base was attacked it was given up and withdrawal ordered by Air HQ Singapore. The Blenheims left in the early morning, the Hudsons and Vildebeests by 4.00pm. Panic evacuation then followed by mostly Australian ground staff, an affair that was the subject of a Court of Enquiry after the war. An Australian Squadron Leader arriving in Singapore in August 1940 wrote:

'Right up until hostilities broke out RAF units, with the exception of one maintenance unit, worked only from 0730 to 1230 each day, with 15 minutes break during the morning … The evident lack of control exercised by senior officers at stations and units, in my opinion, resulted in the disinterested attitude which permeated the whole of the RAF in Malaya.'[4]

An additional problem was rivalry and conflict between the RAF contingent in Malaya, and the RAAF, between whom there was no love lost. When all this is added to poor training of at least some pilots, it is clear that in many respects the RAF in Singapore in late 1941 was a dysfunctional organization. Its capacity to carry out its duties, and even to define what those duties were, was not helped by the hierarchy of government in Singapore and the individuals in power. Sir Shenton Thomas was the last Governor of the Straits Settlements and British High Commissioner for Malaysia: 'Both Pulford and Rear Admiral Jackie Spooner later blamed Sir Shenton Thomas for the absence of air protection provided for Force Z. They were adamant that as soon as Thomas knew of the possibility that fighter aircraft might be diverted from the air defence of Singapore to provide air cover for Force Z, he had protested most vehemently against their use for this purpose.'[5]

Through no fault of his own, Phillips's need for air cover was at risk from the outset:

> '... the Navy would have to request any support from an RAF which had always taken pleasure in thumbing its nose at the senior service. When that pleasure could be justified by a very real shortage of aircraft, the Navy's chances of achieving operational co-operation were not good.'[6]

It is clear that Admiral Sir Tom Phillips did everything in his power, verbally and in writing, to get air cover for Force Z. He had been offered fighter cover only if he agreed for his ships not to go more than 100 miles north of Kota Bharu, and no more than sixty miles from coast at any time, a requirement that was about as sensible as building airfields exactly where the Japanese would find it easiest to capture them and the Army hardest to defend them. In simple operational terms it was an impossibility to tie a raiding force down in this manner.

This brings us back to the question as to why Phillips did not call for air cover. Knowledge of the chaos that was the RAF in Singapore in December 1941 only adds to the obvious answer: *Tom Phillips and everyone who could read a signal on Force Z had absolutely no reason to think that air cover was available.* If it was, why had no one told them? One of the most ill-advised comments on the loss of Force Z is: '... It is reasonable to assume that he [Phillips] knew there were some fighter aircraft available should he call for them.'[7]

Why is it 'reasonable'? Given what he had been told, and what he had not been told, the 'reasonable' position was exactly the opposite. What would have been unreasonable would have been to suppose it was available.

Commentators have also tended to pass over the fact that there were Allied aircraft over Kuantan, which failed to spot Force Z and could have called for air cover if they had. The fact that RAF aircraft sent out to spot an invasion force could not see a battleship, a battle-cruiser and three destroyers is in itself a condemnation of the RAF's being fit for purpose at the time. It was not a mistake the Japanese would make.

The final issue from the Allied side is what difference, if any, the Brewster Buffaloes which we now know were available, but about which no one seems to have bothered to inform Force Z, would have made had they arrived in time.

The Brewster Buffalo was a disaster: 'These had given consistent trouble since their arrival from America, demanding twenty-seven modifications before being either safe or battle-worthy.'[8]

The initial armament of Colt .5-inch machine guns tended to fire one shot each and then cease. The cocking handles for each gun required the pilot to put his feet against something and pull, but as only two of the handles were accessible, there was not much else going on in terms of flying while the guns were being cocked, and even that only gave two more shots. Two of the guns fired through the propeller via an interrupter mechanism, but this was unreliable. '... things used to get out of function and now and again you would punch a hole in the prop.'[9]

Even with the lighter guns, the aircraft had very limited endurance, a ceiling of 22,000 feet on a hot day and up to half an hour to reach that ceiling. Oil seals had a tendency to burst and blot out the pilot's view by spraying oil on the windscreen, and at altitude the aircraft suffered from fuel starvation and supercharger problems. The plane's radios were out of date and unreliable, and the realistic maximum speed of a 270mph (sometimes given as a rarely-achieved 313mph) revealed an aircraft short of several hundred horsepower, and with an unreliable Wright Cyclone engine. At least some of the planes supplied to Britain were given an even less powerful engine than their American counterparts. The purchase of the planes was not a result of their quality, but more Hobson's choice. When appraising the planes the

RAF criticized their armament, engine overheating and poor performance at high altitude. In essence the problem with the Brewster Buffalo was that its airframe was not strong enough to take the more powerful engine it needed to be an effective fighter.

The replacement of the Colts by .303 Brownings gave more reliability of fire but a lighter hitting power and increased chance of blowing a hole in the propeller. As initially designed the Buffalo (known as the 'Bullock' among ground crew) carried no armour plate to protect the pilot. When protection was installed it altered the centre of gravity of the plane. In a dive it was necessary to manipulate the trim tabs, but with one hand off the joystick it was liable to flick back uncontrollably. The Buffalo was totally outclassed by the Zero, but even Japanese bombers could give them a run for their money, largely through the Buffaloes' slow rate of climb.

A factor rarely mentioned is that Buffaloes that had flown at full speed to Kuantan might well have found themselves with limited fuel over the combat zone, suggesting they might have disrupted one attack but not all.

So would the Buffaloes have saved the ships? One senior Japanese officer certainly thought so: 'It was completely incredible that the two warships should be left naked to attack from the skies. Interception of our level and torpedo-bombers by British fighters might have seriously disrupted our attack and perhaps permitted the two warships to escape destruction.'[10]

Flight Lieutenant Tom Vigors led the Buffaloes that arrived just as the battle was over. He too was vociferous about what might have been: 'Six fighters could have made one hell of a mess of even fifty or sixty slow and unescorted torpedo bombers.'[11]

Those who believe the Buffaloes could have saved the day have further evidence in their favour in terms of the aircraft used by the Japanese, the Mitsubishi Type 96 G3M3 Nell and the Mitsubishi Navy Type 1 G4M1 Betty. Both types sacrificed armament and protection for the crew in favour of range, altitude and speed. They were prone to exploding fuel tanks, and their crews had a notoriously high mortality rate. However, with all this being said, they could fly at a significantly higher altitude than the Buffalo, and at high altitude their speed was not greatly below that of the Buffalo.

There are a number of contrasting factors that suggest the arrival of what was a relatively small force of Buffaloes would not have saved the ships.

Newly Qualified Tom Phillips.

Admiral Sir Tom Phillips.

Admiral Phillips and Churchill.

Tom Phillips Tour of Command, probably
HMS *Aurora*.

Captain Leach.

Captain Tennant after the sinking.

Tennant as Vice-Admiral.

Churchill negotiating with Blanche, *Prince of Wales*'s ship's cat, with US destroyer alongside.

Admiral Stark, Admiral Pound and Admiral King.

Admiral Palliser and Admiral Phillips at Singapore.

Admiral Palliser and Admiral Phillips at Singapore in more relaxed mode.

Admiral Phillips and Admiral Palliser on the quayside as *Prince of Wales* docks in Singapore.

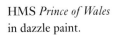

HMS *Prince of Wales* in dazzle paint.

Prince of Wales's Walrus aircraft.

5.25" guns, the main anti-aircraft defence of *Prince of Wales*.

The secondary anti-aircraft defence of *Prince of Wales*, her 'pom-poms'.

5.25" guns firing on *Prince of Wales*.

Prince of Wales's solitary, stern-mounted Bofors gun.

Chief Engineer's Control Room, *Prince of Wales*.

Engine Room, *Prince of Wales*.

Damage to *Prince of Wales* after the *Bismarck* action.

Boiler Room, *Prince of Wales*.

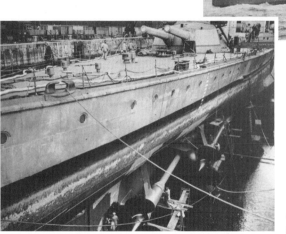

HMS *Repulse*.

Repulse in dry dock, showing her rudder and propellors.

HMS *Electra*.

HMS *Tenedos*.

HMS *Express*.

The Japanese cruiser *Chokai*.

Prince of Wales docking at Singapore.

The final photographs of both vessels, leaving Singapore for the last time.

Prince of Wales and *Repulse*: Japanese photograph of the action.

Japanese photographs of the attack.

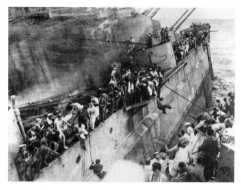

Electra alongside *Prince of Wales*.

Captured Japanese 'Betty' aircraft in RAF livery.

Flight Lieutenant Vigors, a young Australian pilot, is best known for making a fool of himself in flying over the scene of the sinking and reporting men in the water as waving and cheering, when in fact they were almost certainly cursing the RAF for the late arrival over the scene of their planes:

'I witnessed a show of the indomitable spirit for which the Royal Navy is famous … as I flew round, every man waved and put his thumb up as I flew over him … I had seen many men in dire danger waving, cheering and joking, as if they were holiday-makers at Brighton waving at low-flying aircraft. It shook me, for here was something above human nature. I take off my hat to them, for in them I saw the spirit which wins wars.'[12]

One has to be careful not to confuse those who win a war of words with those who win the real thing. There were veterans of the Battle of Britain in Singapore, but the majority of the pilots were inexperienced, and vastly so when it came to aerial combat and the defence of capital ships against air attack. Vigors was a brave young pilot, but he had been ordered from Kallang to command 453 squadron and was shot down in flames on his first sortie. Though wounded, he survived being machine-gunned by Japanese aircraft as he hung from his parachute. Thus the man who claimed his aircraft would have carved up the Japanese attacking *Prince of Wales* and *Repulse* was himself carved up early in combat. Buried in the only book to have been written about the Buffaloes in the Singapore Campaign is a comment from one of the pilots who arrived over the sinking that strikes a different note: 'If there had been Japanese aircraft about there was not a great deal we could have done.'[13]

The same Flight Lieutenant Vigors who professed how easy it would have been for the RAF to shoot down Force Z's attackers was also the officer who discussed air cover for Force Z with the officer responsible from *Prince of Wales*. It was Vigors who suggested the RAF could provide fighter cover to a force whose ships were not to go more than 100 miles north of Kota Bharu, and no more than sixty miles from coast at any time, a condition that was an operational impossibility. One cannot help but wonder, given the fact that there was no love lost between the Services, if this rejection left the RAF feeling it had tried and failed to help, that the whole thing was therefore not their problem.

Certainly there was an alternative Japanese view that the Buffaloes would have made little real difference: '... assuming our attack squadrons were intercepted by the ten Buffalo fighters when we attacked Force Z, we would still have sunk the two battleships, although the damage and losses would have been increased to some extent.'[14]

This assessment is based partly on the assumption that the Buffaloes would have gone first for the Nell bombers, which the pilots would have known were slower than the Bettys and whose 20mm canon had a limited range of fire. The Bettys would also have been first in line for the Buffaloes as they were flying at a higher altitude than the Nells, and no Buffalo pilot liked to lose altitude when it took him so much time to regain it. However, the Bettys would have been flying in tight formation for mutual protection, and were sufficiently well trained to continue their bombing run even when under attack. The Nells would have been the easier target, and were the most lethal to Force Z, but there is no reason to think the pilots were trained to spot this, concentrate on a target *before* it launched its torpedo, or choose individual targets rather than 'ganging up' on a few aircraft. It has to be deemed likely that pilots untrained in this kind of operation, even had they reached the low-level torpedo-bombers, would have been attracted to attacking the torpedo-bombers when they were most vulnerable, after they had launched their torpedo and were struggling to gain height. The Buffalo pilots had been trained to destroy enemy aircraft, not protect surface ships. The absence of radio communication or any combat air patrol direction from the surface ships also meant the aircraft could not be directed on to the most immediate target. These were pilots untrained in the task they would have had to do, and in effect from the moment they sighted the enemy it would have been every (inexperienced) man for himself. This could not have been in starker contrast to the Japanese. Whilst the Allied pilots were inexperienced in combat, and inexperienced in defending capital ships, they were facing arguably the best-trained and most potent anti-surface aircraft and aircrew in the world:

'All through the summer of 1941 Rear-Admiral Sadaichi Matsunga's 22nd Air Flotilla had been carrying out an intensive sea-attack training programme from their airfields in South Formosa. Many of the pilots had already seen action in China and had carried out attacks against Chinese shipping. Their future targets were likely to be more heavily and skillfully defended, however, and this prolonged course was intended to prepare the crews for the time when they would have to meet the fire of British and American warships and fighters.'[15]

Much later in the campaign it was reported that the Buffaloes' guns were still jamming, and if, as seems to be the case, some were using only the two wing-mounted guns, then their capacity to do serious damage would have been limited. An earlier extract showed that the radios were not working, which would have ruled out any coordinated attack, even had the pilots been trained for it. Buffalo tactics were to dive down on the enemy, fire a three to five second burst and then try to get away – very similar, in fact, to the tactics used by German fighters low on fuel in the Blitz over London. The nightmare for a Buffalo pilot was to be caught at low altitude. It could take up to half an hour for the Buffalo to reach its operational ceiling. Had the planes arrived earlier and concentrated on the bombers it would have been completely the wrong target. Given the lack of armour-piercing or even heavy bombs available to them, the Japanese had planned to reduce the upper works and superstructure of the two capital ships, thus reducing their anti-aircraft power, and then attack with torpedoes. This might have brought into play another weakness of the Buffalo, and one of the strengths of the Betty. The Buffalo presented a large head-on target because of its big belly, and the Betty had a tail-turret that unpleasantly surprised many American pilots. The likely attack position for the Buffaloes would have presented their weakest point to the Japanese aircraft's strongest point.

Rarely reported are the pilots who saw sinking capital ships, were convinced they were Japanese and flew home triumphant: 'Without any Japanese aircraft in the air, [we] turned and headed back ... [we] had no radios, but waved happily to each other. That must have been one hell of a fight, with the Japanese Navy taking it right where it hurt most.'[16]

Yet actually the whole thing is a sterile and dry academic debate. 'What if the Buffaloes had arrived in time?' is undeniably an interesting question, but it is not the crucial one. The fateful, crucial decision was taken before the first Brewster Buffalo could or did take off. It was to decide not to signal Admiral Tom Phillips that some fighters at least were available – if one is to believe their commander, with the pilots actually sitting in their cockpits waiting to be scrambled.[17] Seen in this light, it is not true that: 'The heaviest responsibility for the Force Z calamity … must be borne by the RAF … An obsession with the heavy bombing of Germany, approved and even encouraged by Churchill, resulted in not a single modern aircraft being allocated to the Far East.'[18]

It was not the RAF that had decided not to send modern fighters to Malaya, of course, but Churchill, an action bitterly opposed by Tom Phillips at the time. Yet the heaviest responsibility lies with the individuals or individual who kept news of the available fighter support away from Phillips. The finger must point at Palliser. It was he who had told Phillips in an appallingly worded signal that fighter cover was not available, he who had signalled the likely prioritization of air cover for the defence of Singapore. He took no risks of revealing the whereabouts of Force Z by sending a signal. He should have known where it was heading because it was his signal, false as it turned out, that sent it there, but either way he knew Force Z was heading home and should at least have told Phillips the limits of available cover, thus allowing Phillips to decide if it was worth calling for the cover. And if he did not know that the Buffaloes were waiting on the runway? Then it was exactly his job to find out, never mind badgering the RAF into providing cover whether they liked it or not.

There are some footnotes that need to be added to the discussion about air power. Firstly, we have seen that Phillips was aware of the importance of air cover. Yet the fact remains that high or medium-level bombing was a threat that had been overcome by surface vessels, even those stuck in port and unable to manoeuvre. Between March and July 1941 RAF, Bomber and Coastal Command had flown 1,875 sorties and dropped 2,000 tons of bombs on *Scharnhorst* and *Gneisenau* in Brest. There were nine hits causing only superficial damage and thirty-four aircraft were lost. 'It must be recognized,' wrote Churchill to the Chief of Air Staff in April 1941, 'that the inability of

Bomber command to hit the enemy (battle) cruisers in Brest constitutes a very definite failure of this arm.'[19]

Phillips set sail in the belief that his threat from the air would consist of high to mid-level bombing of the type that in the Mediterranean Royal Navy capital ships had been able to cope with, and which had visibly failed in France in attacks on stationary targets. Phillips did not invent this definition of the threat; it was simply what he had been told by the intelligence arm of the service he loved and trusted.

He and the Royal, Dutch, Australian and United States navies were all badly let down by the dismal inaccuracy of intelligence agencies in assessing Japanese strike potential. The Royal Navy took as its benchmark the performance of its own antiquated Swordfish torpedo bombers, which could drop a torpedo at a maximum speed of 90mph from a maximum height of 50ft, and assumed 200 miles as the reasonable range for such an attack, and 400 miles as the outside limit. In fact Japanese aircraft could double the speed and height of a torpedo drop, reducing the run-in time and therefore the vulnerability of the attacking aircraft. When on the approach of the torpedo bombers that to all intent and purposes sank his flagship Phillips said, 'There are no torpedo aircraft about' he was merely telling the truth as the Royal Navy saw it.

Phillips was the victim of a far wider failure of Intelligence. A makeshift Intelligence group had been formed in Singapore, and following research into a Zero fighter shot down in China meant that it had a good grasp of the quite frightening superiority of the Zero against the Buffalo. It appears that the information was passed on in late September to Air Command, but buried in a pile of other material and so ignored:[20]

> 'The general impression in Malaya was that Japanese aircraft were made of rice paper and bamboo shoots; and, except for the Zero incident, Combined Intelligence Bureau supplied no information to the contrary.'[21]

It also needs to be recorded that the figure for the percentage of bomb hits in the attack on *Prince of Wales* and *Repulse* – nine per cent of those dropped – confirms the relatively low threat posed by such attacks. Even the figure for torpedo hits – twenty-two per cent – needs to take into account that after the catastrophic hit that sheered off *Prince of Wales*'s 'A' bracket, the Japanese were aiming at a sitting duck, and were freed to give their attention to *Repulse*. That ship's remarkable feat in avoiding nineteen torpedoes also suggests that in hindsight it was not the torpedo as such that sunk both ships, but one torpedo in particular, in that once *Prince of Wales* was disabled the Japanese were able to concentrate on *Repulse*, thus more or less ensuring her destruction.

What is certainly untrue and unjust is a comment such as: 'Phillips, and only Phillips, was responsible for the ships being where they were, and he seems to have been almost alone in totally dismissing at least the *possibility* of torpedoes being used against him.'[22]

Responsibility for the ships being there starts, in descending order, with Roosevelt, and goes on down through Churchill, Pound, Palliser and Tennant. Nor was Phillips alone in dismissing the idea of a torpedo attack. Responsibility for that lies with the inadequacy of British Intelligence. It is extremely unlikely that any other of the Admirals mentioned in connection with the attack as having more seagoing and combat experience – Cunningham. Somerville and Layton are the obvious three – would have any more reason than he to predict torpedo attack.

It all comes down to the same point I have laboured throughout this work. We cannot judge the actions of Admiral Sir Tom Phillips on the basis of what we now know, but only on what he knew at the time he agonized over taking out his two capital ships, and when he decided to call off his mission. On the basis of what he knew, it was certainly a high-risk mission, but so a justifiable one; after all, what was at stake was Britain's Far Eastern Empire.

Chapter 10

Struggles for Power: Admiral Sir Tom Phillips and the Royal Navy in 1941

T he most senior Admiral who consistently defended Admiral Sir Tom Phillips after the loss of *Prince of Wales* and *Repulse* was his erstwhile boss, Dudley Pound. Pound died in 1943, leaving the field clear for other admirals who were not supporters of Phillips, most notably Admirals Layton, Cunningham and Somerville. Their criticism of Phillips has provided easy ammunition for those who blame him for the sinking of Force Z, and has coloured the way successive historians have written of Phillips. The reputation of an Admiral is, of course, built on their actions. It is also built on their ability to defend themselves once the fighting is over and the post-mortems start. It is perhaps no accident that the three senior figures whose actions have either not been properly recognized or misrepresented all died during the war. Phillips was the first to go, and was the most senior naval officer killed in action. Pound was next, and Admiral Sir Bertram Home Ramsay, whose planning of the naval side of the 1944 invasion was absolutely crucial to its success, was killed in an air crash in 1945.

There were general reasons why the Royal Navy in general did not rally round and defend Tom Phillips, and reasons specific to individuals. As regards the culture prevalent in the Royal Navy at the time among its fighting admirals, Phillips was not popular among some of his contemporaries. 'I shudder to think', Admiral Somerville wrote to Admiral Cunningham, of '... the pocket Napoleon and his party. All the tricks to learn and no solid sea experience to fall back on. They ought to have someone who knows their stuff and can train that party properly on the way out.'[1]

News of Phillips's appointment to Force Z straight from a long string of staff postings was not popular in naval circles. Admiral Cunningham commented: 'What on earth is Phillips going to the Far Eastern squadron for? He hardly knows one end of a ship from the other. His only experience is as RAD [Rear Admiral Destroyers] and then he had the stupidest collision. However, if you have a seat on the board you can generally manoeuvre yourself into a good job – I did!'[2]

These comments illustrate a number of ways in which Phillips had made himself unpopular. Firstly, Phillips had received a double promotion, over the heads of a number of his contemporaries. Such promotions provoke jealousy in any organization, but more so in one that at the turn of the century trained and educated its officers in terms or years at the *Britannia* training college (actually two hulks moored together off Dartmouth) of less than 100 young men, in an intensely competitive environment. The result was that each new generation of naval officers knew each other extremely and perhaps even too well. It is as if the boys at a public school (to which *Britannia* bore many resemblances) had left that school all together to work at the same job for the same company, and a company that practised a fiercely competitive system of promotion that meant the majority of those young men would not get to a top job. It gave rise to close friendships, but could also lead to bitter enmities and jealousy.

Secondly, Phillips was seen as a Staff officer, not a real sailor or seaman. The Japanese navy was relatively unusual in prioritizing staff work for its most brilliant young officers, at the expense of seagoing experience. Contempt for staff officers (by definition non-combatants) is a long-standing military tradition. Hotspur uses it as an excuse for his behaviour to King Henry IV in Shakespeare's *King Henry IV Part One*. Hatred of Phillips was not helped by his perceived closeness to Winston Churchill. However, technology has introduced a new level of friction between commanders at sea and the Admiralty and its staff officers back home. The radio allowed the Admiralty much more knowledge of what was going on at sea than had ever been the case before. This issue first raised its serious head in the Norwegian Campaign, when several commanders at the sharp end felt that interfering signals had been sent out by the Admiralty. This needs another book to answer, but the truth probably lies halfway between the opposing parties. There were serious mistakes made on the front line, but the Admiralty had not learnt to use its new communication capacity to best advantage and sometimes did more harm than good. Whatever the rights and wrongs, the

Admiralty gained a reputation for unwarranted interference, and as VCNS and Pound's right hand man Phillips was seen as part and parcel of the problem.

Part of the resentment against Admiralty interference sprang from the Fisher reforms to the Royal Navy, which were also to do away with the original *Britannia*. Phillips, who became a Midshipman in 1904, was one of the last cadets to graduate from the two hulks moored in the Dart which formed the then Naval College. Admirals of Phillips's generation saw as Midshipmen and junior officers some of the greatest changes ever to affect the Royal Navy. In particular, Fisher's 'calling home of the legions' saw the centre of the Royal Navy move to home waters, the abolition of the Pacific Station, the amalgamation the Australia, China and East India Stations, and the similar amalgamation of the South Atlantic, North America and West Africa stations. Phillips's generation were the last to experience the dash, daring and eccentricity only achievable on ships that were for long periods out from under the eye of any Fleet Commander. Cunningham remembered these days with affection, from when he was a Midshipman on the cruiser *Fox* on the Cape Station in 1898: 'It was before the days of wireless ... our captain ... was monarch of all he surveyed.'[3]

A comment made in 1945 reveals an attitude that was quite widespread, and which though it had originated with the Fisher reforms had long outlived them:

> '... it was POUND and PHILLIPS, with their storekeeper minds, who quenched all the spirit in the fleet. Everything was scheduled; even a snipe shoot in a Greek swamp went into a book because ships were told to report full details of all sport when cruising independently.'[4]

In fact neither Pound nor Phillips were responsible for an individual commander's loss of freedom: radio, the demise of the type of battle fleet that fought at Jutland and the extremely fast movement of events that typified the Norwegian and the Greece/Crete Campaigns simply meant maritime conflict had to be commanded more from the centre. A crucial additional factor was ULTRA and the fact that the Admiralty frequently knew far more about what was happening, because they had cracked German codes, than did the commander at sea. It was essential that knowledge of ULTRA was on a strict need-to-know basis, and the information gleaned from it had to be used so as not to reveal to the Germans that Britain was reading its most secret signals. It meant that apparently gnomic or interfering orders from Whitehall could seem very different to those whose view was seas breaking over the bow of a battleship than it did to those whose view was the script of a decoded signal.

Thirdly, Phillips ran up against a body of opinion and a culture that valued physical prowess and seamanship more than intellectual ability. The emphasis on seamanship is understandable. It is, after all, at the heart of what sailors do. Phillips certainly had less time at sea than some of his contemporaries, but the allegation that he did not know one end of a ship from the other is simply stupid bigotry. Phillips commanded a destroyer for a year and a cruiser for three years, and the collision Cunningham refers to, between *Encounter* (a vessel which was to recur in the story as one of the 'crocks' Cunningham sent to reinforce Force Z) and *Furious,* did not even provoke a Board of Enquiry. There is no evidence that Phillips was a bad seaman, and even if he had been the best in the world it would not have saved *Prince of Wales.*

As for physical prowess, the Navy's emphasis might seem contradicted by the fact that *Britannia* had an extremely demanding entrance examination that all applicants had to pass. Despite this, *Britannia* followed the public school model by placing a great emphasis on competitive sport. Not only did it tire out a potentially extremely feisty group of young men. It encouraged all sorts of qualities that were a decided advantage in a military setting – physical fitness, personal bravery and courage, the ability to take pain and injury, the ability to be a team player and the will to win. For some whose physical stature did not allow them to excel at team sports, competitive sailing was an effective substitute, and a skill acquired by both Tom Phillips and A.B. Cunningham. 'Muscular Christianity' was not only the preserve of Rugby School's Thomas Arnold. It was, and is, a besetting sin of all-male establishments, which will insist on giving more credit to physical ability than intellectual prowess. It was another feature of the Royal Navy bearing many resemblances to the public schools of the time – or perhaps an inevitable feature of primarily all-male institutions – where athletic prowess was far more highly regarded than intellect. A fellow Admiral seeking to praise Captain Henry ('Trunky') Leach of *Prince of Wales* automatically turned to praise of his physical prowess: 'Navy standard at lawn tennis, and indeed he could hit any ball that moved, let alone being a fine shot.'[5] Apparently one of *Prince of Wales*'s best officers established himself by becoming known as Tarzan because of gymnastic expertise in the Mess. In reading memoirs and letters of the time, one is reminded of Edward Thring, Headmaster of Uppingham School, who as a new arrival is reported to have strode up to the crease with cricket bat in hand, dispatched his first ball for a six and proudly declared: 'Now I am Headmaster!' Only the very brightest passed out at the top of their year from *Britannia*, the Royal Navy's training ship, but intelligence was not the most highly regarded virtue in the Royal Navy in 1941. Phillips may have been the brightest intellect of his generation, noted at Dartmouth for his restless intelligence, and the letters written to his family after his death show how invaluable that intellect was at the Admiralty, and how impossible it was to replace. Yet that ability won Phillips little credit outside the charmed circle of the naval staff, Dudley Pound and Churchill. None of Phillips's enemies praised or even acknowledged his ability. Bravery, toughness and tenacity in the face of the enemy, and a bluff manliness, were the most obvious virtues, not intellectual ability. It was summed up by one Navy description of him as 'all brains and no body'.[6] The overwhelming concern for the body as distinct from the brain was shown by the number of naval officers who were near obsessive about physical exercise – even the undeniably bright Admiral Ramsay may have suffered heart strain from driving himself too hard physically as a Midshipman.

Phillips did not therefore fit into the same mould as many of his contemporaries, who gave their approval more to the man who having won the inter-services rugby cup for the Navy could steer *Ark Royal* stern first into Malta Harbour at full speed whilst avoiding a full-blown Stuka attack than to the man who could think why the ship was there in the first place. The answer, of course, is that both have their uses.

As regards individuals who have blackened Phillips's reputation, Vice Admiral Sir Geoffrey Layton was perhaps the one least qualified to make an objective judgment, as a clear case of sour grapes. Commander in Chief of the China station, Phillips had been promoted over his head, and Layton was not pleased about it. After the sinkings, he commented to his Secretary: 'I don't know exactly what's happened. But I always said he would make a balls of it, and he has.'[7] An analogy would be a Judge who commented he had not heard the evidence, but knew the defendant was guilty anyway. Layton seemed an obvious choice to many for the Far Eastern command. He had been a successful sub-mariner in the First World War, and had commanded the Fifth Cruiser Squadron in the North Sea at the start of the Second World War. He was a fighting admiral, very much the salty old sea dog. Cunningham wrote to Admiral of the Fleet Sir Algernon Willis:

> 'What do you think of the Far East? What about P of W & *Repulse*? Why & o why did they not send out someone of experience or at least have Geoffrey Layton who is a well-tried sailor & full of determination.'[8]

Yet on closer analysis it is clear why Layton was passed over. It was a little rich for those who supported him to justify his appointment on his seamanship. He ran aground his submarine *E13* off the Danish coast in 1915, and a German warship destroyed the boat and killed half the crew the next morning. Layton himself was interned, but managed to escape back to the UK. On the scale of things this was a far more serious incident than the collision between two destroyers which Phillips had held against him. However, Layton was unsuitable on other grounds. Layton could get on with officers from other navies, but his diplomatic skills were suspect. Roskill tells the following story in a footnote in his book *Churchill and the Admirals*:

> 'When I was investigating Admiral Layton's activities as C-in-C, Ceylon I was told an amusing story about how the recently appointed Civil Defence Commissioner Mr (later Sir Oliver) Goonetilleke complained that the Governor (Sir Andrew Caldecott) that Layton had called him "a black bastard". To which the Governor replied "My dear fellow that is nothing to what he calls me!"'[9]

Amusing? No doubt Mr Goonetilleke thought it hilarious. However, the speed and ease with which Layton was passed over gives strength to the idea that what Churchill and perhaps even the Admiralty needed for Singapore was a diplomat and a negotiator with the Americans, and someone whose known friendship with Churchill would only add to his credibility. The need for a fighting admiral came second and, as has been discussed, when called on to fight rather than negotiate Phillips showed himself to have the aggressive spirit of Layton without his unyielding personality.

Layton may have had a toughness that impressed some other senior officers, but it was allied with a massive insensitivity. Phillips has been criticized for being aloof. Layton seemed to find it quite easy to do far worse than appear as aloof. Hurriedly recalled to Singapore on the death of Phillips, Layton addressed the survivors of the two ships after an inspirational speech by Captain Tennant of *Repulse*. Layton's speech was 'thoroughly depressing'[10], and he told the survivors that they would no longer be known as the ship's company of *Prince of Wales* or *Repulse*, but would be used in whatever way seemed best to fight the forthcoming battle for Singapore. *Repulse*'s crew were tight-knit anyway, *Prince of Wales*'s drawn together by the catastrophe. The news they were to be split up and denied survivors' leave was a crushing blow to morale. Layton was unsympathetic towards a small number of former crewman from *Prince of Wales* who had been sent to man ferries under fire who walked out and took themselves back to Singapore, men who nowadays would have been immediately diagnosed as suffering from post-traumatic stress disorder, but his biggest disaster was the signal he sent out when he left Singapore just in time to avoid capture:

'Layton's apparent inability to express himself cogently was demonstrated by the signal he sent to the men of the Eastern Fleet a few weeks later when he was appointed C-in-C Ceylon – a signal dispatched at a time when the Japanese army was at the gates of Singapore and the future held only the prospect of death or captivity for all who were still on the island:

With your heads held high and your hearts beating proudly, I leave the defence of Singapore in your strong and capable hands. I am off to Colombo to collect a new fleet.

... the matelots who received the signal paraphrased the unfortunate choice of wording to mean: '*Pull up the ladder, Jack. I'm all right!*' As a message of farewell from their Commander-in-Chief it did not go down well.'[11]

There is nothing to suggest that Layton would have fared any better than Phillips with Force Z. The support given him does point to some of the least attractive features of the Royal Navy in 1941.

Admiral James Somerville was another person with an individual axe to grind. He had been successful in command of Force H, but had fallen foul of Churchill in the Battle of Spartivento and was possibly still smarting from the fact that his ships had had to open fire on units of the French fleet at Mers el Kebir, and despite this had allowed the battleship *Strasbourg* to make good its escape, whilst Cunningham a few days later persuaded the French fleet in Alexandria to disarm peacefully. He could realistically have expected the Far Eastern command that was given to Tom Phillips, as he was indeed given it after Phillips's death. His already-quoted comment: '... the pocket Napoleon and his party. All the tricks to learn and no solid sea experience to fall back on. They ought to have someone who knows the stuff and can train that party properly on the way out,'[12] is as unjust as Cunningham's comment that Phillips did not know one end of a ship from another. Apart from the fact that training a ship's company was the responsibility of the ship's Captain, not the Admiral flying his flag in that ship, *Prince of Wales* lacked any training on working with *Repulse*, a fact that given the latter ship being in a different ocean much of the time would have made it impossible for God himself, never mind Somerville, to train the two crews together. Somerville must have known that the gaps in the training of *Prince of Wales* in particular could not be remedied on the voyage to Singapore. In particular, the absence not only of aircraft but even of towed targets denied *Prince of Wales* the training in anti-aircraft fire that would have stood it in good stead. Nor, given the necessary speed of the trip out and the small number of ships involved, was it possible for *Prince of Wales* to do much about coordinating an anti-submarine screen of escorts or minesweeping operations.

Somerville was invalided out of the Navy with active TB in 1939, as the result of what was almost certainly a mistaken medical diagnosis, and, as was Ramsay, reinstated when war broke out. Somerville made light of this; his family believed it cut him deeply.[13] My own sense is of a man with a deep distrust of what he saw as the Naval Establishment, of which he saw Tom Phillips as a member. That distrust may not have had as its prime motivation that he was sent packing by the Navy on the grounds of an illness that had gone by the time he got home. More likely was his resentment at being ordered to open fire on the French by the Admiralty, when he persuaded himself that with more time he might have brokered a peaceful outcome; the refusal of the Admiralty to allow enough training time for Force H; the accusation emanating from the Admiralty that he was guilty of cowardice at Spartivento. Such feelings were never going to recommend Phillips to Somerville, because Somerville saw Phillips, not altogether justly, as sitting at the centre of the Establishment that undercut him and threatened his reputation.

Somerville spent most of his time as Commander in Chief of the Far Eastern Fleet avoiding the Japanese, and succeeding in this by a mix of sound judgment and plain good luck. It was an impossible job he was given, but his management of the fleet Tom Phillips might have had if he had survived does nothing to suggest Force Z under his command would have fared any differently from how it fared with Phillips. For example, Somerville was an inveterate risk-taker, though to his credit as a human being a number of the risks he took were in order to save his own men. Somerville led an attempt to locate the Japanese fleet that most authorities believe would have led to the loss of his two carriers had it succeeded. It was certainly no less audacious than Phillips's mission with Force Z, but was arguably more foolhardy. Somerville was an early advocate of aircraft in naval operations, and both knew about and was keen on technology, rather unusually so for Admirals of the time. It did not stop him risking two prime carriers against the Japanese, and Somerville at least had the carriers to call on, unlike Phillips.

However, the clash between Somerville and Phillips may simply have been one of personalities. Somerville was another example of someone who placed a high value – perhaps too high a value – on physical exertion. He drove himself too hard physically, nearly dying from illness as a Midshipman and again in 1924. He was described as having a near-obsession with rowing a small boat round the ships under his command (when arriving at one ship unannounced at an ungodly hour he responded to being asked to identify himself by saying he was the Commander in Chief, to which the Quartermaster replied: 'And I'm fucking Churchill!')[14] Somerville had a greater sense of humour than most of his contemporaries, but it was often obscene, lavatorial or sexual: '... Somerville's staff sometimes found his peculiar brand of bawdy humour, and his repartee heavily laced with obscenities, tedious and overdone.'[15]

Somerville changed in his career from being a shy man into an extrovert with '... a conscious urge to be the centre of the stage and to act the unorthodox Admiral who was talked about at all levels.'[16]

Tom Phillips was no prude, neither was he short of social skills, but his personality was such as would take little joy and considerable distaste in a foul-mouthed colleague, and one who was seen at times as striking a pose.

However, Layton and Somerville have only dealt a by-blow to the standing of Tom Phillips, their private comments regarding him and Force Z used as ammunition by writers hostile to Phillips who have plenty more ammunition to fire. A more crucial figure, and something of an enigma, is Admiral Sir Andrew Cunningham. We have seen Cunningham's private view above. Apart from this, Cunningham largely kept a public silence on the sinking of Force Z, allowing it only a few lines in his extremely long autobiography:

'The loss of the *Prince of Wales* and *Repulse* off Malaya on December 10th, about which I need make no comment, had a profound effect upon our sailors, who rather took the view that these two ships, because of their inexperience of air attacks, should never have been sent out. However, that is not for me to discuss.'[17]

This is typical Cunningham, cloaking at least one of his views by ascribing it to others, and then closing with a throwaway line. I doubt very much that the hot topic on the lower deck was the victim's inexperience of air attack. Yet it is not this sideways swipe that has damaged Phillips's reputation. Cunningham emerged from the war as perhaps the most heroic of all British naval leaders and the victor of Taranto and Matapan. He was the only one of the major British Admirals to produce an autobiography. It is self-valedictory and shares with Churchill's writings that it is not so much history as one man's version of history. What it does not share is Churchill's willingness to admit that this is the case. As well as an autobiography that is not short on self-justification, Cunningham was the subject of a largely eulogistic biography.[18] It is not so much that Cunningham said much bad about Tom Phillips. Rather, it is that he failed to say anything good; had he done so, his status would have ensured that the world took note. Even more reason for it to do so is that the official Naval historian, Captain Stephen Roskill, favours Cunningham hugely in his books, and if Cunningham had led he might have followed.

It is possible to discern a degree of hypocrisy on Cunningham's part. Cunningham was a seriously political animal, as well as a brave and charismatic leader. Two Admirals in the war – Phillips and Admiral Tovey (pronounced 'Tuvvy') placed their careers and their prospects at risk by daring to disagree with Churchill on a point of principle. Cunningham disapproved of the expedition to Greece, but backed down in the face of political pressure. The Fleet suffered terrible losses and, to his credit, it was Cunningham who held them together. So bad was the impact of the campaign on the Royal Navy's ships and men that it is true Cunningham offered his resignation, albeit in a manner and at a time that made it certain it would not be accepted.

There is an alternative view of Cunningham that sees his two great victories at Taranto and Matapan as having little to do with him. He was not a fan of the Fleet Air Arm, and Taranto was planned by others, and may indeed have arisen from a suggestion from the Admiralty. In August 1939 Pound wrote to Cunningham: 'When we attack Italy itself ... then I think there is a great deal to be said for making an attack by air on the Italian fleet at Taranto.'[19]

Matapan only happened as it did because of the Royal Navy's aircraft and *Valiant*'s radar, the latter another gadget of the type Cunningham was never keen on. It can be argued that Cunningham's policy of total up-and-at-'em aggression failed for the first time in Greece and Crete, and revealed the limitations of a man whose only tactic was the offensive. However, his greatest sin was his failure to oppose the evacuation of Greece and the defence of Crete. He was one of the few people who might have tipped the balance in favour of sanity, and his importance is confirmed by the fact that Churchill sent no less a person than Anthony Eden to persuade him into acquiescence. Cunningham's failure was that he sensed the truth summed up by one commentator: 'It is difficult to judge which was the greater folly, the British decision to defend Crete or the German decision to seize the island'[20] but let the folly happen, as well as ending the evacuation early and so leaving 10,000 men stranded. It is possible that, if he knew that Phillips had taken the more honourable option by sticking to his cause, it rankled deeply.

This book is only partly about a series of historical events. Inevitably it touches also on how history is written, the hidden machinery of opinion and comment that underpin all published history. In terms of the reputation of Tom Phillips, it is tempting to ask what the effect would be on Cunningham's reputation if his career was subject to the same hostile scrutiny, the same close analysis of every word spoken and every action taken. As one example, Cunningham would emerge as late as December 1939 as believing that mobile surface ships were proof against air attack. Writing to Pound in December 1939 he noted:

'I hope your view about battleships v. aircraft is unduly pessimistic. As far as I know not a single hit has been made on a moving target and surely our battleships have been constructed and reconstructed to stand up to a bomb hit or two?'[21]

This is a stronger justification of the battleship than any on the record from Phillips.

Cunningham was renowned for his parsimony and unwillingness to spend money, one of his favourite phrases used in reaction to expenditure on anything he deemed a luxury being: 'It's too velvet-arsed and Rolls-Royce for me!' His staff were used to being met with the cry: 'That's right – make the war expensive!' Cunningham was bored by administration, and as bad to work for on shore as he was good to serve under at sea:

'...the questioning of administrative decisions taken by the Staff becomes very frustrating and wearing, leading sometimes to definite rows. So eventually I arranged with the Secretary, A. P. Shaw, to issue administrative instructions to the Fleet by memorandum instead of by signal, which I signed "For Admiral" and his Secretary undertook not to let the C-in-C see them. Very improper, but this seemed to be the only way to get necessary things done without the constant criticism.'[22]

One of the biggest disasters to befall the Mediterranean fleet under Cunningham's command was the sinking of the battleships *Queen Elizabeth* and *Valiant* at their moorings by Italian midget submarines. The visual effect of the sinkings was lessened by the fact that the ships did not capsize but were able to settle upright on the seabed, to a cursory glance appearing still to be afloat. It may be that Cunningham's parsimony was partially responsible for the success of the attack, in his refusal to augment harbour defences. In particular, Rear Admiral Cresswell, in charge of security at Alexandria, had asked for an Extended Defence Officer for the harbour boom, but had his request turned down by Cunningham because of what Cunningham saw as Cresswell's 'insatiable' demands for officers.[23] Cunningham was also at fault in that when two Italian divers were found clinging to *Valiant*'s anchor chain, Cunningham ordered the bottom of his two battleships' hulls to be chain swept, but crucially did not order them to get steam up and move. Cunningham's comment to Pound after he had locked the stable door was: 'It is costing a lot, but we must have this harbour secure.'[24]

Yes indeed, but the excuse is startlingly cheeky for a Commander in Chief so obviously closing a stable door long after the horse had gone. A more correct message grammatically might have been: 'We ought to have had this harbour secure.'

What is most interesting about Cunningham in the context of Phillips is Cunningham's tendency to blame others for mishaps. *Barham* was torpedoed and blew up because a destroyer 'pinged' the attacking submarine but did not take the correct action subsequently. Cunningham blamed the destroyer, whilst admitting his ships were under-trained in anti-submarine work. According to Cunningham, Crete was lost because the Army did not use the time the Navy's sacrifice had bought them. Cunningham summed up rather self-admiringly what became a standard part of his management technique: 'I have had to deal with many technical gadgets in my time and when one has gone wrong I have found there are two things I could do, either get a new technical gadget or a new technical officer, and I have invariably found that the more satisfactory alternative was to get a new technical officer.'[25]

Cunningham's first response to any failure was to dismiss subordinates, starting with a succession of First Lieutenants he dismissed from *Scorpion* when he was in command. His post-war image succeeded in blotting out some of his defects: 'There were those who could not stand him, considering him a bully and careless of other people's opinions and feelings.'[26]

Neither was he as popular with the ordinary sailors as much history has made out. A Signalman commented: 'I could never understand why he was not more popular with the lower deck.'[27]

One reason was the comparison with his friend James Somerville. When Somerville took risks, it was often to save the lives of his men. During Operation Tiger in the Mediterranean, Somerville turned his whole fleet back to escort the destroyer *Fortune* which was restricted to twelve knots: 'I couldn't leave my little boats unprotected, though I suppose in cold blood I ought to have. If Dad does not take a chance in helping the boys, the latter will inevitably lose confidence.'[28]

When Cunningham took risks, it was more likely to lose lives.

Perhaps the most telling comment of all was contained in a letter from a contemporary written to the historian Arthur Marder:

'There was probably a considerable element of jealousy in the dislike [by Cunningham of Phillips]. I often noticed, with surprise a strong streak of jealousy where other 'up and coming' Flag Officers were concerned. Surprising in a man of such sterling qualities.'[29]

Cunningham was a deeply flawed figure, and a close analysis of those fellow Admirals he selected for special praise have a common denominator. They posed no threat to Cunningham's career. It is unfortunate that he has become the Second World War Admiral whose credibility rides most high, and his failure to speak out in favour of Tom Phillips is something that should do more damage to his own reputation than to that of Phillips.

What emerges from a study of the human context of the loss of *Prince of Wales* and *Repulse* is a sense of some very murky waters indeed, and no small amount of scrabbling for cover. The most influential Admirals of the day, in the sense of those most listened to after the war, did not like Tom Phillips before the sinking of Force Z and offered his reputation no support after his death. Another individual was a classic case of sour grapes. There is at the very least a serious question to be asked over whether or not there was ever any actual commitment from the Admiralty to send *Indomitable* to join up with Force Z, and if there was not what we have witnessed since 1941 is a classic cover-up to hide the guilty parties.

One individual who could have put this right was the writer of the official history of British naval operations during the war, Stephen Roskill. Unfortunately Roskill can be accused of lacking proper objectivity. Roskill was actually a serving naval officer during the war, and at times is a little too keen to tell the reader of his own importance to the war effort. In a footnote to one of his books he writes regarding the Navy's decision to form a Gunnery and Anti-Aircraft Warfare Division, and appoint a new Assistant Chief of Naval Staff to supervise Weapons Development:

> 'The author this history can claim to have had a share in these developments ... During a quiet visit to my home the need for a Gunnery and A-A Division was agreed and its organization outlined.'[30]

Roskill is at pains to dismiss Phillips's suitability for the Far Eastern Command:

> 'Early in November Churchill telegraphed to General Smuts ... that Phillips was on the way to the Far East in the *Prince of Wales*. "He is a great friend of mine and one of our ablest officers", he added, and having been VCNS since the beginning of the war "he knows the whole story back and forth". This was of course a great exaggeration of Phillips's experience, which had been entirely confined to Whitehall.'[31]

This statement does not stand up to scrutiny. Firstly, Phillips had had a long and distinguished career as a naval officer, which included seagoing commands: his experience had not been 'entirely confined to Whitehall'. Secondly, Churchill does not refer to Phillips's experience, but rather to his knowledge of what was going on in the naval war. From his position at the nerve centre of British naval operations, no one other than Dudley Pound himself had more knowledge of naval operations and what was going on than

Phillips. If one believes that Phillips's mission was less to deter the Japanese than to cement a united Anglo–American naval alliance in the Far East, Churchill's comment that Phillips knew 'the whole story back and forth' takes on a potential new significance.

Roskill had a falling out with Tom Phillips: 'Rear-Admiral Tom Phillips, the Deputy Chief of Naval Staff, who had no first-hand experience of the deadly effect of unopposed dive-bombers on warships, insisted that all that was needed to deal with them effectively was greater courage and resolution; and he took it very badly when told that such ideas were unjust to those officers who had the experience, and were in fact far from the truth.'[32]

The footnote appended to this comment suggested a more accurate statement might have been 'took it badly when told by Roskill': 'I had a stormy interview with Phillips on this matter when I brought back to the Admiralty first-hand reports of the effect of bombing off Norway in April 1940. Phillips would *not* accept that it was suicidal to send warships to operate off an enemy-held coast without air cover.'[33]

We know that Phillips had changed his mind by December 1941, and the letter to Arthur Marder quoted earlier suggests Roskill did too, though he never issued a correction. Official historians really should not let their being given an earful by one of their superiors act as the basis of history. Possibly the objectivity of official histories is compromised if the author was ever in a position to receive such a telling-off. Very few Admirals in any war I know of took kindly to being told they were wrong by a junior officer, and it was a brave and even foolhardy person who told A. B. Cunningham that he was wrong. However, Cunningham was as popular with Roskill as Phillips was unpopular. Another footnote reads:

'In 1944 I was serving in the British Mission in Washington, and was sent back to London to explain the difficulties we were having with King to Admiral Cunningham. After hearing me out Cunningham said, "Roskill, we'd get on better if you'd shoot Ernie King!" To which, knowing "ABC" quite well, replied "Is that an order, Sir, or merely a suggestion?", whereupon he good humouredly turned me out of his office.'[34]

Ho ho. Granted, this and other asides do not form part of the official history, but are found in Roskill's private publications, which his status as the official historian guaranteed a publisher. However, there are grounds for suggesting that Roskill was too willing to pursue personal vendettas. He is hostile to Churchill, who in an unprecedented action, delayed publication of the official history as he objected in part to the way it treated him. Roskill also reacted at length to what he clearly perceived as writing critical of Roskill's stance by the historian Arthur Marder. Ironically, Churchill's attempted censorship has done wonders for Roskill's reputation, suggesting he was a victim of an attempt to restrict academic freedom of comment. No one seems to have thought that Churchill may have had a point in seeing in the work not a cause celebre of academic freedom, but rather a simple case of personal bias.

There was no military, political or career advantage in exonerating Admiral Sir Tom Phillips during or after the war. The rather heroic attempts to do so were confined, after the death of his friend Dudley Pound, to junior officers who had served with Phillips, and who had the first-hand experience so praised by Roskill in his own case. I hope it is fitting to end this chapter with one of those attempts, a letter to the *Daily Telegraph* from Captain S. E. Norfolk, written in response to reviews of the Middlebrook and Mahoney book *Battleship* which was so critical of Phillips:

'The attempt by the writers of the articles on the loss of the *Prince of Wales* and *Repulse* (Sept. 25 and Oct. 2) to put the blame on Admiral Sir Tom Phillips and their portrayal of him as a stiff-necked, obstinate, outdated old sea dog is utterly untrue. He was a clear-thinking, up-to-date, reasonable, and approachable man, devoted to the Service.

'Accepting, regrettably, the overall responsibility of Winston Churchill, the man with the professional responsibility for the loss of the ships was the then First Sea Lord, Admiral Sir Dudley Pound, on two counts – he gave way to Churchill's pressure to send the ships to the Far East against the advice of the Naval Staff led by Admiral Phillips, then Vice Chief of the Naval Staff; and he failed to give the necessary order for putting into effect the accepted policy for the disposition of naval forces in the Far East in the event of a

Japanese attack on Singapore, which required naval surface units to be withdrawn to a secure base to pose a potential threat to the Japanese lines of communication.

'The failure sealed the fate of Force Z, which Admiral Phillips must have known, as he had been the architect of the policy for dealing with this eventuality when he was Director of Plans at the Admiralty in 1937.

'But as Admiral Phillips said to me in 1937, for obvious reasons the implementation of this policy could not be left to the man-on-the-spot; it would have to be ordered by the Admiralty. In the event Admiral Phillips was the man-on-the-spot, and the order was never given.

'Having left Force Z to face the full weight of Japanese naval and air power there could only be one outcome. The tactical details of the action, though of professional interest, are of comparatively little relevance.'

The letter again emphasizes the crucial point. Force Z should have been withdrawn from Singapore once war broke out. The failure to do so sank the ships. Whether or not Tom Phillips made a mistake in ordering the two ships to stick together during the first attack or whatever is of purely academic interest. Winston Churchill had decided that in the worst-case scenario it was acceptable for Great Britain to lose Singapore. Even if that was indeed necessary, it was totally unnecessary to sacrifice *Prince of Wales* and *Repulse* along with Singapore. If the reason for the recall not being sent was a Prime Minister who worked late and slept late it adds an element of black comedy to the whole disaster.

Chapter 11

The Loss of *Prince of Wales* and *Repulse*: A Revaluation – the Preliminaries

S o what is the true story of the loss of *Prince of Wales* and *Repulse?* What did actually happen before and on 10 December 1941? The account that follows in many cases simply summarizes the conclusions reached in chapters above, and whilst reproducing some of the content of Chapter 2 adds to and amends them. Again, I apologise for the element of repetition in this summary of what has gone before. The justification is that this is, to my knowledge, the first ever summary of its type of the case for Admiral Sir Tom Phillips. What follows is a compendium of all the research that has been undertaken into the engagement, and my best stab at giving an accurate and fair account of the events that led to the sinking of *Prince of Wales* and *Repulse.* It is in effect, an executive summary of the case for Phillips.

The Preliminaries

The Royal Navy in 1941 was straining hard to find the men and the ships to fight the European war on one front, never mind opening a second front in the Far East. Yet it was clear that the possibility of war with Japan was rapidly developing into a probability. Regardless of the Malayan Peninsula being a major source of rubber and tin for Britain, British prestige, its ability to maintain an Empire and its obligations to Australia and New Zealand and a military alliance with the United States all demanded that some show of naval force would be required in the Far East in the event of war with Japan threatening to break out.

The situation was rendered more bleak for the Royal Navy by a range of factors. Much of its supposed naval superiority over other nations was formed of worn-out and obsolete ships. The effectiveness of the relatively small new build it had been able to afford was seriously reduced by design restrictions imposed by the various inter-war Naval treaties, designed to stop or at least curtail a new naval race, and by bad design. A manpower crisis provoked by all-out war, and the urgent need for ships, meant that too many were sent out to war too quickly, with their crews not worked up and their weaponry not tested. Heavy losses in the invasion of Greece and the evacuation of Crete had come near to crippling the Navy and added to the shortages of escorts in particular. Late 1941 also saw a crisis in the availability of aircraft carriers caused by sinkings, battle damage and the need for refit and repair if the vessels were to remain in service. Unbeknown to the Admiralty, a number of the new weapons developed in the inter-war years to meet the threat of modern naval warfare would not prove as effective as had been hoped. Also unbeknown to them, they were woefully ill-informed about the power and strength of Japanese weaponry and the men who used it, something for which the Naval establishment of the 1930s, of which Tom Phillips was an influential member, must take a degree of responsibility. Regardless of political or any other issues, it could only be a scratch force that was sent out East in the event of war looming in the Far East. The popular cry 'Main Fleet to Singapore!' reflected the belief that Britain's 'impregnable fortress' could and would have to survive for ninety days before the Fleet arrived. It was a myth; there was no Main Fleet to send.

Historians are best-advised not to crouch in defended positions and seek to pour a withering fire on their enemies and so destroy them. That is the task of those they write about. There is rarely total certainty over an historical event. It can therefore never be proven beyond all reasonable doubt that Winston Churchill had concluded that Britain's Far Eastern Empire was indefensible by available British force of arms, and that such few spare military resources as there were should be sent to Britain's one undefeated ally in the European war, Russia, also on the grounds that if Britain lost its Far Eastern Empire it lost prestige and profit, but if it lost the war in Europe Britain lost its very existence. It can, similarly, never be proven beyond reasonable doubt that Churchill's solution to Britain continuing to hold ground it could not hope to keep by virtue of its own military resources in the Far East, was to cement a military alliance with a country he believed did have the necessary resources – the United States of America – and make

American and British interests in the Far East one and the same thing, as symbolized by Singapore becoming a joint naval base for the British and American fleets. Neither Churchill's having given up hope of Britain alone defending the Far East nor his hope that it could only be done alongside America can be proven beyond reasonable doubt. What there is is sufficient evidence to suggest it as at least a possibility, something rendered stronger by the fact that this theory goes some way to explain what are otherwise inexplicable features in the sinking of *Prince of Wales* and *Repulse*. Of course, the sending of *Prince of Wales* and *Repulse* to Singapore as a gambling ploy in a game which had as first prize a secret alliance with America was entirely capable of running parallel with the reason most historians have plumped for, namely to act as a deterrent to Japanese aggression: the two were not mutually exclusive. This latter was certainly the line Churchill was to take post-event.

There was a clear clash between the Admiralty, led by Admiral Sir Tom Phillips as Vice Chief of Naval Staff, and Churchill over what ships should be sent out to Singapore. Supporters of Churchill would argue that he took a close interest in naval affairs throughout the war. Critics would argue that he interfered remorselessly, and often to bad effect. The Admiralty wished to send out a force of 'R' class battleships, possibly reinforced by the slow but heavily-armed and armoured battleships *Nelson* and *Rodney*. In sheer weight of firepower this looked an impressive force. The 'R' class battleships each carried eight 15-inch guns in tried and tested mountings, while *Nelson* and *Rodney* carried the largest main armament ever placed on a Royal Navy battleship, nine 16-inch guns in three triple turrets mounted forward of the bridge. The turrets had problems as a result of excessive safety precautions but had been good enough to punch holes in the thick armour of the *Bismarck*. If a clear attempt was being made to prove Britain's seriousness of intent to the Americans, those in the know in the Admiralty (which would certainly have included Phillips) might have hoped that sheer numbers and weight of firepower of the proposed force might have made a powerful statement. Probably a more compelling reason was that the 'R' class battleships were those the Royal Navy could most easily spare. *Prince of Wales* and *Hood* had proved no match for the *Bismarck*, and with her sister ship *Tirpitz* and the powerful battle-cruisers *Scharnhorst* and *Gneisenau* unsunk, the Admiralty was understandably concerned to keep a superior or at least equivalent force in northern waters to counter a break-out against Atlantic convoys.

The Admiralty's preferred option was overturned by Churchill. He pointed out that the 'R' class were obsolete and slow floating coffins, badly-ventilated and unsuitable for tropical service, and that apart from aging machinery they were neither armed nor armoured to cope with modern warfare. His wish was for the modern *Prince of Wales* to go out as the main element of a fast raiding force, but primarily as a deterrent. Is it coincidence that it was *Prince of Wales* that had taken Churchill to meet President Roosevelt, and that of all symbols of British naval might this ship might be calculated to most impress the American President? Certainly Churchill had holes punched in his argument when it was pointed out that one of his arguments against using the 'R' class applied equally if not more to the KGV (King George V class) to which *Prince of Wales* belonged. The class not only had inadequate ventilation, being designed primarily for service in cold northern waters, but it was known that a crucial piece of machinery essential for the working of the main armament was liable to failure in tropical heat. Furthermore, *Prince of Wales* had never had the time to work-up its crew properly. It was seen as a jinxed ship in the Navy, largely as a result of it having been in the company of the symbol of the Royal Navy, HMS *Hood*, when it was blown up by the *Bismarck*, and been forced to retire from the action or face its own destruction. Nevertheless Churchill's wish carried the day, with the old battle-cruiser *Repulse* added to the force.

There is no hard evidence to suggest that Churchill, faced with his former ally Phillips presenting a forceful argument on behalf of the Admiralty for not sending out *Prince of Wales,* took Phillips aside and into his confidence regarding Churchill's hopes for a secret alliance and hence the need to impress by sending out Britain's newest battleship, and sweetened the pill by offering Phillips the role of chief negotiator. It is an unfortunate fact of history that many of the conversations historians would most like a record of are those that the participants took the most care of to ensure that there was no record. Yet if such a conversation took place it would at least explain why one of the most cogent opponents of Churchill's plan suddenly gave it the most tangible support possible, by agreeing to be its Commander. Equally, it may just have been that no Admiral in the Royal Navy was ever likely to refuse a fighting command.

For seventy years or more it has been assumed, largely on the word of those responsible for assembling the force, that it was intended to add to the scratch force the modern carrier *Indomitable*, an improved *Illustrious* class vessel that retained an armoured flight deck, but could carry a significantly larger number of aircraft than *Illustrious*. *Indomitable* was working up in the West Indies, but grounded on 3 November, and had to be sent for repair in the United States. However, a recent book[1] has pointed that even had she been ordered there on the day she grounded she would not have made it in time. Until firm evidence is found that *Indomitable* was ordered to Singapore it seems best to assume that, whilst there may have been a thought to equip Force Z with a carrier it was never a firm intention, and was adopted post-event as the party line to protect those likely to be blamed for the sinkings. *Indomitable* was ordered to the Far East after completing her repairs in twelve days, and having to sail back to Kingston to pick up her aircraft, but did not arrive until January, suggesting her posting was a classic case of being wise after the event, or part of a more sinister cover up.

The loss of *Indomitable* to Force Z raises other questions. An absence of any particular record of complaint or worry from the Admiralty might be explained on the grounds that there was a major crisis over carriers at the time – *Illustrious* had been seriously damaged in the Mediterranean, *Victorious* was needed for the Home fleet and *Ark Royal* for the Mediterranean, though she was to be sunk on 13 November 1941. A string of other carriers were either in refit or due for repairs, and the Admiralty was hardly going to welcome their most modern and effective carrier being sent out as part of a tiny raiding and deterrent force to the Far East. However, Pound and others at the Admiralty, including Phillips, were immensely loyal to the service they loved and had devoted their professional lives to, and along with that loyalty and devotion went no small measure of judgment and skill. One did not have to have risen to the top of one of the most outstandingly professional navies in the world to realize that *Prince of Wales* and *Repulse* constituted an appallingly unbalanced force. Admiral Sir Tom Phillips we know had persuaded himself of the importance of air cover for surface ships, and the most surprising absentee from the complainants about the absence of a carrier was Phillips himself. In none of the published comments by Phillips that I have read, and in none of the private papers held for so long by the Phillips family, is there a reference to the body blow that the loss of *Indomitable* was to the fighting and defensive strength of Force Z. This can only suggest that Phillips for one never expected to be reinforced by *Indomitable*, and confirms the suggestion that sending her out was never a serious Admiralty intention. But this then raises a further question: why not? Wars and the decisions taken in them are frequently not rational, but one of the few rational explanations for the apparent ease with which senior officers accepted the dispatch of a chronically unbalanced force (rendered even more unbalanced by the paltry number of escorts it could call on and the absence of any cruisers) is that it was never intended that Force Z should actually have to fight, and that its being sent was essentially a diplomatic mission to impress the USA with Britain's seriousness of intent. This would also explain why Tom Phillips was chosen to command Force Z. There was no shortage of fighting admirals available, with Geoffrey Layton already out in the Far East as Commander in Chief Station, and James Somerville another obvious candidate. Yet Layton was too angular to be an effective diplomat; as referred to above, he had once called a colonial administrator a 'black bastard'[2] and was almost the stereotype of the salty old sea dog. James Somerville had been forced to open fire on the French fleet at Mers-el-Kebir having failed to persuade the French Admiral to disarm, and as a result his reputation as a negotiator was at an all-time low. He also had a deserved reputation for lavatorial humour and language, a quality a sailor could get away with but an ambassador could not.

Phillips had not had any combat experience himself, and for this reason alone was a surprising choice. Historians have in general stopped at this point, and not noted a further area in which, outwardly, the appointment of Phillips was bizarre. Phillips was widely recognized as having the best brain of any senior officer at the time. He had clearly made an immense impact on the quality of Staff work at the Admiralty, was widely seen as irreplaceable and was also highly valued by the beleaguered Dudley Pound, who used him as his right-hand man. There were a number of other British Admirals in 1941 who had shown they could fight, in addition to Layton, Somerville and Cunningham: Harwood, the victor of the Battle of the River

Plate, was another. Yet something prompted the powers-that-be to send the country's most intelligent Staff officer to command a highly vulnerable force that contained one of the Royal Navy's most valuable *materiel* assets, the 'unsinkable' *Prince of Wales*, with one of its most valuable human assets – its most brilliant Staff officer – on board it. The most common explanation is that Churchill, who had fallen out with Phillips over the bombing of Germany and the Greece/Crete Campaign, had repeated his behaviour of the First World War when he had fallen out with Sir Doveton Sturdee, and sent him to an overseas command. It is a theory whose main strength lies simply in its having been repeated so much over so many years. It offers much more of an explanation of why the appointment was made if Phillips was chosen on his political and diplomatic skills, not on his ability to mix it with the Japanese. If there was the hope of what has been called a 'secret alliance' – one that would come into effect before hostilities and either act as a deterrent or, in the event of war breaking out, see Britain and America acting as one, it was political dynamite for the strong isolationist lobby in the States, and if mishandled could have done serious if not indeed lethal damage to Roosevelt's Presidency. Tom Phillips could claim to have moved in the company of Britain's political leadership and be in their confidence, know their minds and act as their spokesman and messenger. If this was why Phillips was chosen, Churchill and the Admiralty got two for two for the price of one; their diplomat seems to have found it quite straightforward to change overnight into an aggressive raiding force leader.

Three further facts give strength to the idea that the sending of Force Z was conceived more as a diplomatic than a military mission. Firstly, it has been accepted without comment as unremarkable by historians that on his way out to Singapore Phillips stopped off and had a private conversation with South Africa's leader at that time, General Smuts. But why did he do so? Why was this meeting deemed important enough to delay the arrival of the Commander of British naval forces to an increasingly troubled region? Brilliant man though he was, Smuts was hardly in a position to advise a British Admiral on how to handle his ships or meet the military threat of the Japanese. Such a meeting, and the importance attached to it, makes much more sense if its purpose was to discuss wider strategy and the intricacies of a defence pact with the United States with the man Churchill admired above all other leaders of the time, and one of the few he trusted enough to know his real mind. Smuts thought highly of Phillips when they met (most people who had one-to-one conversations with him did), but his comments are usually given as proof of the idiocy of sending out Force Z, with Smuts being cast as the prophetic voice who predicted disaster. Smuts sent a telegram to Churchill after he and Phillips met in Pretoria:

'Admiral Tom Phillips has been here for most useful talks and will reach Cape Town before noon today. He has much impressed me and appears admirable choice for most important position... In particular, I am concerned over present disposition of two fleets, one based on Singapore and other on Hawaii, each separately inferior to Japanese navy which thus will have an opportunity to defeat them in turn. This matter is so vital that I would press for rearrangement of dispositions as soon as war appears imminent. If Japanese are really nippy there is here opening for first class disaster.'[3]

This signal makes perfect sense if Phillips had made it clear that his mission was to forge a pre-emptive alliance between the USA with both fleets having their main base at Singapore and a forward base at Manila. Smuts is in effect agreeing with what may have been Churchill's plan, but telling him to hurry up with it and seal the knot *before* hostilities broke out. What is rarely commented on in the many books that refer to this telegram is that it does not suggest joining forces as such, but seems to accept that it is contrary to good strategic sense to have the two fleets in separate bases. In other words, Smuts does not suggest a united fleet at Singapore as a new idea, but argues for the early completion of an idea already in place.

Secondly, Phillips's first action on arriving in the Far East was to rush to see the American Admiral Hart in Manila. Was this the action of someone whose prime job was to bring a fighting force up to full readiness? What was so important to Phillips to mean that out of everything else it was the Americans who could not wait?

Thirdly, after being silent about the ships he had been supplied with, the moment war breaks out Phillips asked for an 'R' class battleship, detached the cruiser *Exeter* from convoy duties to join him, and asked for the Australian cruisers *Achilles* and *Hobart*, as well as complaining of a serious lack of modern cruisers at his disposal. The inevitable reaction of an Admiral to a war situation? Or the actions of an Admiral suddenly having to assemble a fleet that might have to fight rather than merely impress?

Whatever the truth of Phillips's mission, his appointment was unpopular within the Navy. Admirals Layton and Somerville were scathing in their criticism, but both could reasonably have expected to have been offered Phillips's command. Admiral A. B. Cunningham was also critical. Part of this may have been connected to Cunningham's dislike of anyone he saw as a rival: 'There was probably a considerable element of jealousy in the dislike [by Cunningham of Phillips]. I often noticed, with surprise a strong streak of jealousy where other "up and coming" Flag Officers were concerned. Surprising in a man of such sterling qualities.'[4]

But Cunningham probably shared other reasons for his disapproval with senior officers. Phillips was a Staff officer, and Staff officers rarely win popularity contests among those who are not privileged. He had been a friend of Churchill's, a cause for suspicion amongst some. Phillips, a small man, did not fit into the very masculine worship of physical prowess that was part of the naval culture of the time. He was closely associated with an Admiralty resented by a number of fighting admirals for its supposed interference in naval operations. He was also accused, probably unjustly, of being a bad seaman. Part of the problem may have been the jealousy, perhaps inevitable in a relatively small and very close-knit service, of a man who had received promotion so young and so rapidly. Ironically, Phillips had fallen out with Churchill over the latter's support for the bombing of Germany and over the evacuation of Crete, whilst one of his critics, Admiral A. B. Cunningham had caved in to Government pressure to withdraw his opposition to the Greece and Crete disaster.

Phillips not only lacked relevant experience in the eyes of the Navy. A number of historians made much of what they saw as a reputation as a difficult personality to work with, and someone unwilling to listen to anyone who disagreed with him:

'Sir Tom Spencer Vaughan Phillips, KCB, aged fifty-three, had been behind a Whitehall desk since 1939 and he had last experienced action in 1917. A very small man – he needed to stand on a box when on the compass platform and was nicknamed "Tom Thumb" – he was notorious for his angry impatience and, more seriously, his strong conviction that aircraft were no match for properly handled warships, arguing that only greater resolution on the ships' commanding officers was needed to defeat the dive-bomber. He had always refused to listen to anyone who tried to persuade him that fighter protection was necessary for all ships operating within reach of enemy bombers.'[5]

On a minor point, the comment about Phillips standing on a box on the bridge seems little more than reporting a joke by 'Bomber' Harris as fact. On more important matters, it is now clear that Phillips had changed his mind about the vulnerability of surface ship to air attack by mid-1941, following the massive damage suffered by Royal Navy warships from German aircraft in the battle for Greece and evacuation of Crete, in which his own son had been heavily involved. It is simply untrue to write: 'Yet it is probable that Phillips's views were considerably more out of touch and mistaken than those of most of his contemporaries.'[6]

Admiral A. B. Cunningham, Phillips's most famous contemporary, wrote in favour of the battleship and was an opponent of technology, and intellectually if not experientially is one of many Admirals who might reasonably have under estimated the threat to surface ships. Commentators have applied the benefit of hindsight to the loss of *Prince of Wales* and *Repulse* to culpable levels. In particular, they have underestimated an action in which *Prince of Wales* was herself involved, Operation Halberd, or the successful attempt to get a convoy through to Malta in September 1941. It is true that the three battleships included in the escort had the benefit of the aircraft carrier *Ark Royal*, but the ships fought off brave and persistent bomb and torpedo attacks from the Italian air force, which itself was the service arm of a modern nation state. Only one merchant ship was sunk. *Nelson* took a torpedo hit, but all it did was slow her down, and 'there was no hint that well-fought battleships had much to fear from aircraft.'[7] Phillips was *not* a dinosaur when it came to shrugging off the dangers of air attack, though it makes a better story if he is portrayed as being one.

Furthermore, it is probable that no one knew more about what had been learnt about naval matters and tactics since the start of the war than Tom Phillips, sitting as he had at the nerve centre of Royal Navy operations.

What Phillips and no-one else knew was that his flagship contained far more flaws than the superstitious dislike of the Navy for a ship that had broken off the action against the *Bismarck,* or a crew who had never had the chance properly to work up. The 14-inch main armament quadruple turrets were never made to function properly in any ship of the class. The 5.25-inch secondary armament was too heavy for anti-aircraft work, and lacked tachometric directors and fire control. The short-range anti-aircraft armament tended to be effective only after an attacking aircraft had launched its munitions load, and jammed in tropical heat because the ammunition separated out. The ship was too small for its 'torpedo-bulge' protection to be fully effective, and aspects of the design made the class prone to flooding. A bomb falling between the ship and the dockside in 1940 may have weakened a section of the hull significantly more than was realized at the time. The class had a large turning radius, making them more vulnerable to bomb and torpedo attack. Most crucially, the ship's electrical systems and hence its ability to defend and save itself were particularly prone to battle damage.

As important as anything else was the fact that as a result of a failure of Intelligence, Phillips and the Royal Navy in general did not realize the range, hitting power and efficiency of Japanese aircraft. There is also some evidence that the Admiralty and Singapore may have known that there were Japanese torpedo-bombers in range, but failed to pass this on to Phillips. Phillips was also sailing to a military base whose organization descended in to near-chaos when hostilities broke out and whose command structures were confused and riven by jealousies. In particular, the RAF was vulnerable to Japanese invasion and had aircraft more suited to a museum than a forward front. Phillips and his ships were going largely to be on their own.

Phillips's ships were initially designated 'Force G', later changed to 'Force Z'. *Prince of Wales* set sail from the Clyde at 1308 hours on 25 October 1941, with the destroyers *Electra* and *Express* who were to accompany her, and *Hesperus* as additional protection for the first part of the voyage through dangerous northern waters. *Repulse* was already in Far Eastern waters. It appears that the Admiralty had intended *Prince of Wales* to halt its journey at Cape Town to allow for a review of the situation in the Far East. No document trail has been found that explains why this plan seems to have been dropped, with the result that the ship steamed on to Singapore. The most common assumption has been that the cautious Dudley Pound saw a South African stopover as a last chance to review the mission, but was overruled by Churchill and the ships hurried on and through.

Phillips refused the chance to acquire a carrier, albeit a lesser one than the *Indomitable*, a decision for which he has been criticized:

> 'Yet on the very day that the *Prince of Wales* departed from South African waters the veteran carrier *Hermes* had arrived at Simonstown. She carried only 15 aircraft and her maximum designed speed was a disappointing 25 knots. But she had the ability to provide a modicum of seaborne air support in the shape of Swordfish torpedo-bombers and reconnaissance machines. And even a little was better than none.'[8]

This criticism is entirely unfounded. *Hermes* had not just 'arrived' at Simonstown. She had docked there for what was technically a refit, but which in all practical terms were serious repairs, including to her old and ailing engines. She was old, slow and unarmoured, and such serviceable aircraft as she carried would have been no use against the modern, fast and high altitude Bettys and Nells. For once, it does not matter what Phillips's role actually was. *Hermes* would not have impressed the Americans, deterred the Japanese or fought them. As for the latter, adding *Hermes* to Force Z would have been akin to asking a boxer to take his aged aunt in to the ring alongside him. For much the same reason, Phillips also refused further reinforcement, this time of an older battleship that the Admiralty had wished to form the core of the Far Eastern fleet:

> 'For the second time in ten days Phillips had chosen not to strengthen his force with another major warship. *Revenge*, a vintage battleship dating back to 1916, had been berthed in Ceylon when Force G arrived, but the Admiral was content to leave her behind when the other ships sailed for Singapore.'[9]

Again, the addition of *Revenge* would simply have slowed Force Z down, a force whose only chance of success or survival was to use its speed to surprise an enemy and then to get away quickly. Speed was the only true advantage Force Z had over its enemy. As it was, *Prince of Wales* met up with *Repulse* in Ceylon, with Admiral Phillips ordered to fly on to Singapore ahead of his ships in a Catalina flying boat, to discuss the situation regarding the Japanese with Singapore High Command and, if possible, meet Admiral T. C. Hart, Commander in Chief of the American Asiatic Fleet, in Manila.

Force Z sailed into Singapore on the afternoon of 2 December, with Tom Phillips there to meet her on the quayside, with much fuss being made of *Prince of Wales* and her name and presence released to the media, in order to enhance the deterrent effect. In practice, this gave vital Intelligence to the Japanese, and was the direct cause of them making available the very aircraft that sank *Prince of Wales* and *Repulse*. The publicity given to the arrival of a naval force also made it almost impossible for Phillips not to respond to Japanese aggression and be seen to sail. To the intense annoyance of her crew, *Repulse* was not named in the publicity, it being thought that silence on the number and nature of the other ships might serve to exaggerate their power to the Japanese. There were many who thought the arrival of the ships in Singapore was a triumph for the British: Singapore had been told it might have to wait ninety days for the Navy to arrive, and here it was before a single shot had been fired.

The Admiralty appeared concerned that Phillips's ships would be caught in harbour by Japanese aircraft, and signalled him on 1 December, the day a state of emergency was declared in Malaya, that he might take his ships out to cruise east of Singapore 'to disconcert the Japanese', and again on the 3 December to suggest the two ships should get away from Singapore. This was probably the result of Intelligence sightings of twelve Japanese submarines heading in the direction of Singapore, presumably to bottle Force Z up in the event of war. Critics have cited these signals as the Admiralty realizing how weak Force Z was and suggesting it hide in the islands. In fact the signals were more likely to show a post-Taranto fear and a desire to give Force Z freedom to steam where it willed, rather than being trapped in Singapore by the submarine threat. Phillips compromised, pointing out that he was detaching *Repulse* on a good will visit to Darwin that would get her out of Singapore.

What has not often been seen as significant is Phillips's request to the Admiralty at this time for all four 'R' class battleships to be sent now, and a request that *Warspite* could call in at Singapore for a week on its way back from repair in the States, to give a further impression of strength. It clarifies little as regards the 'secret alliance' issue. Phillips, in his later discussions with Hart, negotiated a deal whereby four of his destroyers stationed in Dutch Borneo would sail to Singapore, but only if the three British destroyers at Hong Kong transferred to Singapore. Presumably the presence of no less than six British battleships in Singapore and a battle-cruiser could have given Phillips considerable bargaining power in the tit-for-tat world he seemed to be in, particular if *Indomitable* would also shortly be arriving. Equally, if hostilities were going to break out, the more ships Phillips had at his disposal the better, and he was pragmatist enough to ask only for the ships he knew he was most likely to be granted.

Phillips has been accused of being 'insufficiently alert to the pressing realities of the strategic situation in which he was involved.'[10] He had gone to Manila to talk to his opposite number Admiral Hart of the US Navy on 4 December for a meeting on the 5 December which went through to the next day when the alarm was sounded, and *Repulse* was on her way to Australia for her flag-waving visit. Phillips left for Singapore within the hour and *Repulse* was called back, but the result was that Force Z set sail too late to have a significant impact on the Japanese invasions. Phillips, it has been said, thus missed a major chance to disrupt the Japanese invasions by a lackadaisical response, and failing to act at the start of the attacks when the Japanese were at their most vulnerable:

> 'If the Eastern Fleet had been able to sail immediately the sighting reports were received and had successfully intercepted the Japanese invasion force at sea there is a good chance that the enemy might have been persuaded to turn back, for the stakes were high and the Japanese had not anticipated being discovered quite so early in the game.'[11]

'During a vital period, neither Phillips nor his capital ships were ready for action.'[12]

This is unjust criticism. *Prince of Wales* was undergoing boiler cleaning and having her bottom scraped, both essential housekeeping if a ship that had just completed a very long passage was to remain at full operational efficiency. As it was, the pictures of *Prince of Wales* leaving Singapore on her last voyage do not reveal that she could steam on only four of her eight boilers, the remainder not being able to be fired up until she was in the open sea as the result of them being closed down for cleaning:

'The point is that the four pairs of boilers were then in different stages of cleanliness. The loss of efficiency (there is no record of how much power was lost through the dirty boilers) was regrettable, yet it is doubtful whether the ability of *Prince of Wales* to make better speed would have been enough to get her "out of the hole" on the fatal 10 December. For certain, though, it did not help her.'[13]

What has emerged since the above was written some time prior to 1981 is that *Prince of Wales* was disabled and caused to be sunk by a torpedo hit on her stern whilst she was turning, and that if that torpedo had struck a few feet off where it did she might well have survived. Rather than Phillips not being ready to attack, it is more likely that circumstances forced him to take his ships to sea before they were fully ready.

A further factor was that at the time the alarm was first sounded, Force Z was not authorized to attack the Japanese, and to do so without authorization would be tantamount to a declaration of war. It is one of the absolute commandments of military life that commanders in declaring war do not act on their own initiative. We have seen that the absence of *Repulse* had a sound strategic reason behind it, the visit to Admiral Hart even more so. One does not need to believe that Churchill's agenda in sending out his most modern battleship was to help America declare its alliance with Britain against Japan before war broke out. The avowed purpose of Phillips's visit, to broker a consolidation of the two fleets and a rationalization of their bases, could have saved Singapore and changed the whole nature of the war in the Pacific had it succeeded. It was important enough to merit Phillips's absence.

It is difficult, even with hindsight, to blame Phillips, and indeed most armed forces and their governments, for failing to realize just how fast the Japanese would move. Their plan was staggeringly ambitious, almost ludicrously so. Any naval officer in the Royal, Dutch or American navies who predicted no less than five surprise, out of the blue offensives (Pearl Harbor, the Philippines, Guam and associated islands, Hong Kong and Siam, Malaya and Singapore) would be launched at the same time would have been laughed out of court. Who dared won, at least at the outset.

Those who criticize Phillips for not being able to sail immediately reports of Japanese activity were received also fail to recognize the chaos that was prevalent at this time, the uncertainty as to what was actually happening and the danger of sending the two ships on a wild goose chase. Bad monsoon weather had meant that only fleeting glimpses had been caught of Japanese ships, and the RAF crews lacked experience in what they were doing. Neither did the Japanese lie back and wait to be spotted, shooting down a Catalina reconnaissance flight.

Chapter 12

The Loss of *Prince of Wales* and *Repulse*:
A Revaluation – The Action

8 December

By 8 December Phillips could be in no doubt that Britain was at war with Japan. The night before, his time, the Japanese had bombed Pearl Harbor and bombed Singapore. He had four options: sail out to attach the Japanese invasion barges; retreat to Darwin; hide out in the islands and attempt to exert the same sense of menace that *Tirpitz* did so effectively in northern waters; stay in Singapore. The final option – retreat from Singapore – was not in his gift, but could only happen in response to a direct order from the Admiralty.

Phillips called a conference on board his flagship at 12.30 on 8 December primarily for ships' Captains, and asked his commanders for their views:

> 'The atmosphere was calm and quietly thoughtful – fatalistic perhaps. To the best of my recollection I remember Admiral Phillips saying, "Gentlemen, this is an extremely hazardous mission and I would liken it to taking the Home Fleet into the Skagerrak without air cover. Nevertheless, I feel we have to do something."'[1]

Phillips asked for comments. The silence was broken by Tennant, the captain of *Repulse,* who said they had no option but to set sail in search of the enemy. There was no disagreement. An increasingly ill-looking Tom Phillips was reported as summing up: 'We can stay in Singapore. We can sail away to the East – Australia. Or we can go out and fight. Gentlemen, we sail at five o'clock.'[2]

Though there has been some criticism of his decision to attack – 'Still, there is a point where a decision ceases to be courageous and becomes rash, and

Phillips's decision came close to that point'[3] – the majority of commentators recognize that he had little option. The impact on local morale of the Royal Navy sitting tight in harbour would have been disastrous, apart from the inevitable accusation of cowardice that would have been made against Phillips had he failed to take any action. There was a real chance to disrupt Japanese actions, and perhaps change the course of the war before it had properly begun. Nor was there any certainty that any attempt to hide his ships would not have been discovered. He had clearly signalled his intention to set sail and attack to the Admiralty, and by the conventions of the day the failure of the Admiralty to gainsay this amounted to their permission and support. On 7 December the Admiralty had sent Phillips a 'prodding' signal, asking what action it would be possible to take against Japanese forces, a clear indication that they expected some action to be taken.

Just as importantly, the only way that Phillips could have led his ships into hiding would have been on a direct order from the Admiralty: 'Lacking either a plan of action or a balanced force, The *Prince of Wales* and *Repulse* should have been ordered away from Singapore and out of harm's way. That is not, however, what happened.'[4] And: 'Given that the Admiralty had sent the prodding signal... the only thing that would have stopped him from sailing to attack the Japanese would have been a direct order from London to take his ships out of harm's way: to do otherwise would have seemed like running away.'[5]

The significance of the 12.30 meeting held in the Admiral's day cabin on board *Prince of Wales* is greater than has sometimes been acknowledged, and agreement with the plan to attack seen as a mere formality in a service where people were expected to obey orders, not challenge them. This is a misrepresentation. The silence that greeted Phillips's outline of his plans was not mere servile obedience to orders, but born of a realization of how dangerous was the mission on which they were to embark. Unlike historians, these men's lives depended on what action they took, and the lives of many others, and such circumstances tend to focus the mind on more than obedience. Phillips's conference was also excellent man-management. It meant that this was an agreed mission and that he had his commanders united behind him – would that someone had achieved the same unity among the other defenders of Singapore – and further testimony to that unity is that not one of those commanders subsequently broke ranks to be critical of Phillips. Indeed, there was remarkable support for him and his actions from all the officers who actually fought the battle. Criticism came from those who fought the battle from their armchairs.

How risky was the mission? Highly so, but so were Pearl Harbor, Dunkirk, Overlord and the German Channel Dash. Other factors undoubtedly influenced what we would now call Phillips's risk assessment. He had some good intelligence, both from the Americans and from RAF reconnaissance that had worked, and he knew that there were no Japanese aircraft carriers near enough to launch an attack on his ships, and that other Japanese surface units involved were inferior to his firepower. He knew also the whereabouts of the recently-laid Japanese minefields off Singapore. His ships were fast enough to out run submarines – *Prince of Wales* had done just this when she had crossed the Atlantic unescorted carrying Churchill to meet Roosevelt – whilst the bad monsoon weather, which had made British reconnaissance so difficult, would cloak his force from discovery as it had cloaked Japanese forces from the British. He believed he was out of range of Japanese land-based torpedo aircraft, and the record to date of battleships resisting air attack successfully, and particularly high-level bombing, was good. The key was surprise, the stakes a massive and crucial victory that could affect the whole course of the war. Another key, of course was air cover.

There has been debate about the discussions Phillips had over air cover before the departure of his ships, which will never be fully resolved unless startling new material emerges, for the simple reason that any meetings were unrecorded and those who were there are now dead. However, Phillips sent a telling signal to the Admiralty late on 7 December. It is not clear how much Phillips actually knew about the nature of the Japanese offensive at this time, though he certainly knew an offensive had been launched:

'If the relative strength of the enemy force permits, endeavor will be made to attack the expedition by night or by day. If we are inferior in strength a raid will be attempted and the air force will attack with bombs and torpedoes in conjunction with our naval forces.'[6]

What this clearly shows is that Phillips was hoping to undertake action as a joint striking force with the RAF. The inevitable conclusion was that the subsequent lack of support was not the result of Phillips not wanting or dismissing it, but rather the result of the RAF's inability to supply it. This is confirmed by the conversation with Phillips reported by one of his aides:

> "'I'm not sure", he told Captain Bell, his senior aide, "that Pulford realizes the importance I attach to fighter cover over Singora on the tenth. I'm going to write him a letter stressing the point, and asking him to let me know for certain what he can do.'"[7]

Force Z was ready to go to sea, but Phillips showed judgment and skill in delaying the departure until the evening, meaning that the speed and direction of his attack would be hidden in darkness from the Japanese. The two destroyers *Express* and *Electra* had been out much of the day practising minesweeping, something perhaps not to be expected of a force commanded by an Admiral who did not know one end of a ship from another, and further proof of Phillips's ability to move from diplomat to combat leader.

There is one other area where Phillips has been criticized where perhaps the criticism has been allowed to stick rather too easily. When Japanese bombers made their night attack on Singapore, why did Phillips not realize that he was clearly in range of Japanese land-based aircraft, whose bomb load could be exchanged for torpedoes? The simplest answer is that no, he did not realize, any more than anyone on the British side realized the ease with which Japanese aircraft could switch weapon. More telling was the fact that despite the two British warships lying at anchor in the face of the air force that had just launched the most devastating attack by torpedo on battleships ever in history, there was no hint of torpedo bombers in the force that attacked Singapore. Surely the Japanese of all people would have sent them if they had them? Finally, heavy cloud and bad weather meant that of fifty-four bombers on the mission only seventeen actually reached Singapore, giving a false impression of Japanese strength. It was reported even that some in Singapore thought the attacking aircraft were from carriers, which if it was the case would presumably have high-tailed it out the minute they recovered their aircraft. In any event, the raid was as ineffectual as Singapore's defence and contained nothing to warn Phillips or anyone else of the lethal power of Japanese aircraft.

Force Z slipped its moorings at 1735, its original intention to attack Japanese invasion barges off Singora. In company with the two capital ships were four destroyers – *Electra, Express* and two First World War veterans, *Tenedos* and the Australian *Vampire*. There is perhaps one cruiser Phillips might have been able to take, but in the event he prioritized mechanical reliability and speed. Two destroyers detached to him from the Mediterranean fleet were 'crocks' – one taking on a major list when full of oil, and the other described as having a 'corrugated bottom' – and were too damaged to sail, so Phillips's escort was the bare minimum. Admiral A. B. Cunningham must therefore bear some responsibility for weakening the defences of Force Z.

Phillips asked for air reconnaissance ahead of his force on 9 December, and reconnaissance and fighter cover off Singora on 10 December. As Force Z sailed it was flashed a signal from the Changi signal station from Pulford saying: 'Regret fighter protection impossible', at which Phillips is said to shrug his shoulders and say: 'Well, we must get on without it.'

Eight hours after they set out Palliser signalled to Phillips that Kota Bharu airfield had been abandoned, the military situation there was unclear, a Catalina flying boat could provide reconnaissance on 9 December. Ominously the signal warned of large numbers of Japanese bombers based in southern Indo-China and possibly Thailand, and that the Americans had been asked to use their long-range bombers to attack these airfields. Unfortunately, the Japanese had mounted a pre-emptive strike and destroyed most of the American aircraft. What is perhaps the crucial part of the signal read: 'Fighter protection on Wednesday 10th will not, repeat not, be possible'.[8]

This signal has caused much controversy. It is usually thought to be an error, in that what it should have added was the key phrase 'off Singora'. However, a great many less people would be convicted at law if they could claim as a defence what they ought to have done. What Palliser did was send an unequivocal signal that stated, and repeated, that air cover was not available and that therefore one of the key ingredients for a successful mission was no longer in place, surprise being the other. Furthermore, Palliser's signal was the second one Phillips had received stating that fighter cover was not available. Two unequivocal signals are surely enough to persuade any man, or group of men, that what the signals say is true. Phillips (and, for that matter, the much-praised Tennant of *Repulse*) did not call for fighter cover because they had been told, unequivocally and categorically, that there was none to be had, and been told by their own people.

On receiving the signal that no air cover was available Phillips decided to head for the nearer Kota Bharu, rather than Singora, which is 120 miles further north. We know that he was far from dismissing the risk from air attack. He had even made it clear to his ships that this was a hit-and-run mission. The decision to stay at sea had been criticized:

> '... although the information available to Phillips gave him no reason to foresee the full extent of the threat from Japanese aircraft, there was clearly *some* danger from air attack, and his decision to continue on and to hazard two very valuable capital ships, rather than returning to Singapore or sailing elsewhere, was a very risky one.'[9]

> 'Early on 9 December Phillips was told by signal ... that the Royal Air Force would not be able to provide air cover, because all the airfields in northern Malaya were being evacuated. Nevertheless he elected to press on. Lack of experience, his belief, despite all the evidence of the past two years of war, in the invincibility to capital ships, and his own temperament led to this unwise decision.'[10]

The case against Phillips at this point is that once he knew air cover was not available he should have called off the operation. Yes, it was a risky decision: battles usually are. No, it was not the result of inexperience. No-one in the Royal Navy had experienced this situation before. No, he did not believe capital ships were invincible. As for the decision being a function of his own personality, it was not challenged by the numerous other personalities on his bridge and the bridges of his ships. Rather than a personal decision, it has all the hallmarks of one that was a practical inevitability. In fact, the decision Phillips took was a compromise. The fine weather had broken and there was low, heavy cloud with frequent rain storms. Phillips could make use of the cover this provided to steam north on 9 December, and if not spotted by

Japanese aircraft, make a dash to attack Japanese invasion forces and make a high-speed retreat thereafter to Singapore.

The morning of 9 December broke to low cloud, mist and rain. Phillips handled Force Z well. He sent *Electra* ahead to sweep for mines and ordered a zigzag course and speed of 17.5 knots, fast enough to put the ships beyond anything except a lucky shot from a submarine but economical enough on fuel to keep the maximum number of options open, reaching Japanese invasion areas in twenty-four hours but leaving plenty of fuel for a top-speed dash back to Singapore.

At 0620 on 9 December a single lookout on *Vampire* spotted a solitary aircraft. Phillips called for clarification, and decided to disregard the sighting:

'Phillips remained unconvinced and, adopting the attitude of an ostrich beset by danger, he metaphorically buried his head in the sand and shrugged off the warning.'[11]

Phillips is sometimes cited at this point as believing simply what he wanted to hear, choosing to disbelieve a lookout because he was the bearer of bad news. This seems unlikely. The lookout believed he alone had sighted a plane through a gap in the clouds for no longer than a minute. There was no certainty either that it was Japanese or that it had sighted Force Z. It would have been far more likely, had the ships actually been spotted, that any aircraft would have come in for a closer look. Philips was bound to check with *Prince of Wales*'s radio room to see if it had picked up a sighting report. In the absence of any such, he took a judgment call, and he was right. The aircraft has never been identified, and if it did exist it sent no sighting report.

At 1300 the promised RAF Catalina appeared, and signalled a Japanese landing at Singora, one of the few times that Force Z saw friendly aircraft. At 1343 the Japanese submarine *I-65* reported sighting Force Z. At 1550 it lost the ships in a squall, found them again at 1652 but finally lost them again when a Japanese float plane threatened to attack and force it to submerge, finally signaling at 1710 that it had lost contact. Force Z steamed on, unaware it had been spotted. Perhaps at this moment if Force Z had had the extra two destroyers Cunningham was ordered to send the enlarged escort might have 'pinged' the Japanese submarine.

'This [being spotted by I.650] was the cruellest of luck for the British. If their course had carried them just a few miles more to the east, *Prince of Wales* and *Repulse* would not have been spotted.'[12]

The Japanese Admiral Ozawa only received the sighting report at 1540, and ordered cruisers to send out search planes. Something approaching panic took place as reconnaissance over Singapore confirmed the two ships were no longer there, and planes were scrambled willy-nilly, despite imminent nightfall. However, the weather cleared at around 1700 and Force Z was sighted by a search plane from cruiser *Kinu*, then by search planes from *Suzuya* and *Kumano*. It was, by any standards, remarkable bad luck. Force Z was only a few hours away from nightfall, and only a few miles away from being outside the Japanese planes' search umbrella. Despite finally knowing it had been spotted by the Japanese, Force Z maintained radio silence. *Tenedos*, short of fuel, was detached, and ordered to signal Singapore next day at 0800 that Phillips was breaking off the attack against Singora. What Phillips did not know is that the path of Japanese warships returning from escorting the invasions would bring them extremely close to his forces.

At this point, the argument goes, Phillips knew that he had been spotted. There was no longer any reason to maintain radio silence, yet still he made no signal of his intentions to Singapore. Yet there was little point in any such signal. There were no ships in Singapore or heading there that could help him in time, except as anti-submarine escorts in the final run-in to Singapore. He had been told twice there was no fighter cover available, and Palliser had neither corrected his earlier signal to say there were, nor told Phillips that a squadron of Brewster Buffaloes were on stand-by. Furthermore, knowing he had been spotted, Phillips swung his force west at 1900 and increased speed to 26kt, to giving the impression he was heading to Singora. Having then hopefully told Japanese attackers where he was heading, he planned to turn south for a high-speed run to Singapore. What was the point of a signal to Singapore, when the signal he had arranged for *Tenedos* to send next morning said all he needed to say with no risk of giving away his position?

It is rarely pointed out that Phillips's skillful changes of course and speed very nearly succeeded in allowing Force Z to evade the Japanese attack squadrons sent out to hunt them.

What then followed was one of the more bizarre incidents of the engagement. Much has been made of the risks Phillips took, less of the risks the Japanese took. One of the latter – hurriedly launching a multitude of aircraft to attack in the dark enemy ships whose exact position was not known, in an area where their own ships were operating – nearly ended in farcical disaster. At around 2000 Japanese bombers searching for Force Z mistook a force of Japanese cruisers and destroyers searching for Force Z for Force Z itself, and preparatory to attacking dropped a flare over the cruiser *Chokai*. Following some frantic signaling, an attack was narrowly averted. For a long while it was assumed that Force Z had seen the flare the Japanese aircraft dropped over *Chokai*, and immediately turned away. Modern research[13] suggests that if seen at all the flare was only seen on the extreme wing of Force Z's progress, and that when at 2015 Force Z, under cover of darkness, turned south for the run to Singapore, this was simply a planned manoeuvre. There has been some speculation as to what the outcome would have been had Force Z engaged the Japanese forces which one writer claims were only five miles distant, but another says were over twenty miles away. The British force was superior in terms of raw firepower, but a night action would have injected an element of uncertainty into the whole business. What is certain is that Phillips sent out by signal lamp at 2055 a message to Force Z marking the effective end of the mission as it had been planned:

> 'I have most regretfully cancelled the operation because, having been located by aircraft, surprise was lost and our target would be almost certain to be gone by the morning and the enemy fully prepared for us.'[14]

Phillips was reportedly much cheered by receiving a signal from Tennant of *Repulse* appreciated how difficult the decision had been, but supported it fully. It was a difficult decision to throw in the towel, and a brave one, as recognized even by one of Phillips's most savage critics: 'The decision [to cancel the operation] ... showed a great deal of moral courage.'[15] And by others: 'Phillips's action, in ordering the return of his force to Singapore, was perhaps the most courageous in a brilliant and distinguished career.'[16]

Ominously for Force Z at 2238 the moon rose and the rain stopped. At 2302 Palliser signalled saying that enemy bombers were undisturbed, and could attack Force Z five hours after sighting it. He also said the northern Malayan airfields were becoming untenable, and hinted that Air Chief Marshal Sir Robert Brooke-Popham might order the concentration of all air efforts on Singapore. To this writer, but apparently to no other, it seems quite extraordinary that having sent one signal stating there could be no fighter cover Palliser sends another in effect confirming the absence of air support when in fact a squadron of aircraft were on stand-by.

Yet it is only extraordinary if Palliser knew of this squadron. It seems totally bizarre, if not surreal, to question if the RAF had actually told the Navy of the available support. The more one reads about the tragi-comedy that was the fall of Singapore, the more one realizes that of all combat zones in the Second World War Singapore was the one where such an event was at least possible.

At 2335 Palliser sent the signal that could be deemed to mark the start of the downfall of Force Z. It read, simply enough: 'Enemy reported landing at Kuantan'.

Kuantan was of vital strategic significance, and its capture would allow the Japanese to cut British forces in half. It was in effect on Force Z's way home to Singapore and 400 miles away from the Japanese air bases, a distance at which Admiral Phillips had every reason to believe, on the Intelligence of the day, he was out of range. It also put Force Z clearly out of range of the two Japanese carriers, which Phillips had been told were off Saigon.

In effect, the signal meant that Phillips had no option but to stop off at Kuantan, and is likely to have welcomed it as offering Force Z a belated chance to make a difference. Not to have stopped off at Kuantan would have meant the Royal Navy turning an unacceptable blind eye to the very situation it was tasked to fight. In fact the report of a landing was false. Palliser must bear responsibility for not keeping a weather eye on the situation to stop Force Z going on a wild goose chase. He must also take responsibility for yet again not telling Phillips that air cover was in fact available, if indeed he knew. Most important of all, he must take responsibility for in effect sending Force Z to Kuantan, warning the RAF and not seeking at least some air cover over Kuantan. Apologists for Palliser have argued that expecting him to realize his signal would send Force Z to Kuantan would have required Palliser to be telepathic:

> 'One cannot but feel that Admiral Phillips's belief that air cover would meet him off Kuantan, when he had given Singapore no hint that he was proceeding there, demanded too high a degree of insight from the officers at the base.'[17]

It did not demand too high a degree of insight, merely a normal level of intelligence. It did not need insight to realize that a commander at sea in the most hostile possible environment would not send signals that could reveal his position. After all, the whole plan for the survival of Force Z hinged on persuading the Japanese it was heading to Singora. It did not need insight to realize that, short of ordering Phillips to Kuantan, which Palliser did not have the power to do, the signal was the nearest thing possible to an order. Phillips was also justified in thinking that if Kuantan was being attacked it would, given its strategic importance, have whatever air cover was available over it, as indeed it did, in small measure. The efficiency of the RAF is highlighted by the fact that their aircraft failed to spot a battleship, a battle-cruiser and three destroyers off a spot reportedly being invaded by the Japanese.

At 2352 the Japanese submarine *I-58* sighted Force Z. A faulty tube hatch delayed its attack, but eventually five torpedoes were launched at *Repulse*. All missed.

10 December

At 0052 on 10 December Force Z changed course south-west for Kuantan. No signal was sent to Singapore. Phillips did not know he had been spotted, had surprise as his only ally for an attack on Kuantan and as discussed above would have been mad to risk giving his position away. It was reasonable for Phillips and his staff to believe that he was two hours south of where the Japanese thought he was, and steaming in the opposite direction. He had already arranged for *Tenedos* to do what was necessary in the morning, at a safe distance from *Prince of Wales*.

A bizarre signal was received from the Admiralty during the night, apparently reminding Phillips of the dangers of ships being attacked by torpedoes in harbour. This slightly surreal signal – Phillips was confused by it and said something about the First Sea Lord going off at half-cock – is important not for its rather silly nature, but rather as a hint that the Admiralty knew that Japanese land-based bombers had a torpedo-carrying capacity. If they did have this information no-one had passed it on to Force Z.

The Japanese received *I-58's* sighting report at 0211 – the famed Japanese military efficiency did not cover the quick handing-on of sighting reports in this action – and ordered the 22nd Air Flotilla to attack the ships later in the day, giving up on the idea of a surface attack following the near fiasco with *Chokai* and her force. Failure to report-on sighting signals meant that the Japanese did not realize Force Z was steaming south-west, not south directly towards Singapore. Force Z sailed on through the night. Unbeknown to it, eleven Japanese search planes from 22nd Flotilla were dispatched at 0455, and at 0625, 0644, 0650, 0800 eighty-five Japanese bombers flew off from their land bases.

Action Stations was called just before dawn at 0500. A tug and three barges were briefly investigated at 0515; Force Z was nearly at Kuantan and bigger targets were in prospect. A solitary aircraft was spotted from *Repulse* at 0630, but no action was taken, and the aircraft's identity remains something of a mystery. It is possible it was identified as British, but in any event Force Z was hoping to announce its presence in the most dramatic way possible in a few minutes, and if Kuantan was indeed being attacked it was hardly a surprise to see an aircraft flying over it. At 0720 *Prince of Wales* launched its Walrus aircraft to reconnoitre Kuantan; it was directed to land at Singapore, as was *Repulse*'s aircraft, launched later for anti-submarine reconnaissance. Capital ships were very vulnerable if they had to stop to take back on board their aircraft, one reason why the provision for carrying aircraft was progressively removed from the KGV class as the war went on.

The Walrus reported that all seemed calm, and at 0845 the destroyer *Express* was sent ahead, and reported 'complete peace'. Some versions have it saying that things were, 'As quiet as a wet Sunday afternoon.' Force Z dawdled whilst some barges and small craft were investigated, at the suggestion of Captain Tennant of *Repulse*. This delay has received severe criticism, it being argued that it showed a complete lack of urgency and a failure to realize the seriousness of the situation Force Z found itself in. As usual in this story, it is not as simple as that. If the Japanese had actually landed on Kuantan and dug in, the 14-inch guns of *Prince of Wales* and the 15-inch guns of *Repulse* were the only British weapons in the Far East capable of digging them out. If Japanese troops were in possession of this crucial interchange, they were hardly likely to announce themselves to two British capital ships, much more likely to keep their heads down and hope the ships would go away. As for the small force of barges, they could merely have been the advance party for a larger force. Most important of all, both Phillips and Tennant (and the delay at Kuantan must be a shared responsibility) believed they were out of range of Japanese land-based aircraft. Perhaps most crucially of all, there has been no evidence offered to suggest that had Force Z kept on its way to Singapore it would have been less likely to be spotted.

Whatever else may have been wrong with Admiral Palliser, he was not shy about sending signals. The problem was rather that he sent the wrong ones. At 0952 he reported fifteen Japanese transports and an aircraft carrier off Singora '… further reinforcing the obvious, that no one in Singapore had expected Force Z to arrive off Kuantan that morning.'[18]

The question is not whether they had expected it, but whether they should have expected it. Meanwhile, *Tenedos* had sent off her signal at 0800. It is believed it was received at Singapore, but the timing has not been established beyond doubt. We have to assume that, at the very least, Singapore knew sometime after 0800 that Force Z had abandoned its mission to Singora. '… but there [Singapore] it was only inferred that the Admiral's plans had changed and that he could not have gone as far north as Singora.'[19]

One is tempted to ask just how well qualified one has to be to work out that an Admiral who is now heading south and has been told of an enemy landing on his way is likely to head to the reported site of that landing.

The Engagement

Throughout the engagement that was to follow both *Prince of Wales* and *Repulse* faced continual problems with the ammunition for their short-range anti-aircraft weaponry separating out and jamming the guns. It is not possible to give exact figures, but the comments of survivors suggest it caused a major diminution in the ships' short-range firepower.

The battle started at 0952 when *Tenedos* was sighted and attacked by a Japanese reconnaissance plane searching for Force Z. It launched two bombs, both of which missed. At 0955 it reported the attack. At 1030 *Tenedos* skillfully avoided nine bombs, and sent off signals at 1005, 1020 and 1030. It is unclear whether or not these were received in Singapore, though they were received by Force Z. Meanwhile, at 1015, a Japanese Nell search plane, piloted by Ensign Hoashi Masane, sighted Force Z, and sent a report. *Repulse* detected the plane on radar. The Japanese bomber and torpedo squadrons were low on fuel and about to reach their point of no return. At 1020 Force Z made its first visual sighting, and at 1030, on receipt of the signal from *Tenedos*, Phillips ordered first–degree readiness for air attack, an increase of speed to twenty-five knots, and a change of course for Singapore.

It is at this point that there is the most unity among commentators in condemning Phillips. It is frequently pointed out that had he sent a report to Singapore when he knew he had been spotted the squadron of Brewster Buffaloes reserved for covering Force Z could have been at the scene of the attack by the time the first torpedoes were launched.

The signals from *Tenedos* have been recorded as having happened in all accounts of the engagement, but their true importance has not been commented on. Lost and vanished records and the death of all the senior figures involved, if not in the sinkings then of old age, mean that certain issues can never be proven beyond reasonable doubt. Did Singapore fail to receive *Tenedos's* signals stating she was under air attack, even though they were received on board *Prince of Wales?* Those signals made it clear there was still a sizable force in the air. What is certain is that Singapore sent out no aircraft in response to *Tenedos's* request. Either Singapore did not indeed receive the signals, or it did and there was a monumental cock-up in notifying those who could have sent air support. Historians have worked backwards from the fact that Singapore did not dispatch aircraft either to support *Tenedos* when it had signalled it was under air attack, and did not dispatch any aircraft to find and provide support for Force Z (no organizer of a lottery would have made knowing where Force Z was the jackpot winner: too many people would have won). It seems appalling even beyond the tragi-comedy of the fall of Singapore to contemplate that such crucial signals might not have been passed on, but is it any more appalling than the fact that equally crucial sighting reports on the Japanese side were not passed on for hours to those who could act on them?

I have not been able to verify one statement by a recent historian:

'In Singapore, Admiral Palliser had still heard nothing from Admiral Phillips. At some point, perhaps after receiving the signals from the *Tenedos,* Palliser sent Phillips a signal informing him that he had two aircraft and asking for instructions on where to send them. Admiral Palliser received no reply, and sent the aircraft off based on what he thought Phillips would do; unfortunately, his guess was not correct, and the aircraft went to the wrong location.'[20]

The primary fact remains that Phillips and his staff had been informed unequivocally that fighter protection was not available, once from Pulford and once from Palliser, a message that was not challenged in any of the numerous signals received subsequently. Its unavailability was confirmed by Force Z seeing only one friendly aircraft for the whole length of the mission, and a complete absence of air cover over a supposed invasion area. Had any fighter protection been available Phillips might reasonably assume the *Tenedos* signals would draw it out, and had no reason to think that its signals received by him were not being received by Singapore. As it was, yet again Force Z had appallingly bad luck:

'By 11.00am all ninety-five aircraft of the 22nd Air Flotilla were on their return leg, with fuel gauges registering well below the half level, and with hopes of finding the battle fleet almost abandoned. Many of the crews, in fact, were preoccupied with endurance calculations rather than the enemy, and several squadrons had determined to set course for Kota Bharu rather than risk the longer sea passage to Cape Cambodia. Then at approximately 11.05 am Ensign Hoashi ... on the last leg of his sector search, caught sight of several unidentifiable vessels between a gap in the clouds.'[21]

The Japanese aircraft had been sent out with over an hour and a half between the first and the last squadrons taking to the air, and had been in the air for several hours. The divided force attacked as and when it spotted its enemy. The first attack was by bombers on *Repulse*, from Lieutenant Yoshimi Shirai's eight Nell bombers. One bomb hit. It detonated against an inch of deck armour she had gained in one of her many refits (the bomb, at 250kg, was a relatively light one, as all the available heavy armour-piercing bombs had been allocated to the Pearl Harbor attack), and Shirai's squadron did not even have the 500kg bombs the other Japanese bombers carried, but appalling injuries were caused to some of the crew by burst steam pipes. In the cruel language unlikely to be appreciated by someone skinned alive by superheated steam, 'her fighting efficiency was not impaired'.

Tom Phillips has been heavily criticized for his initial order for the two ships to manoeuvre together by flag signal, which totally confused both ships' fire control systems and masked their fire. 'Admiral Phillips had made a fiasco out of his first handling of ships in action …'[22]

He soon realized his mistake, and allowed the ships to operate independently. Events proved his orders to be a mistake, but it is rarely pointed out that there was a sound reason behind them. *Prince of Wales*'s 5.25-inch guns were state-of-the-art, *Repulse*'s equivalent antediluvian. Phillips's orders brought *Repulse* under a protective umbrella. The vulnerability of *Repulse* was confirmed by the Japanese attackers, who flew over *Prince of Wales* to attack the weaker *Repulse*.

At 1132 Force Z was sighted by sixteen Nells of the Genzen Air Group, with the first attack, by nine Nells of Lieutenant Ishihara's squadron, made on *Prince of Wales*. The *Express* signalled 'Planes approaching have torpedoes'. An officer on bridge of *Prince of Wales* said: 'I think they're going to do a torpedo attack.' Admiral Phillips is reported to hear the remark, turn round and say: 'No, they're not. There are no torpedo aircraft about'. These famous almost-last words have been used against him, but if they are to be used against anyone it should be against the British Intelligence who had given him the information:

'I could see a formation of about ten planes skimming low on the water towards us. I … awaited with excitement the massacre of this echelon monster that would frighten the life out of lesser mortals. But, no, not us; let them get nearer, catch them on the upsweep. A deafening crescendo of noise erupted into the heavens. Eight 5.25's fired simultaneously. I watched the shells burst – but not a plane was hit. To me they seemed well *off* target. The planes came on remorselessly as all the pom-poms, machine guns and the Bofors gun opened up. All hell seemed to be let loose at once but nothing seemed to stop them ...'[23]

One Nell was discomfited by *Prince of Wales* making a sharp turn to port, and switched its attack to *Repulse*, but eight torpedoes were launched at *Prince of Wales*. The destroyer *Express* may have been the reason some torpedoes were dropped relatively early (another reminder as to what difference might have been made if Cunningham had supplied Force Z with two seaworthy destroyers), and one torpedo appears to have exploded as it hit the water. Survivors did not realize that the ship was hit at the stern by two torpedoes, as one hit produced a plume of water but the other was masked by the overhang of the stern.

The effect of these initial hits on *Prince of Wales* was catastrophic. In a tragic and ironic echo of the fate of her erstwhile opponent *Bismarck*, her fate was sealed by a single torpedo hit on the stern. The bracket securing the port outboard propeller shaft to the hull sheared, and the unsecured revolving shaft tore a gash in the hull along the length of the shaft. Earlier damage to the hull sustained as the result of the near-miss bomb in dock may have exacerbated the damage, creating a 'fault line' in the plating. Within seconds the ship took on an immediate list of 11.5° to port. With only the two starboard shafts operating, speed dropped from 25kt to 16kt. Flooding and shock damage disabled much of the ship's electrics. As a result four of its eight 5.25-inch turrets were put out of action, as was her steering. Lighting, ventilation and communication were lost below decks, where damage control was most needed, and much of the ship's capacity to pump out water was also disabled. Just as crucially, much of the ship's counter-flooding capacity was lost. *Prince of Wales* was one of a new type of warship, designed from the outset to be worked by electricity, but not as it turned out designed to ensure the continuation of her power supplies following a major blow to the hull. Everyone on the ship appears to have realized that something frighteningly extraordinary had occurred. Various unattributed comments include: 'It was as if the ship had collided with a very solid object coupled with a leap in the air', 'The ship appeared to be on springs; it lifted into the air and settled down again' and 'the ship's structure whipped violently like a springboard.'

At this one moment a number of factors came together in effect to sink *Prince of Wales.* Hull weaknesses, a single hit in just the wrong place and a design that proved horrendously susceptible to a body-blow to the hull turned this 'unsinkable' ship into a sitting duck. The torpedo hit rendered *Prince of Wales* useless as a fighting vessel, but did not sink her. Critics comment that even at this stage, when his ship could have been kept afloat, Phillips did not signal to Singapore for air support. Of course. Why should he when he had been told there was none?

It seems likely that what was meant to be a pincer attack failed to coordinate because one squadron believed it might be Japanese ships that were being attacked, and held back. In any event, it was some ten to twelve minutes after *Prince of Wales* had been disabled that a combined bomb and torpedo attack was launched against *Repulse*, which, magnificently handled like a destroyer by Captain Tennant, managed to avoid seven torpedoes and six bombs, acting now as the focus of the Japanese attacks as her consort was so clearly wounded. Critics of Admiral Sir Tom Phillips usually fail to point out that at this point in the action *Repulse* seemed a convincing example of the capital ship's ability to resist air attack.

In the brief lull that followed the last attacks on *Repulse*, Captain Tennant decided he should manoeuvre closer to *Prince of Wales* to see if he could offer assistance. He was reported as being horrified to be told that *Prince of Wales* had made no signal to Singapore reporting the attack, and immediately made his own at 1158. Received in Singapore at 1204, it resulted in the scrambling of eleven Buffalo fighters of 453 Squadron, at 1225, under the command of Flight-Lieutenant Tim Vigors.

It is about as wise for a historian to say there is no evidence for something as it was to claim that a ship is unsinkable. Suffice it to say that I am not aware of any evidence that Tennant was 'horrified'. It is extraordinary what a spin a writer can put on an action by the simple use of an adjective. The suggestion that Tennant was horrified by the failure to call for fighter protection (which is what the story has become) requires interrogation on a number of fronts. Firstly, *Prince of Wales*'s radio aerials, always a fragile part of any warship delivering or receiving heavy blows, had been partially affected by the torpedo explosion. Secondly, we know that a room crucial to her signals structure had to be evacuated quickly as a result of the hit. Thirdly, the assertion that the ship's signalling capacity was intact until the end, when tracked down, appears to hinge on the word of one Petty Officer Telegraphist. Tennant was certainly concerned; one of his first questions by signal lamp, as he moved over to *Prince of Wales*, was whether or not her wireless was out of action. As well as aerial damage, we know how badly the ship's electrics were affected. I find it difficult to accept that there might not have been difficulties with the ship's ability to signal. Phillips was no fool, and nor were his Staff and Captain Leach. Why should he not signal when there was nothing to lose by it? Even if Phillips had had a rush of blood to the head there were enough people on the bridge of his flagship to put him right. It has to be left as at least a possibility that Phillips did not signal Singapore because he could not do so. Fourthly, at no time following the sinkings did Tennant criticize his flagship's failure to signal.

At 1210, *Prince of Wales* hoisted two black balls, the international signal for a ship not under control. At 1218 twenty-six Bettys of the Kanoya Group, low on fuel, spotted a seaplane (probably *Repulse*'s Walrus), and then spotted Force Z. These aircraft carried a heavier torpedo than their predecessors, the so-called 'Model 2' with a 204kg (450lb) warhead. Six aircraft were first to launch at *Prince of Wales*, at point-blank range. *Prince of Wales* could not steer, and could only manage some 15 knots on her starboard engines. Four out of the six torpedoes hit along virtually her whole length on the starboard side, from bow to stern. Pictures taken of the wreck show a hole punched right through her bow. Damage was increased as a result of compartments on this side having been filled with water for counter-flooding, the effect of an explosion on these being far greater than on an air-filled compartment. *Prince of Wales* was reduced to eight knots, down to one out of her four engines, and had only two of her eight dynamos producing the electricity she needed to help her stay afloat. It is estimated she had taken in nearly 18.000 tons of water.

At 1220 *Prince of Wales* signalled she had been hit, and asked Singapore to send destroyers. This signal has been seen by many commentators as showing

Phillips's contempt for air cover: '… it is incredible that the Admiral should ask for destroyers rather than fighter aircraft.'[24]

It is only incredible if Phillips knew fighters were available. He called for all that he thought there was in the way of possible assistance.

At 1223 a new Japanese attack saw three planes break off from attacking *Prince of Wales* and turn on *Repulse*, when she had already taken evasive action to comb the tracks of eight torpedoes launched at her from relatively long range. *Repulse* was hit by one torpedo on her torpedo bulge, and shrugged off the hit, continuing to steam at 25kt. As for *Prince of Wales*, the last hit on her stern was probably decisive, as it negated all damage control in that area. By this time, and perfectly understandably, some people were cracking under the strain:

'… to make matters worse, a commissioned gunner had needlessly and without orders decided to flood several magazines, presumably to prevent an explosion. Stopped by the ship's engineer officer, Commander L. J. Goudy, this nevertheless caused yet more water to enter the ship …'[25]

At around 1223 *Repulse*'s luck finally ran out. Caught in a pincer movement led by the last group of Kanoya aircraft under Lt Iki, she took three torpedo hits on her starboard side, one to port. Her rudder was jammed, and she took on a list of 30° to port. Hit by four torpedoes in four minutes, the old girl had received her death blows, and Tennant, realizing the end was inevitable, ordered 'Abandon Ship'. She sank at 1233.

The last attack on *Prince of Wales* took place at 1243. A 1,100lb bomb hit the cinema flat, causing horrific injuries to the wounded gathered there in large numbers. The explosion also damaged uptakes and downtakes to her last operating boiler room. The ship stopped, dead in the water. At 1305, at considerable risk and showing magnificent seamanship, the destroyer *Express* came alongside *Prince of Wales* to take off survivors.

Prince of Wales rolled over and sank at 1318. Shortly after, two Buffaloes arrived, possibly sent by Admiral Palliser, then 453 Squadron. The death toll was twenty officers and 307 ratings from *Prince of Wales*, twenty-four officers and 486 ratings from *Repulse*. Neither Admiral Phillips nor Captain

Leach of *Prince of Wales* survived, though the most recent commentator believes, 'Admiral Phillips had not tried "to go down with the ship"'.[26]

One account has the last words Phillips was heard to utter as, 'I cannot survive this.'[27]

Majority opinion holds Phillips to have a very significant responsibility for the disaster:

> 'Apologists for Phillips have claimed that the admiral was upholding the fighting traditions of the Royal Navy by taking Force Z in to the South China Sea to look for Japanese shipping. If Phillips's foray had been well timed and executed that line of argument might have had some validity. But Force Z's final cruise was launched too late to be effective and was riddled with operational mistakes. Two capital ships and many lives were wasted.'[28]

In fact the timing of the departure was largely out of Tom Phillips's control. The only real 'operational mistake' Phillips made was to manoeuvre his ships in close order for the first attack, but there was good reason to do so and he changed the order as soon as a problem became apparent. Whilst operating in close order no damage was done to either of his ships that reduced their fighting ability.

The Judgment of History

So who was to blame for the loss of these two ships and their officers and men? The finger points at three people in particular. Winston Churchill's major failure was not to support the reinforcement of Singapore more strongly in the 1930s, or agree to more modern weapons and aircraft being supplied to it. He may have been proved wrong, but his failure to make the defence of Singapore a priority can be justified on the basis that 1930s Britain simply could not meet all its obligations. Nor was his failure to dispatch Force Z to Singapore. It was a gambler's throw, but the gambler in question could justify it by pointing out the weakness of his hand, and that in the circumstances this bluff was his only option. His failure rather was not to recall the ships when his bluff was called. In his defence, it matters little whether he sent out Force Z as a deterrent, to reassure the colonies or to bring America in as the defender of Britain's Far Eastern colonial empire. The latter would have been an extraordinarily outrageous plan, but Churchill was an extraordinarily outrageous man. Furthermore, he was expert at producing plans that were brilliant in their conception but fell down on detail and execution: the Dardanelles was just one such. In any event, there is one common denominator in all three reasons for Churchill to push for *Prince of Wales* to be sent out: none of them would require the ship actually to fight. It was a diplomatic mission, one good reason for putting a brilliant thinker who was quick on his intellectual feet in charge rather than an up-and-at-'em sea dog. The change to it being a military mission came about as a result of Pearl Harbor. There are tantalizing snippets to suggest that Roosevelt may have known more about the likelihood of the attack on Pearl Harbor being launched than he admitted at or after the time, but no hint that Churchill knew more than anyone else who was surprised by the speed and venom of the Japanese assault. Churchill was playing for high stakes. If his aim was to impress America or frighten Japan with his commitment he was right to send them *Prince of Wales* rather than a collection of obsolete rust buckets. Churchill may have been instrumental in taking the decisions that put the two ships in harm's way. There was good reason to do so. There was much less reason for not ordering them out of it.

Dudley Pound, the First Sea Lord, must bear equal responsibility for the ships not being recalled. When things in the Far East went, as Admiral Somerville would undoubtedly have said, 'tits up', it could be argued that it was Churchill who should have issued the orders to get Force Z out of Singapore. Yet the person whose office set him up to give that order was Dudley Pound, ally and sponsor of Tom Phillips and the person most responsible for his early promotion. Churchill was a politician. Pound was a sailor in the service of the world's proudest and oldest fighting navy. A politically possible mission became military suicide the minute war actually broke out, and it was the military arm who should have done what soldiers and sailors are employed to do, stick by their guns and win the day. Fair enough, perhaps, that Pound had not dug his heels in and threatened to resign when Churchill overrode the Admiralty and sent the Navy's newest battleship out, rather than some of its oldest. It was not so fair that he failed to insist on the ships being pulled out when Churchill's bluff in sending the ships out was called. Phillips could not pull himself out of the action: it could only be done on the basis of an order from the Admiralty, an order that never came. Courage takes many forms. One form is that in which one risks death and dishonour by taking ships out against a far superior enemy. Another form is that whereby one places one's career and livelihood on the line by insisting that such a risk does not have to be taken, and sadly it was this form of courage that was found wanting in Pound when the moment came. Just as Churchill had been stopped from prosecuting Admiral James Somerville on a trumped-up charge of cowardice by the threat of resignations from senior officers, so it is difficult to see how Churchill could have failed to ignore a threat of resignation from his First Sea Lord if he did not order the ships to safety.

A third finger of blame points at Admiral Palliser. He made six crucial errors that contributed a significant amount to the sinking of Force Z. One: He told Phillips, quite categorically, that there was no fighter protection available, and then repeated it for good measure. Two: He sent a subsequent signal confirming his first by suggesting that any available aircraft were likely to be reserved for the defence of Singapore itself. Three: He sent a signal erroneously reporting a landing at Kuantan. Four: He failed to keep himself abreast of events and signal or spot that this was a false report: in either event, he was highly culpable. Five: He failed to realize the inevitable result of his signal in sending Force Z to Kuantan. Six: He failed to tell Phillips, or find out, that fighters were on stand-by for Force Z.

As for Phillips, he seems the least guilty of all. He was party to the pre-war tendency to underestimate the likelihood of war with Japan, for which he must bear a share of the responsibility, but his actions elsewhere – arguing for modern aircraft to be sent to Singapore, opposing the bombing campaign against Germany, opposing the Crete and Greece actions – showed him to have excellent overall judgment and the courage to stand up for his convictions. He was given an unbalanced and wholly inadequate strike force, with his best ship not fully trained. His grasp of the realities of war was clear through his emphasis on the importance of air support, and his call for reinforcements. He set sail as soon as he reasonably could in the best and unavoidable traditions of the Royal Navy, handling his flawed fleet with

skill and dash. He was man enough to start the mission, man enough to
call it off when he lost his only advantages, surprise and bad weather. He
did everything he could to arrange air cover. He could not know that the
ship he was in was a sinking waiting to happen, or that his Intelligence on
the range and capacity of Japanese aircraft was hopelessly inaccurate. He
failed to call for air cover because his representative ashore and liaison with
the RAF had told him there was none to be had. The failure of a fellow
Admiral saw him sail short of escorts, the decisions of the Admiralty left
him to fight an advanced enemy without the aircraft carrier that would have
made a balanced force, and that same Admiralty failed to recall him or send
him into hiding when that was all that could have saved him and his ships.
A few miles and a few minutes either way and he might well not have been
spotted. A few feet away and his ship might have avoided or at least absorbed
damage and fought on: it was effectively the torpedo hit that sheered off
Prince of Wales's 'A' bracket that sealed the battle, and looked at from any
angle Phillips had appallingly bad luck.

Should he have set sail, without air cover? Apart from the fact that he
would have faced a court-martial if he had not, betrayed every tradition of
the service he loved and destroyed the morale and standing of Britain with
every inhabitant of Singapore, there was good reason for doing so. He had
surprise and the monsoon weather on his side, and if he could bring his
force into contact with the Japanese invasion forces he could have changed
the course of the war. Tom Phillips was too clever a man to think that any
ship was unsinkable, but had no reason to think his ship would sink as easily
as it did. If he did make an error in having *Repulse* too close to him on board
Prince of Wales amid the opening shots of the battle then it was for good
reason and did no serious damage before it was changed. He may not have
signalled that he was being attacked because he could not do so, but more
likely because with the information held at the time it could serve no useful
purpose to do so.

In so many areas Tom Phillips was the victim of other people's mistakes
– those who sent him out there, those who failed to order him back, those
who he left behind in Singapore, those who had failed to equip Singapore
with modern aircraft, those who had provided so-called Intelligence in the
inter-war period, those who designed *Prince of Wales*, those who failed to

send him ships that were fit for purpose. His own death and inability to defend himself meant that those same people were able to use him as a front and a cover, and for over seventy years have done so to such good effect that it is still Phillips who is deemed guilty of a crime he did not commit, rather than them.

A jealous Navy which had never quite known how to handle a man whose skills were so much intellectual rather than physical, the premature death of his greatest ally in the Royal Navy who also bore a large share of the responsibility for the disaster and the hostility of the most influential naval historian of the Second World War were not the reason Tom Phillips was knocked to the ground, but helped to keep him down when he fell.

Unfortunately he has also been a victim of the trait whereby one must never let the truth stand in the way of a good story: an unreformed senior naval officer hoist by his own petard *is* a better story than a man who was the victim of circumstances he could not control. Phillips has also suffered, not from the School of Armchair History that has damned so many other brave commanders, but from the School of Hindsight, where so many have insisted that because we know a squadron of clapped-out death-traps were on stand-by to defend his ships, he too should have known.

There were others who should have been held to account for the sinking of *Prince of Wales* and *Repulse*. What books have been written about the design team responsible for a battleship that was not fit for purpose? Why do we not know the names of the Intelligence officers who failed so woefully to ascertain the true qualities of Japanese aircraft, and may have failed to tell Tom Phillips that he was within range of Japanese torpedo-bombers? Why has Tom Phillips's name been dragged through the mud when Admiral Palliser told Phillips no fighter cover was available, failed to tell him that it was available when it clearly was and sent him off on a wild goose chase to the landing that never was? Why has no one been blamed for the biggest failure of all, the failure to pull back the two ships when it was clear that deterrence had failed? Who gained most from the circulation of the story that what was actually no more than a thought that *Indomitable* might be sent to join Force Z was in fact a firm intention? Is it right that the official historian could write on Phillips when he had had a clear falling-out with him, and is it right that the same historian should admit in private that Phillips had had a change of heart about the air threat to surface ships, but never admit so in public?

It is time the record was put straight. Admiral Sir Tom Phillips was no more perfect than any other mortal, but the things that ensured the command of Force Z was a poisoned chalice were none of them of his making. He has been made a classic scapegoat for the failings of others.

Notes

Chapter 1: The Military, Political and Historical Background

1. Richard H. Hough, *The Hunting of Force Z. Britain's Greatest Modern Naval Disaster* (1963) Collins, London, 88.
2. PRO, PREM 163/3.
3. Quoted in *Old Friends, New Enemies. The Royal Navy and the Imperial Japanese Navy*, Arthur J. Marder (1981) Oxford, Clarendon Press, 28.

Chapter 2: The Loss of *Prince of Wales* and *Repulse* The Action: The Case Against Tom Phillips

1. Martin Middlebrook and Patrick Mahoney, *Battleship. The Loss of the Prince of Wales and Repulse* (1977) London, Allen Lane, 305.
2. Edwin Gray *Operation Pacific. The Royal Navy's War against Japan 1941–1945* (1990) Leo Cooper, London, 23.
3. Ronald Bassett, *Battle-Cruisers. A History 1908–1948* (1981) Macmillian, London, 228.
4. Middlebrook, 58.
5. Lord Ismay, *The Memoirs of General The Lord Hastings Lionel Ismay* (1960) Heinemann, London, 240.
6. Quoted Richard Hough, op.cit. 174 and others.
7. Gray, 24.
8. Ibid. 25.
9. Ibid. 35.
10. Sir Andrew Gilchrist, *Malaya 1941* (1992) London, Robert Hale, 163.
11. Alan Warren, *Singapore: Britain's Greatest Defeat* (2002) Hambledon and London, London/New York, 55.
12. Arthur Nicholson, *Hostages to Fortune. Winston Churchill and the Loss of the 'Prince of Wales' and 'Repulse'* (2005) Sutton Publishing, Stroud, 71.
13. A comprehensive and verbatim list of all signals relevant to the action can be found in Nicholson, op.cit. 192–223.
14. Ibid. 105.
15. Julian Thompson, *The Imperial War Museum Book of the War At Sea. The Royal Navy in the Second World War* (1996) Sidgwick & Jackson/Imperial War Museum, London, 134.
16. Gray, op.cit. 40.
17. Stephen Roskill, *The War at Sea, Volume 1: The Defensive* (1954) London, HMSO, 565.
18. Arthur Nicholson, op.cit. 117.
19. Ibid. 118.
20. Ibid.
21. Martin Middlebrook, op.cit. 175.
22. Ronald Bassett, op.cit. 248.

23. Nicholson, op.ci. 136.
24. Ibid.137.
25. Middlebrook, op.cit. 304.
26. Gray, op.cit. 57.
27. Alan Warren, op.cit., *Singapore: Britain's Greatest Defeat* (2002) Hambledon & London, London/New York, 78.
28. Middlebrook, op.cit. 305.

Chapter 3: Admiral Sir Tom Phillips
1. Michael Arnold, *The Sacrifice of Singapore. Churchill's Biggest Blunder* (2011) Marshal Cavendish, Singapore, 40.
2. Bassett, op.cit. 232.
3. Admiral Sir Tom Phillips to TVG Phillips, 11 November 1941. Phillips Papers.
4. Ibid. 25 July 1941.
5. Bassett, op.cit. 232.
6. Commander Michael G. Goodenough to Lady Phillips, 6 June 1947. Phillips Papers.
7. Nicholson, op.cit.143.
8. Ibid. 148–149.
9. Letter, Arthur Marder to TVG Phillips, 2 February 1979. Phillips Papers.
10. Marder, op.cit. 388.
11. Post-war Memoir by Admiral John Godfrey. Phillips Papers.
12. CA RMSY 2/45.
13. Marder, op.cit. 31.
14. A.V. Alexander to Lady Phillips, December 21 1941. Phillips Papers.
15. Hough, op.cit.166.
16. Letter Dudley Pound to Lady Phillips. Phillips Papers.
17. Gray, op.cit. 31.
18. Captain L.H. Bell, letter to Arthur Marder, 24 March 1975. Marder Papers. Quoted Nicholson, op.cit. 25.
19. Field-Marshal Smuts, PRO, PREM 3 163/3.
20. Nicholson, op.cit. 25.
21. Quoted Marder, op.cit. 397.
22. Letter Captain (later Admiral Sir) Ralph Edwards to Lady Phillips, December 19 1941. Phillips Papers.
23. Letter, Marjorie Armitage to Lady Phillips, December 1941. Phillips Papers.
24. Letter, Harry V. Markham to Admiral Dudley Pound, 11 December 1941. Phillips Papers.
25. Letter, Gerald Warner to Lady Phillips, 12 December 1941. Phillips Papers.
26. Letter, Stephen King-Hall to Lady Phillips, 26 December 1941. Phillips Papers.
27. Letter, Robert Cassidi to Lady Phillips, 7 September 1942. Phillips Papers.
28. Letter, Neville Napier to Lady Phillips, 17 December 1941. Phillips Papers.
29. Copy of Letter to Winston Churchill from Lieutenant F.A. de Vere Hunt, RNVR, 1 February 1942. Phillips Papers.
30. Letter, Captain L.H. Bell to Lady Phillips, 12 December 1941. Phillips Papers.
31. Letter, Sidney E. Gobler to Lady Phillips, 14 December (1941). Phillips Papers.
32. Letter, Captain Tennant to Lady Phillips, 9 January 1942. Phillips Papers.
33. 'Staff Work, August to December 1934', undated note. Phillips Papers.
34. Letter, 'Tam' to Lady Phillips, 17 December (1941). Phillips Papers.

35. Letter, Admiral Sir Tom Phillips to Mildred Barker, 30 November 1941. Phillips Papers.
36. Letter, to Mildred Barker, 14 February 1942. Phillips Papers.
37. V.E. Tarrant, *King George V Class Battleships* (1991) Arms & Armour/Cassell, London, 101.

Chapter 4: Singapore and Signals

 1. Hough, op.cit.181.
 2. Letter, Lady Phillips to Captain Russell Grenfell, 28 Nov 1950. Grenfell Papers, Churchill Archives.
 3. Roman Bose, *Singapore at War. Secrets from the Fall, Liberation & Aftermath of WWII* (2012) Marshall Cavendish, Singapore, 71.
 4. Ibid. 69–70.
 5. Ibid. 71.
 6. Ibid. 74–75.
 7. Letter, Commander Michael Goodenough to Stephen Roskill, 8 May 1951. Phillips Papers.
 8. Letter, Commander Michael Goodenough to Captain Stephen Roskill, 8 May 1951. Roskill Papers.
 9. Nicholson, op.cit.118.
10. Stanley L. Falk, *Seventy Days to Singapore* (1975) New York, G.P. Putnam's Sons, 110.
11. Ibid.
12. Nicholson, op.cit.148–150.
13. Letter, Captain S.E. Norfolk to T.V.G. Phillips, 2 December 1977. Phillips Papers.
14. Middlebrook, op.cit. 210–211.
15. Hough, op.cit. 224.
16. Russell Grenfell, *Main Fleet to Singapore* (1987) Oxford University Press, Oxford,127.

Chapter 5: Churchill, and 'The Secret Alliance'

 1. Quoted in Roskill, *Churchill and the Admirals*, 124.
 2. Lieutenant R. Dyer, quoted Middlebrook, op.cit. 105.
 3. Hough, op.cit. 238.
 4. Bassett, op.cit. 244.
 5. Christopher M. Bell, *Churchill & Sea Power* (2013). Oxford University Press, 249.
 6. One such was from General Sir John Dill, sources for which are given in Bell, op.cit.239.
 7. Quoted Roskill, *Churchill and the Admirals*, 79.
 8. Gray, op.cit. 20.
 9. Bell, op.cit. 239.
10. Bell, op.cit. 232.
11. See Roskill, *Churchill and the Admirals*, op.cit. 25.
12. Winston Churchill, *Complete Speeches* Volume 6, 6, 532, and quoted widely.
13. Nicholson, op.cit. 81.
14. Letter, Churchill to G.R.G. Allen, 2 August 1953. Roskill Papers.
15. Roskill, *Churchill and the Admirals*,100.
16. Ibid. 278.
17. Bell, op.cit. 249–50.
18. Letter, Admiral Sir Tom Phillips to Mildred Barker, 19 November 1941. Phillips Papers.
19. Letter, Churchill to Admiral Sir Tom Phillips, February 6th 1940, Phillips Papers.
20. See Roskill, *Churchill and the Admirals*,182.

21. Hough, op.cit. 169.
22. Letter, Mildred Barker to T.V.G. Phillips, 22 March 1962. Phillips Papers.
23. See Alan Matthews, *The Secret Alliance. Anglo–American relations and the prelude to war with Japan.* Paper in possession of the author.
24. Report by Joint Planning Staff, War Cabinet, Chiefs of Staff Committee, 'Implications of Japanese Penetration of Indo-Chinas and Thailand', 27 October 1940, PRO, COS (40) 873, Cab 80/21.
25. J.R.M. Butler, *Grand Strategy Volume 2: The History of the Second World War September 1939 – June 1941.* (1957) London, HMSO, 424–425.
26. War Cabinet, ADB Conference, American Comments, para. 2(d), Report by Joint Planning Staff, 9 August 1941, PRO, JP (41) 648. Cab 79/13.
27. Admiralty to BAD Washington, Most Secret Glean 150, 5 November 1941, PRO, ADM 116/4877, Appendix V1.
28. See Marder, op.cit. 74–75.
29. Ibid.74.
30. Marder, op.cit.194.

Chapter 6: The Ships: *Prince of Wales*

1. Tarrant, op.cit. 30.
2. Churchill, quoted Nicholson, op.cit. 16.
3. See Tarrant, op.cit.17.
4. Bassett, op.cit. 246.
5. Tarrant, op.cit. 124.
6. R. A. Burt, *British Battleships 1919–1945* (2012) Revised Edition, Barnsley, Seaforth Publishing, 387.
7. Ibid. 388.
8. Martin Middlebrook and Patrick Mahoney, op.cit. 53.
9. Quoted in Burt, 240.
10. For a full discussion of this issue, see William H. Garzke Jnr, Robert Dulin Jnr, Kevin Denlay, *A Re-analysis of the Tragic Loss of HMS Prince of Wales* www.pacificwreck.com.
11. Bassett, op.cit. 245.
12. Nicholson, op.cit .99.
13. Alan Raven and John Roberts, *British Battleships of World War Two* (1981) London, Arms & Armour Press, Third Impression, 313.
14. Garzke, 61–62.
15. Tarrant. op.cit. 25.
16. Public Records Office, ADM, 199/2232.
17. Nicholson, op.cit.170.
18. Tarrant, op.cit. 25.
19. Raven, op.cit. 313.

Chapter 7: The Ships: *Repulse* and Escorts

1. Burt, op.cit. 210.
2. Ibid. 240.
3. Marder, op.cit. 382.
4. Grenfell, op.cit. 95.
5. *Arthur Marder, Old Friends, New Enemies. The Royal Navy and the Imperial Japanese Navy, Strategic Illusion 1936–1941* (1981) Oxford, Oxford University Press, 421.

6. See Nicholson. op.cit. 209.
7. Captain Bell to Arthur Marder, quoted Marder, op.cit. 418.
8. See Nicholson, op.cit., p.p.208–9.
9. Marder, op.cit., 422.
10. James Leasor, *Singapore. The Battle That Changed the World* (1968) London, Hodder & Stoughton, 185.
11. Marder, op.cit. 423.

Chapter 8: Intelligence, SS *Automedon* and 'Matador'
1. Middlebrook, op.cit. 304.
2. Nicholson, op.cit. 91, footnote, 62.
3. Warren, op.cit. 46.
4. Admiral Farnhill, quoted in Marder, op.cit. 418.
5. Ibid.
6. Ibid. 87.

Chapter 9: Aircraft
1. Nicholson, op.cit. 44.
2. Ibid. 41–44.
3. Thompson, op.cit. 38.
4. Brian Cull with Paul Sortehaug and Mark Haselden, Mark, *Buffaloes Over Singapore* (2003) London, Grub Street. 9–10.
5. Ibid. 215–216.
6. Bassett, op.cit. 231.
7. Middlebrook, op.cit. 298.
8. Hough, op.cit. 128.
9. Flight Lieutenant Terry Marra, writing in Brian Cull, op.cit. 6.
10. Cull, op.cit. 56.
11. Quoted widely, but see Cull, op.cit. 56.
12. Ibid. 54.
13. Sergeant George Scrimgeour, Cull, op.cit. 54.
14. Lieutenant Haruki Iki, IJN, quoted in Marder, op.cit. 483.
15. Hough, op.cit. 187.
16. Ibid. 55.
17. Ibid. 56.
18. Bassett, op.cit. 225–226.
19. See Hough, op.cit. 141.
20. Leasor, op.cit. 162.
21. Ibid.
22. Bassett, op.cit. 244.

Chapter 10: Struggles for Power: Admiral Sir Tom Phillips and the Royal Navy in 1941
1. BL ADD 52563, Somerville to Cunningham, 20 October 1941.
2. IWM Wentworth Papers, Cunningham to Wentworth, 12 October 1941.
3. Admiral A. B. Cunningham, *A Sailor's Odyssey. The Autobiography of Admiral of the Fleet Viscount Cunningham of Hyndhope, KT, GCB, OM, DSO* (1951) London, Hutchinson, 20.

4. Letter W. H. James to J. H. Godfrey, CA DUPO 6/1, October 1945.
5. Vice-Admiral Ronald Brockman, quoted in Nicholson, op.cit. 96.
6. Leasor, op. cit. 183.
7. Warren, op.cit. 77.
8. Letter A. B. Cunningham to A. Willis CA, WLLS, 17 January 1942.
9. Roskill, *Churchill and the Admirals*, 203.
10. Nicholson, op.cit. 163.
11. Gray, op.cit. 59.
12. Letter, Admiral Somerville to Admiral Cunningham BL ADD 52563, 20 October 1941.
13. I was able to spend a considerable amount of time with both James Somerville's son, and arrange for the son of Admiral Sir Tom Phillips to have lunch with the son of Admiral Sir James Somerville, in the late-1980s. I also worked with Captain Bill Lapper, who had for a time been Somerville's Secretary. Bill Lapper taught me how to read Somerville's handwriting in his indecipherable diaries. For future researchers I offer the following advice; hold the writing at eyeball height and slant it at 45 degrees.
14. Letter to the author from Captain W. H. Lapper.
15. Roskill, *Churchill and the Admirals*, op.cit. 270.
16. Captain Donald Macintyre, DSO, DSC, *Fighting Admiral: The Life of Admiral of the Fleet Sir James Somerville, GCB, GBE, DSO* (1961) London, Evans, 32.
17. Cunningham, op.cit. 436.
18. See Oliver Warner, *Cunningham of Hyndhope. Admiral of the Fleet. A Memoir* (1967) London, John Murray.
19. Pound to Cunningham, Cunningham Papers, BL ADD 52560, 18 August 1939.
20. Richard Hough, *The Longest Battle: The War At Sea 1939–45 (1986)* London, Weidenfeld and Nicolson, 226.
21. Cunningham to Pound, Cunningham Papers, BL, ADD 52560, 18 December 1939.
22. CA WLLS, 12/1, Memoirs, 18.
23. Warner, op.cit. 199.
24. Cunningham, op.cit. 425.
25. Captain S.W.C. Pack, CBE, *Cunningham the Commander* (1974) London, Batsford, 163.
26. Ibid. 3.
27. Ibid. 9.
28. Macintyre, op.cit.126.
29. Marder, op.cit. 366.
30. Roskill, *Churchill and the Admirals*, 181.
31. Ibid. 199.
32. Ibid. 119.
33. Ibid.
34. Ibid. 234.

Chapter 11: The Loss of *Prince of Wales* and *Repulse*: A Revaluation – the Preliminaries

1. Nicholson, op.cit.
2. Roskill, *Churchill and the Admirals*, 203.
3. PRO, PREM 3, 163/3, but quoted in almost every book on Force Z.
4. Marder, op.cit. 366.
5. Ronald Bassett, op.cit. 228.
6. Middlebrook, op.cit. 58.
7. Ibid. 52.

8. Gray, op.cit. 24.
9. Ibid. 25.
10. Sir Andrew Gilchrist, *Malaya 1941* (1992). London, Robert Hale, 163.
11. Ibid. 35.
12. Alan Warren, *Singapore: Britain's Greatest Defeat* (2005) Hambledon and London, London/New York, 55.
13. Marder, op.cit. 381.

Chapter 12: The Loss of *Prince of Wales* and *Repulse*: A Revaluation – The Action

1. Lieutenant R. Dyer, HMS *Tenedos*, quoted Middlebook, op.cit.105.
2. Lieutenant Commander F. J. Cartwright, HMS *Express*, Ibid.106.
3. Arthur Nicholson, op.cit. 71.
4. Nicholson, op.cit. 47.
5. Ibid.73.
6. PRO, ADM, 199/1149.
7. Bassett, op.cit. 232.
8. A comprehensive and verbatim list of all signals relevant to the action can be found in Nicholson, op.cit. 192–223.
9. Ibid.105.
10. Julian Thompson, op.cit. 134.
11. Gray, op.cit. 40.
12. Middlebrook, op.cit. 123.
13. See Nicholson, op.cit.
14. Quoted widely, but see Middlebrook, op.cit.145 et.al.
15. Middlebrok, op.cit. 144.
16. Hough, op.cit. 205.
17. Stephen Roskill, *The War at Sea, Volume 1: the Defensive* (1954) London, HMSO, 565.
18. Nicholson, op.cit.117.
19. Ibid. 118.
20. Ibid.
21. Hough, op.cit. 215.
22. Middlebrook, op.cit. 175.
23. Ordinary Seaman Derek Wilson, quoted Middlebrook, op.cit.185.
24. Bassett, op.cit. 248.
25. Nicholson, op.cit. 134.
26. Ibid. 136.
27. Ibid. 137.
28. Alan Warren, op.cit. 78.

Select Bibliography

This is not an exhaustive list, but simply one containing those works I have quoted from and which I have found most useful.

Arnold, Michael, *The Sacrifice of Singapore. Churchill's Biggest Blunder* (2001) Marshal Cavendish, Singapore.

Barnett, Correlli, *Engage the Enemy More Closely. The Royal Navy in the Second World War* (1991) London, Hodder & Stoughton.

Bassett, Ronald, *Battle-Cruisers. A History 1908–1948* (1981) Macmillian, London.

Bell, Christopher M., *Churchill & Sea Power* (2013) Oxford, Oxford University Press.

Bennett, Geoffrey, *The Loss of the Prince of Wales and Repulse* (1973) Sea Battles in Close-Up 7, London, Ian Allan.

Bose, Roman, *Singapore at War. Secrets from the Fall, Liberation & Aftermath of WWII* (2012) Marshall Cavendish, Singapore.

Burt, R.A., *British Battleships 1919–1945* (2012) Revised Edition, Barnsley, Seaforth Publishing.

Butler, J.R.M., *Grand Strategy Volume 2: The History of the Second World War September 1939 – June 1941* (1957) London, HMSO.

Cull, Brian, with Sortehaug, Paul and Haselden, Mark, *Buffaloes Over Singapore* (2003) London, Grub Street.

Cunningham, Viscount Hyndehope, *A Sailors's Odyssey* (1951) Hutchinson, London.

Falk, Stanley L., *Seventy Days to Singapore (1975)* G.P. Putnam's Sons.

Garzke, W. H. Jnr, Denlay, Kevin V, Dulin, Robert O. Jnr, *A Re-analysis of the Tragic Loss of HMS Prince of Wales* www.pacificwreck.com, nd.

Gilchrist, Sir Andrew, *Malaya 1941* (1992) London, Robert Hale.

Gray, Edwin, *Operation Pacific. The Royal Navy's War Against Japan 1941–1945* (1990) Leo Cooper, London.

Grenfell, Russell, *Main Fleet to Singapore* (1987) Oxford University Press, Oxford.

Gough, Barry, V. *Prince of Wales and Repulse: Churchill's "Veiled Threat" Reconsidered*; Paper delivered to 2007 International Churchill Conference, Vancouver.

Hack, Carl and Blackburn, Kevin, *Did Singapore Have to Fall? Churchill and the Impregnable Fortress* (2004) Routledge, London.

Hough, Richard H., *The Hunting of Force Z. Britain's Greatest Modern Naval Disaster* (1963) Collins, London. *The Longest Battle: The War At Sea 1939–45* (1986) London, Weidenfeld and Nicolson.

Ismay, Lord, *The Memoirs of General The Lord Hastings Lionel Ismay* (1960) Heinemann, London.

Law, Derek, *The Royal Navy in World War Two. An Annotated Bibliography* (1988) London, Greenhill Books.

Leasor, James, *Singapore. The Battle That Changed the World* (1981) London, Hodder & Stoughton.

Leutze, James, *A Different Kind of Victory: A Biography of Admiral Thomas C. Hart* (1981) Annapolis, Naval Institute Press.

Macintyre, Captain Donald DSO, DSC. *Fighting Admiral: The Life of Admiral of the Fleet Sir James Somerville, GCB, GBE, DSO* (1961) London, Evans.

Marder, Arthur J., *Old Friends, New Enemies. The Royal Navy and the Imperial Japanese Navy. Strategis Illusions 1936–1941* (1981) Clarendon Press, Oxford.

Matthews, Alan, *The Sinking of Prince of Wales and Repulse. A series of personal accounts compiled from crew members.* www.microworks.net/pacific/personal/pow_repulse.htm

Middlebrook, Martin and Mahoney, Patrick, *Battleship. The Loss of the Prince of Wales and Repulse* (1977) London, Allen Lane.

Nicholson, Arthur, *Hostages to Fortune. Winston Churchill and the Loss of the Prince of Wales and Repulse* (2005) Sutton Publishing, Stroud.

Pack, Captain S.W.C., CBE, *Cunningham the Commander* (1974) London, Batsford.

Raven, Alan, and Roberts, John, *British Battleships of World War Two* (1981) London, Arms & Armour Press, Third Impression.

Roskill, Stephen, *Churchill and the Admirals* (1977) Collins, London. *The Navy At War 1939–1945* (1960) London, Collins.

The War at Sea, Volume 1: the Defensive (1954) London, HMSO.

Stephen, Martin, *The Fighting Admirals. British Admirals of World War 2* (1988) London, Leo Cooper.

Stephen, Martin, and Grove, Eric, ed., *Sea Battles in Close-Up: World War 2* (1988) London, Ian Allen.

Tarrant, V. E., *King George V Class Battleships* (1991) Arms & Armour/Cassell, London.

Thompson, Peter, *The Battle for Singapore. The True Story of the Greatest Catastrophe of World War II* (2006) Piatkus/Little, Brown, London.

Thompson, Julian, *The Imperial War Museum Book of the War At Sea. The Royal Navy in the Second World War* (1996) Sidgwick & Jackson/Imperial War Museum, London.

Tsuji, Masanobu, *Singapore: The Japanese Version. London, Constable, 1962* (2002).

Warren, Alan, *Singapore: Britain's Greatest Defeat* (2002) Hambledon and London, London/New York.

Index